THE MYSTERY OF TIME

THE MYSTERY

OF TIME

Jean Mouroux

A Theological Inquiry

Translated by John Drury

DESCLEE COMPANY   *New York - Tournai - Paris - Rome*

This book was first published in French under the title *Le Mystère du Temps* (© 1962, Editions Montaigne).

NIHIL OBSTAT

Austin B. Vaughan, S.T.D.

IMPRIMATUR

✠ Francis Cardinal Spellman

ARCHBISHOP OF NEW YORK

January 22, 1964

The nihil obstat and imprimatur are official declarations that a book or pamphlet is free of doctrinal or moral error. No implication is contained therein that those who have granted the nihil obstat and imprimatur agree with the contents, opinions or statements expressed.

Library of Congress Catalog Card Number : 64-12768

Printed in Belgium

Abbreviations

BJ   *Bible de Jérusalem.*

BLE   *Bulletin de Littérature ecclésiastique* (Toulouse).

DB   Denzinger-Bannwart-Umberg-Rahner : *Enchiridion Symbolorum.*

DBS   *Dictionnaire de la Bible. Supplément Pirot-Robert.*

DTC   *Dictionnaire de Théologie Catholique.*

LV   *Lumière et Vie* (Lyon).

MélSR   *Mélanges de Science Religieuse* (Lille).

NRT   *Nouvelle Revue Théologique.*

PL   *Patres Latini,* Migne.

PG   *Patres Graeci,* Migne.

RB   *Revue Biblique.*

RHPR   *Revue d'Histoire et de Philosophie Religieuses.*

RevSR   *Revue des Sciences Religieuses* (Strasbourg).

RSPT   *Revue des Sciences Philosophiques et Théologiques.*

RSR   *Recherches de Science Religieuse.*

RT   *Revue Thomiste.*

TWNT   *Theologisches Wörterbuch zum Neuen Testament* (G. Kittel).

VSS   *Vie Spirituelle, Supplément.*

The works of St. Thomas are cited in the usual way.

Table of Contents

FOREWORD

This book does not owe its beginnings to any deliberate preoccupation with its subject matter. I had done some research and meditation on hope, the poor little virtue so sketchily presented in our theological texts. But I found myself running into the problem of time at every turn. I was forced, in spite of myself, to write a chapter on the time of faith. This chapter began to expand in all directions before my eyes. It has become the book you are now reading.

I allow myself this reminder because it will excuse me, I think, for having approached, for its own sake, this profound mystery, which evokes so many difficult problems. In countless ways, for the man in the street as well as for the scientist and the statesman, for the poet as well as for the philosopher, time has always been one of the torments of man. My approach is not philosophical, but rather theological. To be sure, I have tried to benefit from the profound attention which modern thought has devoted to this problem again and again. [1] But — without going so far as to share his views — the theologian may usefully consider Heidegger's warning: " Only those epochs which no longer really believe in the true grandeur of theology's task arrive at the pernicious notion that theology could gain something of a so-called revitalization with the help of philosophy. " Theology, which is the work of reason, can always profit from contact with a great philosophy; and it does not dare ignore the march of human thought. But its true source of revitalization is its submersion in the Word of God as taught in the Church, nurtured in time by spiritual activity, and developed by those great Doctors who were both geniuses and saints. When a theologian does his work, it is to this school that

---

[1] An outline of the various philosophical positions on time can be found in J. WAHL, *Traité de métaphysique* (Paris 1953), pp. 219-227, 285-308; and an excellent introduction in the little book of J. PUCELLE, *Le Temps*, in the series *Initiation philosophique* (Paris : P.U.F., 1955).

he returns; and it is from this standpoint that I have attempted to meditate on this difficult problem.

* * *

The book is divided into three parts. The first — God and Time — examines the problems which are posed by the dogma of creation. After having indicated the permanent living source of time, the eternal God (Chap. I), we analyze the significance of time as a dimension of the created world (Chap. II). Then we examine, in terms of the human mind, the passage of time and its significance for man's vocation (Chap. III). There are certain fundamental guiding levels within any theological investigation of time; St. Augustine has attacked them in a perfectly ingenious way. It is absolutely necessary to begin by pointing out these levels (on the basis of Revelation) in order to be able to " understand " Jesus Christ and to be permitted to " teach " in the radically new atmosphere of His mystery.

The second part — Christ and Time — is the heart of this book. It completes the first part and dominates the third, because it deals with Jesus Christ " the heart of the world and the psyche of psyches " (the fine expression of Jules Lequier). " The two Covenants look toward Him, " said Pascal. " The Old views Him as its expectation, the New as its model; both, as their center. " Christ's entrance into Time (Chap. IV), Christ's knowledge and Time (Chap. V), the phases of Christ's temporal existence (Chap. VI), the creative and redemptive presence of Jesus Christ in human time (Chap. VII) — all these try to show that Christ is — scandalously and happily — the Absolute Event in history; that He introduces eternity into time for the salvation of all mankind; that " Christ is exalted more as mankind increases " [2]; that He is the efficacious meaning of all creation — heaven and earth, as well as the new heavens and the new earth. This part of

[2] M. BLONDEL, unpublished text, cited by H. BOUILLARD, *Blondel et le Christianisme* (Paris 1961), p. 200.

2

our study is, therefore, decisive for the full meaning of the mystery and the problems which it evokes. For, if it is true that "the problem of the relationship between time and eternity is the whole of philosophy and at the same time dominates all of human conduct" (Jean Lacroix), then it is also true that in Christ all is resolved, and that in personal relationship with Him, however hidden it may be, everything is resolved daily.

The third part — the Church and Time — extends and "manifests" the second, since the Church is nothing more than "Jesus Christ distributed and made known." One chapter (VIII) describes the major components of the Church's temporality, on its journey among men. A second chapter (IX) attempts to analyze, in a sort of vertical arrangement, the levels involved in the time of the Church. A third chapter (X) situates the personal time of the Christian in the midst of the Church's time. The next chapter (XI) utilizes St. John of the Cross to study the extraordinary time of mystic experience in its personal, cosmic and ecclesial aspects. A brief conclusion points out the precise significance of the time-for-death, and the very hour of death, in the life of a Christian.

* *

The plan of this book recalls the successive historical stages of revelation, of the Covenant and of human redemption. But it is not meant to be a theology of history. It only examines the time of the world and the time of man, the time of God in Jesus Christ, which is the necessary condition, the foundation, and the intrinsic orientation of history itself.

Thus it touches upon a basic dimension of contemporary problems. Marxism, for instance, is an attempt to remold human existence. It has a well-developed view of history and of eschatology. It implies that time is ruthlessly closed in upon itself because it is deliberately cut off from any possible link with eternity. The age of technology creates a new rhythm in human life because it rationalizes, collectivizes and accelerates time. It makes a more urgent demand on men to ponder and rebuild it. World-wide atheism makes time absurd,

3

chaotic, uncontrolled and frightening. Indeed, in this view, man no longer has any time. He will find it again only in Jesus Christ. Many different contemporary philosophies encase man in an extremely shallow temporal reality, which allows only one type of relationship, that of man with the present world. Some noted Protestant exegetes with a large following refuse to link time with its foundation in eternity. They are left with a salvation-period that is fatally segmented. In it there is no dwelling-place for Christ.

The Catholic apostolate is directly concerned with this problem. In order to orientate itself properly, it must fully accept the mystery of time and be acutely aware of two realities : the urgent nature of the problems of evangelization, and God's dominion over the efforts of men, which never succeed except through Him who alone can give the increase to what men have planted and watered.

* * *

The reader should attach great importance to the subtitle of this work : A Theological Inquiry. This book is definitely not a " theology of time. " Such a project would be premature today. Only a rash spirit would attempt it. This work is only an approach to such a theology. It is based on time-honored thoughts which have nourished it and to which it makes but a few references. It only broaches a few essential problems and treats them cursorily. It tries to encompass a mystery which raises a hundred different problems, and recognizes how far it is from the hidden core of that mystery. Finally, it is animated by one thought, which takes on a deeper meaning as the work proceeds, the creative and redemptive presence of eternity in time. Man, who already breathes an atmosphere outside time, can no more shut himself up in time than he can " leap above time. " Before they even become men, they wish to be like God. [3] It is absolutely

---

[3] St. Irenaeus, *Adversus Haereses*, IV, 38, 4 (*PG*, 7, 1108-1109).

necessary for man to encounter, in time, the eternity in Jesus Christ, the Savior in time and in eternity.

It is my hope that in these pages dealing with a single topic, one may glimpse the rich significance of Catholic thought for one of our most urgent problems; that one may hear the call which God sounds for us in the very pulsation of time — the call to pass beyond time, to open up to the day of grace, to be converted to truth and charity, to build untiringly a habitable and fraternal city together with all men. This means we must work day after day in Jesus Christ, the Author and Perfecter of faith. We must pray and struggle in sorrow and patient hope, " for God will not threaten like man, nor be inflamed to anger like the son of man " (Jdt 8, 15). Working in time, we wait and prepare the only city whose foundation is fixed. One day we shall enter it, the city whose builder and maker is God Himself (Heb 11, 10), the Eternal God in Jesus Christ.

Dijon, May 15, 1961

I

God and Time

I

The Eternal God

Open the Gospel of St. John to one of his harshest passages (8, 30-59). In the midst of the temple, Our Lord confronts the Scribes and Pharisees, the haughty offspring of Abraham. [1] He reproaches them for being the spiritual sons of the devil, not of Abraham, and for promoting the works of the devil. Then, in contrast with Abraham himself, He makes a formidable and provocative claim : " Abraham is dead, " but " if any man keep my word, he shall not see death for ever. " Abraham — so many centuries before — " saw his day, " and he " was glad "; thus Christ is *beyond death and time*. When the Jews protest : " Thou art not yet fifty years old, and hast thou seen

---

[1] The texts are quoted from the Douai-Rheims version.

9

Abraham ?, " He replies solemnly : " Amen, amen I say to you, before Abraham was made, I am. " [2]

This sudden confrontation between Being and becoming concludes a long history to which we must return. Here, through the human mind of the Son of God, the mystery of time and eternity is expressed. They are two realities necessarily linked together. They imply and yet exclude each other; they oppose and yet complement each other, they must be viewed together in permanent dialectical action if we wish to account for both. To be sure, we start with time and come to a knowledge of eternity by a process of negation and purification; but, on the other hand, eternity is the foundation and the explanation of time. That is why, since the time of Plotinus and St. Augustine, theologians quite naturally begin a consideration of time with a meditation on eternity.

The Testimony of the Bible

God is not in time. He is eternal. The Bible provides us with our point of departure. Beginning especially with the second part of Isaias, it presents three major ideas on the mystery of eternity, or rather, on the mystery of God as Eternal. Let us just assemble a few texts.

First, in contrast to the world, God is completely beyond any beginning or end : He is without beginning or end. God is *always before*. " Before the mountains were made, or the earth and the world was formed; from eternity and to eternity thou art God " (Ps 89, 2). This is the situation before the world begins, because He is the one and only God : " Before me there was no God formed, and after me there shall be none.

[2] Cf. C. H. DODD, " A l'arrière-plan d'un dialogue johannique, " *RHPR* (1957), pp. 5 ff. Abraham " appears in the first part (of the dialogue) as the ancestor of the Jewish people, in the last part as a venerable figure of the past whose *essentially transitory* role in history emphasizes *the eternal nature of Christ* " (our emphasis).

10

I am, I am the Lord : and there is no Saviour besides me. . . .
You are my witnesses, saith the Lord, and I am God. And
from the beginning I am the same " (Is 43, 10-13). The
Book of Proverbs depicts Him conversing with His mysterious
child, Wisdom, " before he made any thing from the
beginning. . . before the earth was made, " that is, " in the
beginning of his ways. . ., from eternity " (Prv 8, 22-23).
Finally, in the New Testament we read that God loved His
Son and gave Him His glory " before the creation of the world "
(Jn 17, 5.24). And, " before the foundation of the world, "
God chose His own in Christ (Eph 1, 4).

But God is also *always after* all things. He is the one who
has set the end of the world and of time — the day and the hour
of judgment which brings history to a close. The passing of
beings and of centuries does not affect Him. " In the beginning,
O Lord, thou foundest the earth : and the heavens are the
works of thy hands. They shall perish but thou remainest :
and all of them shall grow old like a garment. And as a vesture
thou shalt change them. . ., but thou art always the self-
same, and thy years shall not fail " (Ps 101, 26-28). God can
say : " I am the first, and I am the last, and besides me there
is no God " (Is 44, 6). The Book of Ecclesiasticus will add :
" All things were known to the Lord God, before they were
created : so also after they were perfected he beholdeth all
things " (Sir 23, 29). In short, " The Lord is the everlasting
God " (Is 40, 28); and, *in this sense*, eternity designates God's
duration, " its infinite expanse unlimited in either direction. " [3]

Furthermore, while the world changes and passes away,
God does not. He remains the same. *He perdures.* " Who
hath wrought and done these things, calling the generations
from the beginning ? I the Lord, I am the first and the last "

---

[3] O. CULLMANN, *Christ et le Temps*, p. 34. Eng. trans., *Christ and Time*
(Philadelphia : Westminster, 1950). Note the words of J. PEDERSEN (*Israel,
Its Life and Culture*, I-II, p. 491) : " The sacred authors view eternity as a
primordial time in which the substance of all time is concentrated, and
from which all time derives its content " (cited by H. BOUILLARD, *K. Barth*,
Paris 1957, II, p. 162).

11

(Is 41, 4). And so " a thousand years in thy sight are as yesterday, which is past " (Ps 89, 4). Nothing of God's passes away; neither His word, which " endureth forever " (Is 40, 8), nor His help, which " shall be for ever " (Is 51, 6), nor His promise, because, for those who fear Him, " the mercy of the Lord is from eternity and unto eternity. . . . And his justice unto children's children " (Ps 102, 17). In short — *Jahweh does not change*, He perdures. [4] This expression, which appears throughout the New Testament, comes from the Septuagint writers who used it to express God's permanence. [5] " He is the living and eternal God " (Dn 6, 26). Everything else fades, totters, and crumbles into oblivion. Only God does not pass away. He is " the Lord God mighty for ever " (Is 26, 4). [6]

Finally, what is more significant, God lives. He does not die. *God is.* The central object of Hebrew thought is the living God. Since He lives absolutely, His life is not comparable to the lives of men. He is eternal. He says : " I live for ever " (Dt 32, 40). " I am, I am the Lord. . . from the beginning I am the same " (Is 43, 11-13). " Wast thou not from the beginning, O Lord my God, my holy one ? " (Hb 1, 12). The Second Epistle of Peter (3, 8) will attempt to fathom God's transcendent duration. Psalm 89 had said (v. 4) : " A thousand years in thy sight are as yesterday "; the later epistle presents the striking contrast : " one day with the Lord is as a thousand years. " For man, a day is a day and a thousand years is a thousand years. The ordered march of days and years cannot be accelerated. For God, a passing day and a long period of

---

[4] The Bible certainly says that God changes, loves, punishes, and repents. . . . But these are only frail attempts to express the activity of the living God. St. James will have the last word about the Father of lights (1, 17) *with whom there is no change, nor shadow of alteration*.

[5] Cf. C. SPICQ, *Ép. aux Hébreux*, II, 197 and his references. The epistle takes up the formula and applies it to Christ who " continueth for ever " (7, 24).

[6] Ps 18, 8; 46, 2-3; 114, 4. J. GUILLET [*Thèmes bibliques* (Paris 1951). Eng. trans., *Themes of the Bible* (Chicago : Fides)] proposes the following translation for Is 40, 6 : " All flesh is like grass, its substance like the flowers of the field, while the Word of God alone endures for ever " (p.64, note 60).

time are equal. Both are perishable fragments of time. At times God's plan can be fulfilled in an instant, since " One day is as a thousand years. " At other times it may advance step by step through successive centuries, since " a thousand years are as yesterday. " Obviously, in God's eyes, time is *as if* it were not. He alone is.

There remains the famous passage in Exodus (3, 13-14). God is sending Moses to the children of Israel. " If they should say to me : What is his name? What shall I say to them? " Jahweh says to Moses : " I AM WHO AM. " Then He adds : " Thus shalt thou say to the children of Israel : HE WHO IS hath sent me to you. " The extremely varied interpretations of this passage are well known. [7] It seems more likely that it is partly a refusal to define God, an affirmation of His sovereign transcendence; and partly a mysterious revelation, God's communication with His people. [8] Here we must underline the fact that the mysterious formula attests to the *presence of a sovereign existence in history*. Jahweh signifies the dynamic presence, salvific intervention, and close proximity of " He who is really and truly there. " [9] M. Jacob writes : " Since this name is the expression of the living God, it should reveal some aspect of His life. *El* expresses life as power. *Jahweh* expresses life as duration and presence. Jahweh is truly He who is. But when the Israelites pronounce Jahweh's name,

---

[7] Among the recent studies are : A. M. DUBARLE, " La signification du Nom de Jahweh, " *RSPT* (1951), pp. 3-21; G. LAMBERT, " Que signifie le Nom divin Jahvé?, " *NRT* (1952), pp. 897-915; P. VAN IMSCHOOT, *Théologie de l'Ancien Testament*, I, pp. 15-17; P. M. ALLARD, " Note, " *RSR* (Jan. 1957), pp. 79-85; also the succinct note in the *Bible de Jérusalem*, p. 63, note g. As is well known, theologians are divided on the interpretation of the divine Name. Concerning the opposition between St. Augustine's essentialist interpretation and St. Thomas' existential interpretation, see E. GILSON, *Le Thomisme*, V, chap. 4, pp. 122 ff. [Eng. trans., Cambridge : Heffer & Sons, 1924].

[8] See the apt remarks of H. DE LUBAC on this point in *Discovery of God* (New York : Kenedy, 1960), p. 137 f.

[9] A. GELIN, in *Moïse l'Homme de l'Alliance* (Paris 1955), p. 36 ; cf. H. CAZELLES, *ibid.*, p. 1.

it is the notion of presence, not of eternity, which predominates. Like all Israelite ideas, existence implies a relationship. It is real only in relation to another existence. God is He who is with someone. " [10]

It could not be expressed better. We find ourselves confronting the *most important experience of Israel* : the intervention of God in the history of His firstborn people. It is an unpredictable intervention, but they hope and plead for it. Actually, it is a *series of interventions* which mark the entire history of Israel and indicate Jahweh's *permanent presence among His people*. There is no better biblical definition of eternity. It is the sovereign, ever-close Presence which creates and guides human time by its permanent intervention and establishes the history of salvation by specific interventions. Because He perdures, Jahweh is always present, always before, always after. This is the characteristic dimension of eternity in the Bible, and we must return to it. It cannot be viewed as a reality indifferent to time, completely separated from finite existence by its absolute transcendence. Nor can this kind of eternity be conceived as an unending horizontal line. The *direct connection* between God, His creation, and the time which measures this creation, is essential to biblical eternity, and therefore, to the Christian view of eternity itself. Surprisingly enough, the Book of the Consolation of Israel (Is 40-55), which portrays the transcendence of God the Creator, also portrays *the eternity of the God who acts sovereignly* in the universe and in history. He is the sovereign ruler, not only of the present, but also of the past and the future. The Eternal means the Creator of the world who chose Israel, punished and saved her, and who will redeem and save her and all mankind through His Servant, *the Covenant with the people and the Light of Nations*. As the Creator, Revealer, and Rock of Israel, He inaugurates all the moments of time, directs them and endows them with their spiritual quality. He transforms

[10] *Théologie de l'Ancien Testament* (Neuchatel : Delachaux et Niestlé, 1956), pp. 40-42.

them into awesome and wondrous stages of salvation-history. [11] We can delve into the mystery of this direct relationship *from two starting points*, God Himself, or the history which He inaugurates. But it cannot be neglected or minimized. Indeed, if we are to remain faithful to the Word of God, we cannot exaggerate its importance.

The Septuagint writers " will re-read " this passage and insist on God's absolute Existence and permanence. God is " He who is, " as opposed to idols, which are nothing. [12] The Book of Wisdom (13, 1) will condemn the " vain " men " who by these good things that are seen, could not understand him that is. " [13] In St. John's Gospel, Christ will apply the expression to Himself in a striking manner. He is the one through whom judgment takes place. When a man does not believe " in the name of the only begotten Son of God " (3, 18), he is already condemned. " For if you believe not that I am he, you shall die in your sin " (8, 24). He is the one who is to enter into glory through the cross and thus save the world, condemning the unbelief of the Jews. " When you shall have lifted up the Son of Man, then shall you know, that I am he " (8, 28). He is a prophet, predicting the betrayal of Judas. " At present I tell you, before it comes to pass : that when it shall come to pass, you may believe that I am he " (13, 19). And finally, He utters the most astonishing words of all. They are such a strong

[11] Some texts from Isaias illustrate this : 40, 27-31 ; 42, 5-9 ; 43, 1-3. 11-12 ; 44, 1-28 ; 48, 1-11. 12-22.

[12] In a well-documented study on the work of the Septuagints, P. J. Coste writes : " Whatever the translator of Exodus may have had in mind by translating '*eyeh 'asher 'eyeh* as ἐγώ εἰμι ὁ ὤν, *de facto* he introduced a potential foundation for a philosophy of being inspired by Platonic and Aristotelian principles " (*La Maison-Dieu*, Nr. 53, p. 86). We would rather say that he was stressing an aspect of Revelation where religious reflection encountered the admirable fruit of Greek thought, an aid but also a danger.

[13] We cannot deny the possibility that Platonic thoughts inspired these writers to take up the phrase of Exodus 3, 14. See the comments of P. Tournay in *RB* (April, 1957), p. 609, regarding the book of Ziener, *Thèmes bibliques de la Sagesse*.

15

affirmation of eternity [14] confronting the world of becoming, that the Jews immediately attack it as blasphemy : " Before Abraham was made, I am " (8, 58). In the same vein, the Apocalypse (1, 4) calls God : " Him that is, and that was and that is to come. " This stereotyped formula " expands on the divine name. " [15] " It attempts to express the notion of eternity in terms of time. " [16] It implies that God is eternal because He simply is. Jahweh is the God who existed yesterday with the patriarchs, exists today with His people, and will exist with them tomorrow until His promise is fulfilled. Only one expression describes such a presence — " He is. " Thus Jahweh is *the living unity* of time and history. He transcends them and establishes them at the same time. Far from being alien to history and time, eternity in the Bible inaugurates both and finds sovereign expression in them. They, in turn, find the roots of their existence in eternity.

The God of the Bible is truly the eternal God. [17] And we can conclude this rapid survey with the doxology in the Epistle to the Romans (16, 25-27). There Paul utilizes the full dimensions of his message — " the preaching of Jesus Christ, according to the revelation of the mystery which was kept secret from eternity, and which now is made manifest by the scriptures of the prophets, according to the precept of the eternal God, " with a view of the faith of the gentiles, so that to Him be " glory for ever and ever. Amen. " It is all part of the " now " of revelation. But this " now " is explained by

[14] Here " Christ clearly affirms His divine mode of existence, which transcends time. " J. DUPONT, *Essais sur la Christologie de saint Jean* (Paris 1952), p. 71; also D. MOLLAT, *Évangile de saint Jean (BJ)*, p. 122, note *a*. St. IRENAEUS wrote : " God, the real Being, as the Word said to Moses : I am Being " (*Démonstrat.*, in *RSR* (1916), p. 370, note 2).

[15] E. M. BOISMARD, *Apocalypse (BJ)*, p. 28, note *c*.

[16] A. GELIN, *Apocalypse* (Bible de Pirot, XII, p. 596).

[17] On αἰώνιος see H. SASSE, *TNWT*, I, pp. 208-290. J. COPPENS has shown that the word '*olam* which is frequently used in the texts of Qumran " is always to be translated as ' eternal. ' " (*Nouvelle Clio*, 1953, pp. 6-7.) Cited by B. RIGAUX, *Les Épîtres aux Thessaloniciens* (Paris 1956), p. 631.

what precedes it — eternity, God's everlasting duration — and by what follows it — God's glory forever and ever. All acquires value only from the eternal God Himself secretly arranging this mysterious economy in eternity, revealing it in the now of grace through Jesus Christ, and bringing it to fulfillment in conversion and glory forever and ever. [18] Time is seen to be suffused with eternity. Eternity establishes it, measures it and gives it meaning. Time unfolds through this direct contact. Once more, the eternal God is shown to be the root-source and explanation of human and cosmic time.

The Testimony of Two Fathers

All these affirmations do not constitute a biblical metaphysics. They are not products of deliberate reflection but flashes of an unceasing revelation, taking root and developing in the prayers, the trials, and the hopes of an entire nation. Far from forming an elaborate and rigorous system, they are bright rays which God causes to shine gradually on human minds. To be sure, they provide more rich thoughts than countless theologies, and they imply some metaphysical truths. But they reach this degree of philosophic development only after a long time, after being nurtured in the light of faith and matured in a theology based on scripture, liturgy and spiritual principles. Finally they are rigorously analyzed and find logical expression in analogical propositions. In dealing with such a subject, it is dangerous to try to avoid " the path of reflection " and the demands which it entails. Only after centuries of spiritual experience and reflection will Christian thought be able to formulate a " metaphysics of the Exodus. " We shall content ourselves with citing two patristic witnesses who are important in this process of elaboration.

[18] Cf. K. RAHNER: " He who is ἀινώνιος is not only without beginning or end, but is raised up so high above the earthly world that he was able to enter into it and precisely so make it share in his own upliftedness above the eternal up and down, the eternal inconclusiveness of time. " *Theological Investigations* (Baltimore : Helicon, 1961) p. 113.

17

The Fathers of the Church worked over these themes untiringly and synthesized the biblical data. If God has neither beginning nor end, eternity implies the negation of all temporal limitation. If God does not pass away but rather perdures, eternity is not a process of continuation but a state of concentration and permanence. If God lives and if God is, eternity is nothing but the substantial plenitude of God.

By way of example, here are two texts of St. Augustine. They are not philosophical texts (they refer to the psalms just cited) but go right to the point : " What are the years which do not fail but the years which perdure? Now, if these years perdure, they are a single year; and this single perduring year is a single day. This day does not begin nor does it end; its beginning is not yesterday, its end is not tomorrow; this day endures forever. Call it years, — if you wish; call it a day — if you wish; whatever you call it, it simply perdures. " [19] " God's years are not one reality, and God Himself another reality. God's years are His eternity; God's eternity is God's very substance which does not include change. In Him nothing is past, as if it no longer existed; nothing is future, as if it did not yet exist. What exists in Him? Only : it is; and not, it has been, or it will be. For, what has been, is no more; and what will be, is not yet. But in Him everything purely and simply is. " [20] Here Augustine grasps the eternal instant by contrasting it to the process of becoming; he characterizes this instant as the substantial plenitude of God; and he can find no other phrase to signify all this, except the biblical expression — God is. [21]

[19] *Enarrat. in Psalmos*, in Ps 121, 6 (*PL* 37, 1023).

[20] *Ibid.* in Ps 101, 11, n. 10 (*PL* 37, 1311). On the dialectic between eternity which endures and time which does not, between the *semper stans* and the *numquam stans*, cf. *Confess.* XI, 11-13. The basic reference work on this problem is still J. GUITTON, *Le Temps et l'Éternité chez Plotin et saint Augustin* (Paris 1933).

[21] H. DE LUBAC is perfectly right in noting that the difference between St. Augustine and St. Thomas " is less than is sometimes asserted. The ' eternal Being ' of Augustine does not mean simply ' existing forever. ' Eternity refers to a quality of existence, a deeper element which corresponds to the ' Thomistic notion of being ' " (*op. cit.*).

18

Now let us cite the magnificent text of Gregory of Nyssa which is on an entirely different plane and reveals a typically Greek orientation. Here we see the mind trying to juxtapose time and eternity in order to distinguish created measures from the uncreated measure, to underline our inability to comprehend the divine nature as opposed to our direct understanding of the temporal world. First, there is the *negation of any common measure* between the infinite God and the finite world : " Nothing can possess a common measure with the divine, beatific Life. The latter is not in time; time comes from it. The creature has a clearly defined beginning and is transported to his proper end through segments of time. . . . But the transcendent beatific Life is not accompanied by any segment of time; thus, there is nothing that measures or envelops it. Every created reality has its own proper measure in accordance with the wisdom of the Creator. It is enveloped within certain limits, according to a measure provided for the harmony of the universe. Thus, although the weakness of the human mind makes it impossible for us to transcend the realities of the visible creation, there is no doubt that all things within the bounds of creation are limited by the power of the Creator. "

Secondly, there is the *absolute transcendence of God, who embraces the activity of thought itself* within His inaccessible pale : " But the Power which has created beings contains the reality of creatures in Himself, while He Himself is not contained in anything. Every thought which tries to reach the source of divine life, encloses it within itself; it transcends any curious, prying, querulous attempt to reach the boundary of the infinite Being. In mounting toward eternity and separating itself from time, the soul can only reach the point of realizing the impossibility of the effort. Thus time (αἰών), [22] and everything in time, seems to be the measure and the limit within which human thoughts can work and move; all that surpasses this limit remains inaccessible to our thoughts because it is devoid

[22] On the manifold meanings of such a term in the Hellenistic period, see A. J. FESTUGIÈRE, *La Révélation d'Hermès Trismégiste*, IV (Paris 1954), pp. 153-198.

19

of everything within the grasp of man. In these realities there is no shape, no place, no size, no temporal measure — nothing for us to seize upon. If the mind tries to grasp them, it will follow its natural bent and seek to grasp time-segments and creatures-in-time, and thus it will allow the incomprehensible nature to escape it on every side. . . ''

Finally, Gregory attempts to *juxtapose* the eternal God and the creature-in-time : '' The eternal Nature which lacks nothing and embraces all creatures is not in place or time; it is before and above all that — how, we cannot say; faith alone can contemplate it *in se ;* it is not measured by centuries, it does not know the passage of time; it subsists in itself and is possessed by itself; one cannot view it along the axis of past and future. For there is nothing close to it, or outside of it, which, in passing by, would be past or future. These are states proper to creatures, the basis of hope and of memory, dimensions accompanying a life divided by the passage of time. But in the supreme beatific *power*, to which all things are equally present at every moment, the future itself can only be viewed as mastered by an all-embracing power. '' It is useless to try to grasp the divine substance, because '' it is beyond any beginning; it does not furnish clues to its exact nature; *it is known only by the fact that it cannot be known.* This is its truly distinctive note; it is beyond any attempt of the mind to characterize it. '' [23] Marvelous theology! By a movement that is necessarily both positive and negative, the mind is oriented toward the supra-essence in all its purity. It is within such a theology that we must now attempt to state our thoughts precisely.

Eternity and the One God

Eternity is, first of all, an '' attribute '' of the one God. From this point of view, it designates the absolute fullness of being

[23] St. GREGORY OF NYSSA, *Contra Eunomium*, Book I (*PG* 45, 365B-368). Cf. H. URS VON BALTHASAR, *Présence et Pensée* (Paris 1942), especially Vol. I, chaps I-III and Conclusion; also some apt reflections of J. DANIÉLOU in *The Lord of History* (Chicago : Regnery 1958), pp. 244 ff.

which is proper to God. The world had a beginning and it will have an end; eternity has neither beginning nor end. The world is that which passes away and develops in perpetual sequences of time; eternity does not pass away and does not contain the possibility of sequences. The world is in a process of movement and becoming; eternity excludes movement and becoming. It is that absolute plenitude outside of movement, becoming, and sequences, outside beginning and ending — outside time. It is a plenitude of infinite life, infinite knowledge, and infinite love. In short, eternity is God Himself, absolute plenitude which is always in act, — *Ipsum esse subsistens,* — who lacks nothing, to whom nothing can be added, in whom a transition from potency to act is inconceivable. The essence, the core of eternity is not, then, to be without beginning and without end; time itself might not have had a beginning or end. Nor is it to be beyond movement and change; the angels, by their nature, are beyond such movement. The essence of eternity is to be *absolute plenitude in which everything is at once completely given ;* [24] it is to be the God who possesses Himself, knows Himself, loves Himself and lives in Himself, in short, the God who is.

At this point, the mystery of eternity seems to be nothing more than the mystery of God's Being itself. God is His eternity, and eternity is His very being. " You have not been yesterday, " said St. Anselm, " You will not be tomorrow; but yesterday, today, and tomorrow, *You are.* Or rather, You are not yesterday, not today, not tomorrow; *You simply are,* outside time completely. For nothing exists yesterday, today, or tomorrow, except in time; nothing exists without You, yet You are not in place or time, but all things are in You; nothing contains You, yet You contain all things. " [25] Thus, eternity

[24] Boetius did not invent this idea, as his definition of eternity indicates — *interminabilis vitae tota simul et perfecta possessio.* This is one of the major affirmations of patristic thought. See, for example, the texts assembled by PETAU, *Theologica dogmata,* Book III, chap. iii-iv. The formula was already expressed in PLOTINUS, *Enn.* III, 7, note 3.

[25] *Proslogion,* 19, 4, 6 (*PL* 158, 237).

appears as the dialectical negation of time *to the extent that* time is essentially devoid of being and represents succession and lack of permanence. The triple " ek-stasis " — past, present, and future — which makes up human time, is not applicable to God. His " ek-stasis " — the one God in three Persons — is that perfect plenitude, that absolute inwardness, that total communion, which excludes any possible connection with time. While the created being develops and seeks himself by being placed in time, the eternal Being exists and subsists in Himself, absolutely. He is — and this is eternity.

Thus, eternity is transcendent and mysterious, even as God Himself. Though it may be legitimate to say that time is " the proper measure of being in motion " and that eternity is " the proper measure of immutable Being, " [26] we must handle this notion of measure carefully. [27] This notion has various meanings depending upon the being in question, its degree of perfection and the extent to which it is in act. The human mind, for example, measures " motion " by numbering things as before and after, and thus it construes time. In God, who is perfect Act, there is no before and after, no plurality, no sequence. In God there is no possibility of *number*; the three Persons do not constitute a number, they are the one God. In Him there is no possibility of *measure* by means of enumeration; God is absolute permanence and unity in a Trinity of Persons. In Him the only conceivable " measure " is beyond every type of division, every type of sequence, every type of measure. It is a *measure indivisible by way of unity*; [28] it is the pure unity and

[26] St. THOMAS, *Summ. theol.*, Iª, X, 4.

[27] We shall come across it again in the problem of creation.

[28] St. THOMAS, *II Sent.*, d. 2, q. 1, a. 1, 5; cf. *I Sent.*, d. 8, q. 2, a. 1, 1ᵐ. *Eternity in its essence implies a negation.* For eternity is unity and unity is indivisibility. It is, therefore, the negation of any division, real or possible, in God's plenitude. The immutability of God, far from being a monolithic notion, is comprised of a *triple negation*, a negation of the power to change, of any succession, and even of being numbered as mobile things (cf. CAJETAN, *in Iam*, X, I, 5). On the importance of negation with respect to eternity, Suarez agrees with Cajetan (cf. *Disputationes metaphysicae*, 50, sect. IV, 9 ff. *Vivès*, 26, 928 ff.).

permanence of infinite act; it is God possessing His own plenitude.

Thus, when we consider the eternal Being in relation to the being who is still in the process of becoming, we are forced to say that just as the divine Being is the measure of every act, so eternity is the measure of every duration, but a transcendent *(excedens)*, non-homogeneous *(coaequata)* measure [29]. However, when we consider the eternal God in Himself, we are forced to say that He is " not at all measured, " [30] and that, strictly speaking, even His eternity does not perdure, because duration implies for our minds a " distension, " [31] and this cannot convey the plenitude, the permanence and the simplicity of the eternal God. Beyond all measure and all duration, *God is*.

Eternity and the Triune God

The One God is at the same time a Triune God. In accordance with this line of thought, the eternity of the Christian God acquires new aspects. They are revealed only in Jesus Christ, and we presuppose this revelation when we attempt to ascertain its essential elements. We need not understand the expression " God is " in its purely philosophical meaning, where it is rigorously distinguished from every other concept and reduced to its essential notes. Rather, we must understand its meaning *as expressed by faith*, with all the richness it possesses in the heart of Revelation. Although St. Thomas has expressed its essential meaning in the formula : eternity is " a measure by way of unity, " we must expound on this strictly supernatural unity which we can only glimpse from afar. Before everything

[29] *I Sent.*, d. 19, a. 1, 2^m, and also : " Eternity contains within itself, *in a simple form*, all the perfection which is portioned out among temporal things. For time imitates the perfection of Eternity, insofar as it can " (*I Sent.*, d. 8, a. 2, q. 3, 1^m).

[30] *Summ. theol.*, I^a, X, 2, 3.

[31] " Duratio dicit *quandam distentionem*, ex ratione nominis " (*I Sent.*, d. 8, q. 2, a. 1, 6).

else, we must relate it to the *One God in Three Persons*, and this submerges it in the unfathomable mystery of trinitarian life.

Eternity is, as we know, *permanence*, and the instant in which it is concentrated is a *Nunc Stans*, outside of all becoming. But eternity is also the *presence of God to Himself*. If every present is a presence, the divine present is absolute presence itself, not to another but to Himself. Time, by its inexorable sequences and intervals, renders us absent and distant from ourselves. But eternity is completely beyond sequences and intervals; it is the pure presence of God to Himself, the pure transparence of perfect act to itself, in the *pure relationship* of being, knowledge, and love, which links the three Persons together. In them there is no possibility of distance, because the three Persons are one God; there is no possibility of absence, because they exist only in this absolute reciprocity of relations which unites them and distinguishes them; there is only the purest, most total, most unifying kind of presence, ever new and joyous as the early morn.

Eternity, by its very nature, is the *possession of self*. [32] Insofar as our existence is a process of becoming, it is always an inexorable flight, the endless draining of our being into nothingness. But God possesses Himself in plenitude because He is existence itself, in whom everything is at once completely given — *tota simul et perfecta possessio, totum esse suum simul habens* (*C.G.* 1, 15). He possesses Himself in the fullness of thought which gives birth to the Word, in the fullness of love from which the Holy Spirit bursts forth, in the fullness of life, glory, and happiness which is suffused through the Father, the

[32] St. Thomas found this word in the definition of Boethius. In answering the objection that possession has nothing to do with duration, he says (*Summ. theol.*, I^a, X, 1, 6^m) : " Something which is ' possessed ' is held securely and confidently. Thus, the word ' possession ' is used to designate the immutability and the plenitude *(indeficientiam)* of eternity. " The word is even more apt and significant when it is applied to the Trinity. Furthermore, eternity is the " possession of *life.* " St. Thomas says : " To be eternal is not only to exist, but to *live.* " Here, too, we must go further, because the God of the Christians is Three living in one common Life.

24

Son, and the Spirit. The three divine Persons possess the same divine existence, each according to a definite relation which links Him to the other two. This possession *does not enclose each within Himself*, but *opens Him completely* to the other two, in an act of perfect communication. This is the final, most inexpressible characteristic of eternity; it is a *communion* of life, of light, and of love, that is *always in act;* it is the infinite activity — far above any other activity — in which the three Persons communicate their existence to each other; it is the infinite repose — far above any sort of immobility — in which the three Persons possess each other and belong to each other in joyous plenitude. Eternity is *this* infinite, unselfish *life of communication*, this mutual giving and receiving, this ebb and flow of love in the shoreless ocean of happiness. But this communication is never a process of becoming. It is always in perfect act, without beginning and without end. [33] Eternity, therefore, implies the *absolute plenitude*, not only of divine existence, but also of *divine community*, where the One and the Three exist together in a state of absolute permanence, and in a communication beyond all movement, all processess of thought, and all categories of priority. It is the eternal God, in three coequal, eternal Persons : *Aeternus Pater, Aeternus Filius, Aeternus Spiritus Sanctus.* [34]

Thus, *the God who is, is the living God.* But He is not only the God who knows, loves, and possesses Himself as Father,

[33] Speaking of the generation of the Son, St. Bonaventure writes : " The Son of God has a being which is absolutely permanent and absolutely united to the Principle which generates Him. " Because He is pure Act, " He is always being born, He is always already born, and He is always existing. He never ceases to exist and He never ceases being engendered. Nor does the Father cease to engender Him " (*I Sent.*, d. 9, a. 1, q. 3).

[34] St. THOMAS, *Summ. theol.*, Iª, 63, 2, c : " We must assert that, one only, God the Father, the Son, and the Holy Spirit, exists from all eternity. The Catholic faith holds this firmly. " Only through faith do we assert this, as St. John of the Cross chanted :

> The Three live in one stream of life,
> And each comes from the other,
> We know, but only through the night.

Son, and Holy Spirit. He is also, by His infinite mercy, *the God who reveals the mystery of His eternal love to His creatures*, so that they may share it in Jesus Christ; to ransomed sinners, so that they may become, through the Savior of the world, " God and the sons of God "; to all human beings so that, after being saved in time, they may enter into their eternity, as " the joyful Church " sings on Easter morn when she praises her God for having " opened the gates of eternity once again. " When the Christian raises his eyes to God, it is to say : " Blessed be the God and Father of Our Lord Jesus Christ, who hath blessed us with spiritual blessings in heavenly places, in Christ : As he chose us in him before the foundation of the world, that we should be holy and unspotted in his sight in charity " Eph 1, 3-4). God's eternity is, therefore, the *essential foundation-stone of man's time.* It manifests itself by interventions in history which are unforeseeable because they are perfectly free. They culminate in the absolute mystery of history, Jesus Christ, and allow man to participate in the eternal blessings of God, *in His eternal state.*

In Jesus Christ God has brought about an eternal Redemption (Heb 9, 12). In Christ He calls us to eternal glory (I Pt 5, 10). In Him He communicates eternal life to us (the great theme of St. John). He transforms our earthly trials into an eternal weight of glory (2 Cor 4, 17). He prepares an eternal inheritance for us (Heb 9, 15). In short, the vocation of the Christian is to participate in the bliss of the eternal God — *O beata Trinitas !* And all our energy will be devoted to exploring this communication of eternity. Now we see that in saying that God is, beyond any transition and process of becoming, we are merely *affirming a mystery in our adoration.* By a negation of impermanence, imperfection, and nothingness, we are catching a glimpse of boundless plenitude and limitless communion. We are opening out to the simple mystery of the eternal instant, the fountain of endless time, which surrounds us completely, encircles us forever, and illuminates our power of understanding, to allow room only for the pure song of praise : *Glory to You, Coequal Trinity, One God, before all ages, now, and forever.* [35]

St. John, the contemplative, has woven all these ideas into the prologue of his Gospel. The theme of eternity : " In the beginning was the Word, and the Word was with God, and the Word was God. The same was in the beginning with God. " (1, 1-2); the theme of creation : " All things were made by him; and without him was made nothing that was made " (1, 3); the theme of life : " In him was life, and the life was the light of men " (1, 4). In his own manner, St. John unites the strands of biblical revelation and brings it to its conclusion. After affirming (v. 1-2) the permanence, the communion, and the unity which go to make up Christian eternity, he reveals it as the source of becoming, and thus, the source of the time of creation and of history, the source of the time of cosmic life and of eternal life. " From eternity to eternity, through the entire development of history — that is the meaning of the theology of the *Logos.* " [36]

The Christian contemplatives will come after him. They will find nourishment and joy in the thought and the longing for eternity, and in the infinite richness of the simple phrase: " God is. " For this they will deny and exhaust themselves. Over this they will exult in silent meditation. For Christians in the twentieth century, the most significant example is, undoubtedly, the " Little Flower. " She was only a child, with little culture; yet she lived for eternity with an intensity, a certainty and a determination which were extraordinary. She

[35] First antiphon of Vespers for the feast of the Holy Trinity.

[36] D. MOLLAT (referring to G. STAEHLIN), " Jugement, " *DBS*, col. 1385 : " G. Staehlin has pointed out that John's theology of the *Logos* involves the traditional eschatology. The emphasis on the beginning (ἀρχή) points toward the end; the theology of the Word as Creator points toward a theology of the Word as the Consummator; the theology of creation points toward a theology of judgment. If the world belonged to Christ at the beginning, it must return to Him in the end. History unfolds from eternity to eternity. This is what is implied in the theology of the *Logos.* " Cf. O. CULLMANN, *Christology of the New Testament* (Philadelphia : Westminster, 1959); E. M. BOISMARD, *Le Prologue de saint Jean* (Paris 1953), pp. 23-24.

was convinced from early childhood that she would live for only a short time. She never asked to die young and never feared " a long life. " [37] But God Himself had given her this conviction. [38] As a result, life for this " aged child of twenty " (*L.* 213) seemed to be " an instant between two eternities, " (*L.* 118) and her soul was fixed on eternity from the time she first began to " meditate " in the corner of her room (*M.A.* 79). She was consumed with this thought : " It is a mirage, a dream " (*L.* 158). She loved the words of Psalm 89, 4 : " A thousand years in thy sight are as yesterday, which is past " (*L.* 91); she herself will say : " Two thousand years in the eyes of the Lord are no more than twenty years. . . than a single day. . . " (*M.A.* 245). Life is only a day, " a single day " (*L.* 198, 363), " and tomorrow is eternity " (*L.* 311, 363). It seems to her that life is not only passing but has *already passed*. " The shape of the world is passing. . . . Soon. . . *all will have passed* " (*L.* 115); " even as this year has passed, our life will also pass, and soon we shall say : *it is past* " (*L.* 143).

It would be a serious mistake to see in these words only the trite theme of the shortness of life. In fact the all-pervading significance of " passing " for her is the hold of eternity on time; because Thérèse touches eternity and lives in it, everything else appears to her to be vanishing. At the heart of her life is an *eternal reality*, the reality of Infinite Love. In the important letter in which she recounts her search for her vocation (*M.A.* 226-30), she finds amid the particular forms of vocations — such as soldier, priest, apostle, doctor and martyr — the universal form, which is the summation and the heart of every vocation : Love. With amazing sureness she realized that Love is the *substance* of every vocation, the *only* worthwhile reality, the " *all-embracing* " absolute. " I realized that Love embraced every type of vocation, that Love was everything, and included all times and all places. " And she adds the decisive

---

[37] *Manuscrits Autobiographiques* (= *M.A.*), Carmel de Lisieux, n. d., p. 255.

[38] *Lettres* (= *L.*), Carmel de Lisieux, n. d., p. 424.

phrase: I realized "... *in short, that it is eternal!*" The discovery of eternity, therefore, is the acme of her personal revelation. Love is the measure of everything else and is not measured by anything; it transcends everything by the fact that it is infinite Act. Even the sudden appearance of the present tense in her text amid all the imperfects, indicates that eternity suddenly loomed up as the answer to her search. All this implies that Thérèse identifies her personal love with the love which burns in the heart of the Church and, ultimately, with the Love who is *God Himself*, the living, transforming fire of eternity.

There is only one thing for Thérèse to do; to offer herself as a holocaust to this Love, to let herself be won and carried off by the "eternal Eagle," to fly "on the wings of the divine Eagle to the *eternal furnace* in the bosom of the blessed Trinity " (*M.A.* 236-37, 319-20; *L.* 338). Thus *the meaning of time is transformed, and time itself is profoundly revitalized.* A single instant is enough for God to do his work: "In Your eyes time is nothing; one day is like a thousand years. So, in an instant You can prepare me to appear before You " (*M.A.* 320). Every instant of life becomes weighted with eternity. Jesus plants in souls "the seed which must be developed above," so that " the *essence* of their *being* works in secret " (*L.* 237). The soul is able to love and save other souls by bringing the eternal love within it to fruition (*L.* 135). Life may be a "dream." But " in that dream we can save souls " (*L.* 194).

Finally, life, the fruitful dream, is unified and made eternal by awaiting the "return of the bridegroom " (*M.A.* 194) on that tomorrow, "the day of the eternal nuptials " (*L.* 170), and even more by the passionate desire to *see at last*, unveiled forever, *that hidden countenance*, that Holy Face which is always hidden here below. "A radiance, half-veiled, is emitted from the lowered eyes in the Face of my Fiancé " (*L.* 165); but she will see Him unveiled on the day of eternity. "Soon His shining face will be unveiled in our homeland, and then we shall enjoy ecstasy and glorious eternal union with our Spouse " (*L.* 170). But here again Thérèse enters eternal love only to let others enter, to bring time once more into eternity.

We are familiar with the astonishing words in which she expressed this conviction during the last weeks of her life. Here is the principal text : [39] " I know that my mission is about to begin, my mission to make people love the Good God as I love Him, to give my little way to souls. If my wish is granted, I shall spend my heaven on earth until the end of the world. *Yes, I wish to spend my time in heaven doing good on earth.* It is not impossible, because the angels in the heart of the beatific vision watch over us. No, I shall not rest until the end of the world, so long as there are souls to save. When the angel has said : ' Time shall be no longer ' (Ap 10, 6), then I shall rest and take delight, because the number of the elect will be complete and all will have entered the state of joy and repose. My heart tingles at the thought. . . " Subsequent events have taught us how true these words were. It is precisely because they exhibit the boldness of love — and its reward — that they also indicate the divine sureness with which Thérèse had " grasped " the mystery of eternity, the mystery of the eternal God. It is not a mystery in which one escapes and loses oneself in infinite joy; nor is it a solitary kind of sharing. The *Source of Mystery* is by definition the mystery from which spring created beings, mankind, called, fallen and redeemed. Thus, in entering the eternity of the Father, the Son, and the Holy Spirit, we not only enter eternal happiness, we also receive in our hands the world's process of becoming and we can participate in the redemption of sinners — until the angel says : Time shall be no longer! The words of this little book are better than any learned text in helping us to grasp, in a soul that is completely transparent, *the presence and absence of eternity at the heart of our faith*, the desire for eternity and the refusal ever to anticipate it; — in short, the tension between the Presence and the Absence of the Beloved, in sorrow, in joy, and in peace, which is the mysterious core of Christian eschatology.

[39] *Novissima Verba* (May-September 1897), pp. 81-82.

2

God and Cosmic Time

God is eternal. When creatures appear, time does also. The
Fourth Lateran Council (1215) and the First Vatican Council
declare that God, in His sovereign goodness, power and liberty
" *at the beginning of time,* [1] made from nothing all creatures —

---

[1] *Sessio III,* cap. 1 (*DB* 1783). The text reads : *Simul ab initio
temporis....* The Fathers of the First Vatican Council objected to this phrase,
but Franzelin had already anticipated them. His answer was that in every
respect the creation of the angels preceded the creation of men (" ac *deinde*
humanam "), that the *simul* of the Lateran Council merely indicated that
both angels and men were created, and even if time was implied in the
word, it definitely *did not define* the time of the angels' creation (Franzelin's
text is in *Mansi* (50), 337, note 6. See VACANT, " Ange, " *DTC*, col. 1268).
St. Thomas, writing after the Lateran Council, saw in *simul* only the unity of
the creation-plan (in *I Decret.,* c. II). He considered the simultaneous creation
of the angels and the world more probable (*ST*, I[a], 63, 3) because of *the unity
of the universe.* He certainly pointed out that the angels entered " time " :
" The angel is above time insofar as it measures the motion of the heavens,
because he is above all corporeal motion. But he is not *above time* insofar as
it measures *his course in existence* and his *operations after he has come from non-
being* " (*ST*, I[a], 63, 2, 2[m]). (Note that the non-being referred to is a biblical
notion, the absolute gap between the perfect Being and created entities.)

spiritual and material, angelic and terrestrial — including human beings. " Whatever profound differences there may be between angels, men, and stars, *they are all created.* Their existence is a gift. It is the eternity of God which charts their course in existence. Each of the three has a different type of " duration. " Man is midway between the simple concentrated duration of the angels and the vague evanescence of matter. But each of these durations *is measured* by the Sovereign Creator, and this measure, different for each one, is nothing but time itself. In this broad yet basic sense, time is the *measure of the course* of created things through *existence.* [2] Because our universe reaches its apex in man, the only fully constituted time we know is that which is initiated by human consciousness. And we shall examine it for its own sake. But our universe has been " created in time "; so there is also a cosmic time to which we must attribute a large place in the experiences of mankind. We must, therefore, try to examine it and analyze its religious significance.

Creation in Time

The Rhythm of Time

One of the major doctrines of the Bible and of Christian dogma is that creation occurred in time. The world had a *beginning* and it will have an *end.* The divine act which determines its appearance and disappearance, or transformation, establishes it as a universe in time, an ordered process of becoming, regulated by time which directs it " from beginning to end. " Both poles of the divine act are a strict *mystery.* We

[2] St. Thomas, who systematically treated the theory of angelic duration *(aevum)*, did not hesitate to write, for example, that " the angels are in time, but not in the same way as bodies are " *(Quod.* 11, 4, c). In the *Summa* (I[a], 10, 5, 1[m]) he notes that the angels can be both in time, *aevum,* and eternity. Time is an analogical concept which must be defined in connection with the particular grade of being to which it is applied. Still, time, *in the strict sense,* refers to our cosmic and human world.

cannot attempt to date either one, and so we find ourselves faced with the *paradox* of realities *in time* but outside any exact *chronology*.

The temporal rhythm of the universe is most evident when we note its three essential moments. The universe is created by God " in the beginning, " through His Son. " All things were made by him : and without him was made nothing that was made " (Jn 1, 3). The advancing universe has as its center the Incarnation — " The Fullness of Time " — in which the Father sends His Son, born of a woman, to save men. It has an end, the Parousia of the Risen Lord, with all the events involved in this Return. Thus the world is completely enveloped in God's plan — and concretely *enveloped in Christ Himself*, who sets and arranges its duration, and sustains it by the Omnipotence received from His Father and exercised through the Spirit. Cosmic time, therefore, has primarily a *spiritual significance*. It is a salvation-history. It is *centered in Christ* because He is the source, the center, and the end of its development. The universe does not pass from birth to death. Rather, it passes from birth, through the fall, to rebirth in Jesus Christ. Later we shall examine the problems concerning Christ and time. Now we must analyze the nature and significance of cosmic time *from the viewpoint of creation*.

Biblical Creation and Time

In the Old Testament, creation is a secondary consideration. [3] Israel's primary concern is the saga of the Exodus — the deliverance, the establishment and the purification of the chosen people, " by the strong hand and the extended arm. " But Israel gradually realizes that the God who rules history and the universe is also the God who has created the world and placed it in existence by His omnipotent word; God the *Savior* is also God the *Creator*. This discovery becomes a

[3] Cf. G. LAMBERT, " La Création dans la Bible, " *NRT* (March 1953), pp. 252-282.

major doctrine in Christian Revelation. God thinks of and wills the world and thus the world exists. This is a free divine action, because God does not create out of necessity but out of love. It is an immanent action, because it arises in God's intrinsic decision, and only the end-result is external to Him. It is an eternal action, like all divine operations, because God's willing does not have beginning or end. It is identical with the very substance of God, [4] because the creative plan is really God Himself creating the world. But the end-result of this eternal action is temporal, not only because the world *comes* into being by God's decision, but principally because the beginning of the world is *also* the beginning of time.

Therefore, it is not exact to say that God created the world *in time* — " in the beginning God created heaven and earth. " We are dealing here with the origin of time itself [5] which man cannot see or know, and which he can learn only through the words of God. " Where wast thou when I laid the foundations of the earth? Tell me, if thou hast understanding " (Jb 38, 4). Since time and eternity are linked together, the Bible sets the birth of the world and time in relation to eternity. " Who hath wrought and done these things, calling the generations from the beginning? I the Lord, I am the first and the last " (Is 41, 4). The praise of Wisdom relates this beginning to another, infinitely more mysterious, one submerged in the eternity of God Himself: " The Lord possessed me in the beginning of his ways, before he made any thing from the beginning. I was set up from eternity, and of old before the earth was made. The depths were not as yet, and I was already conceived, neither had the fountains of water as yet sprung out " (Prv 8, 22-24). These magnificent images always point to this fact: before the world, there existed the eternal God. " Eternity precedes the time of creation, " [6] not as one moment of time precedes another, but

---

[4] St. THOMAS, *De Potentia*, III, 3, c.

[5] For the purpose of our discussion, it does not matter whether one translates it as " in the beginning, " " in a beginning, " or " to begin with. "

[6] St. THOMAS, *De Pot.*, III, 14, 6m.

as the fullness of Being precedes and freely establishes creation and its participation in being. [7]

God creates time when He creates the world. Time and the world are *created together*. St. Augustine already pointed this out [8] : The world is not created *in* time, but *with* time. They appear together, because time is nothing but the *proper measure of created being*, of being in becoming, in growth and in decay. Time is also a creature of God. [9] It is a *constituent dimension* of the created world.

The Beginning

God created the world " in the beginning. " The notion of beginning (r̄e'šit, ἀρχή) is extremely important in the Bible. It has *three mysterious aspects*. First, [10] any real beginning defies understanding. We only understand *things which have had a beginning*, not pure beginning itself. A free act itself provides us with an experience of plenitude rather than of begin-

---

[7] " In the Bible, creation implies time and a period in which there was no time. Creation is the beginning of time. " A. NEHER, *L'Essence du Prophétisme* (Paris 1955), p. 130. For St. THOMAS, " before creation " refers to an " imaginary " time, as opposed to the real time of creation (cf. *De Potentia*, III, 10^m; 2, c; 14, 6^m; 17, 20^m, etc.). It is merely *a manner of speaking*.

[8] *Civitas Dei*, XI, 6. Cf. *ST* : " *Simul cum tempore*, coelum et terra creata sunt " (I^a, 46, 3, 1 & 3; cf. 46, 1, 6). On the position of K. BARTH in regard to that of St. Augustine, and on the objections to his view, see H. BOUILLARD, *K. Barth* (Paris : Aubier 1957), II, pp. 180-187. English edition to be published by Desclee, New York.

[9] *De Potentia*, III, 17, c : " God is the cause of time itself. For time also is contained in the totality of things created by God. " A noted scientist, whose frankness should appeal to the theologian, has written : " Space and time are not established and regulated by either theologians or physicists, but by the Creator. One must take them for what they are. Who can do this, except the physicist, who measures them ? " (O. COSTA DE BEAUREGARD, in *Parole et Mission*, 13, pp. 275-276.) Here we find an objectivism and an exclusiveness which are both formidable. And yet it coincides strikingly with the theological doctrine. It certainly poses an unavoidably complex problem.

[10] P. LEVERT is faced with these difficulties in her book, *L'idée de Commencement* (Paris 1961).

35

ning. It is never an absolute beginning, since it presupposes a past, and since liberty is *in* time only to *surpass* time. Secondly, there are *some* beginnings in the Bible, but there the word always represents God's *mysterious initiative*, a spiritual act which establishes a point of time — the beginning of the people of Israel, the mission of Christ, the apostolic preaching, conversion to Christ. [11] These are *salvation-mysteries* introduced in the world supernaturally and *vital moments* in the actual accomplishment of the salvation-work.

Finally, in the first beginning are concentrated all the other mysteries — the beginning of the world, the beginning of salvation-history, the beginning of cosmic time, the beginning of the salvation-period. This is the awesome paradox of the *absolute beginning*. Before it there exists only the Creator who brings about the existence of creatures, but is not numbered or blended with them. He has revealed this to us. God's Word causes the world to appear, and this beginning is impregnated with all the mercies, promises, and marvels which are to blossom in the course of time, and which are to reach their climax in the *yes* of Jesus Christ. The New Testament, which is enveloped in the new beginning wrought by Jesus Christ, is filled with references to the " beginning, " [12] because the latter is the creative moment, par excellence. It is the foremost seed of sovereign Benediction. It directs everything to the " end of

---

[11] Cf. the remarks and references of B. Rigaux, *Les Épîtres aux Thessaloniciens* (Paris 1956), pp. 683-684.

[12] Referring to marriage, Mk 10, 6 and *passim ;* the final tribulations, Mk 13, 18-19 and *passim ;* " the absence " of God and the course of history, 2 Pt 3, 3 ff.; the revelation of God through His works, Rom 1, 20; the eternal existence of the *Logos*, Jn 1, 1. Note the central role played by the act which founded the world. *Before* the foundation (katabole) of the world, the Kingdom was prepared (Mt 25, 34), the Lamb was known (1 Pt 1, 20), the Christians were chosen (Eph 1, 4) and Christ was loved (Jn 17, 24). *Since* the foundation of the world, the mystery has been hidden (Mt 13, 34-35), blood has been spilled (Lk 2, 50), the works of God have been perfected (Heb 4, 3), Christ (if He were only a man) would have had to suffer many times (Heb 9, 26) and men have existed whose names are not written in the Book (Ap 13, 8; 17, 8).

time " inaugurated by Christ and to that eternity where the Word existed with God.   It is a kind of *absolute limit* between what was " before " and what is " since, " i.e., between the pure existence of the eternal Creator [13] and the existence of creation.   It expresses in a simple way *faith in the free creation* of God who called all of us " before the foundation of the world, " in Jesus Christ.

Primordial Time

There is a temptation to say that before any mind acted in the world, there existed only " elements potentially in time, " a *process of becoming* which thought would conceive as time.   This is the typical approach of philosophies which view human consciousness as the true center of the universe.   But for those who base their approach on the biblical concept of creation, this seemingly obvious position is scarcely tenable.   It would empty the *created* character of the universe of all reality.   In saying that cosmic time exists, the theologian does not view time as a *thing*, nor does he attribute too much objective reality to it.   He is merely taking the creation-account seriously, *linking time to a thought* — the creative thought.   He is viewing the universe (outside any " beatific vision ") in its relationship to the divine act which establishes it, regulates it, and orders its beginning, its development, and its end.   He is paying close attention to St. Augustine and St. Thomas, who say that God " creates time " and " ordains its end. "   It is quite natural that the first " level " of time *discovered* and *worked out* by a *living* human mind should be cosmic time.   We must analyze its importance later on.

The actual progress of the universe is measured by the creative thought.   And this notion of *measure* is *essential to a created universe.*   God is the measurer and the measure itself.

---

[13] St. BONAVENTURE indicates the proper precaution to be used in speaking of the eternal Creator by using a typographical device.   One can use " aeternus Conditor " and " Aeternus conditor " (because He *can* create from all eternity).   But one cannot use " aeternus conditor " (because He *does not create* eternally), cf. *I Sent.*, d. 29, dub. 3.

Throughout the Bible we are presented with a measured universe. In Deutero-Isaias where the doctrine of creation is stated explicitly, we read : " Who hath measured the waters in the hollow of his hand, and weighed the heavens with his palm ? Who hath poised with three fingers the bulk of the earth and weighed the mountains in scales, and the hills in a balance ? " (Is 40, 12). Job shows us God contemplating Wisdom when He " made a weight for the winds, and weighed the waters by measure " (28, 25). Wisdom herself abruptly reminds Job that he could not know " Who hath laid the measures " of the earth " or who hath stretched the line upon it ? " (Jb 38, 5). Wisdom says that God has " ordered all things in measure, and number, and weight " (Wis 11, 21). Thus, God ponders the universe and His pondering " measures " the divine participation which He has granted it. [14] And how bountiful and magnificent this measure is! " God makes all things with order and measure, and there is nothing unmeasured beside Him, because everything has its own number. " [15]

Thus God is the *creative and normative* measure of all beings, according to their intelligibility and perfection, their essence and existence. [16] He is the measure of their devel-

[14] The New Testament takes up this theme and applies it to the New Creation. God measures the gift of grace which He gives to men to lead them to their full measure in Christ (Rom 12, 3; Eph 4, 7. 13. 16). At the last judgment He will measure men according to the measure they have used (Mt 7, 12; Lk 6, 38). And the angel of the Apocalypse uses a golden reed to measure the new Jerusalem, the messianic kingdom of heaven (Ap 21, 15-17).

[15] St. IRENAEUS, *Adv. Haer.*, 4, 4 (*PG* 7, 982, 2).

[16] St. Thomas constantly asserts that God is the measure of all things, because He is the supreme existent in whom all the rest participate (cf. *Ver.*, 23, 7, c; *ST*, I^a, 3, 5, 2^m; I *CG* 28, item); that the divine intellect is the adequate measure of all things according to their essence and their existence (cf. *Ver.*, 2, 7, c; I^a, 21, 2c; I *CG* 44, 53, 57); that the human intellect is measured by God and created things, because an objective affirmation is measured by being, etc. On St. Thomas' view of measure, see P. G. ISAYE, " La Théorie de la mesure chez saint Thomas, " *Archives de Phil.*, XVI, I; also the reflections of P. DE COUESNELONGLE, *RSPT* (1958), I, pp. 55 ff. and the note of P. GEIGER, in *Bull. Thomiste*, 10, 57-59, pp. 512-513.

opment and maturation, because He orientates them toward their proper end when He creates them. He is the measure of their own individual movements through which they try to reunite with Him, to imitate Him, and to find their fulfillment in Him by attaining their proper end. This measure is nothing else but the universal hold which divine thought has on creatures. It makes them realities that are essentially measured. [17] Hence man inhabits the universe first as a being *measured by God* and *by His creation.* " O Lord, make me know my end. And what is the number of my days. . . . Behold thou hast made my days measurable, and my substance is as nothing before thee " (Ps 38, 5-6). But what is still more profound, man is the being who is to *discover* the measure of the universe. He in turn is a *measurer* who must lay hold of the universe and bring it to fulfillment. In this sense, to use Heidegger's fine expression, " man ' *inhabits* ' the space between heaven and earth *as its measurer.* " [18] Time is nothing else but the *sovereign hold* of the divine measure on the universe in its process of becoming. [19]

[17] John of St. Thomas did not hesitate to write that eternity was the *intrinsic* measure of things and that it constituted being *in ratione mensurati* (*in* I^{am}, X; *disp.* XIX, a. note 16). Of course, this is not a statement of an " obvious fact " but rather a conclusion reached by deep reflection and critical analysis.

[18] In this fine but enigmatic text from his 1951 conference : " Measure exists for man insofar as the hidden God reveals Himself. God's ' self-revelation ' is the measure by which man measures himself. This revelation lets us see how much is still hidden. It does not lay bare these hidden realities, but rather guards them. Indeed it is a strange kind of measure involving not possession but actions which correspond to the control of this measure. Only this measure provides the measure of human nature. Man ' inhabits ' the space between heaven and earth as its measurer. " (Cited in H. DUMÉRY, *Le problème de Dieu en philosophie de la Religion,* Paris 1957, p. 126, note 1.)

[19] The concept of measure is linked to the concept of a *sacred* universe. It is found in the ancient *Veda* of India : " The sacred rite itself organizes time, and the sacred poet is a ' measurer. ' The word māyā, which comes to assume an important place in Indian thought, originally means ' measuring magic ' " (H. CORNELIS, " Le discontinu dans la pensée indienne, " *RSPT,* 2

The Creator's thought inhabits "things." Because it is within them, it establishes cosmic time. So that, in spite of the apparent paradox, the *intelligibility* and the *temporal nature* of the world are *interconnected*. Intelligibility floods the *created* world. There are no "things," if by that one means realities which are alien and impervious to the spirit; [20] because the simplest "things" exist only through the Creator's thought and they bear within themselves the presence of God Himself. Maurice Blondel was justified in emphasizing the existence of a *cosmic idea* in the very tissue of the world, "a real idea outside every thinker and everything thought." And he described this "cosmic kind of thought" as a living but obscure dialectic between "the noetic and the pneumatic," between a force of unity and universality on the one hand, and a force of diversity and singularity on the other hand. [21] But it is also true that no matter how active this intelligibility may be, it remains purely potential and dormant as long as the human mind does not activate it and develop it.

The same is true for time. In its development, the created world is measured by time. But its temporal quality lies *dormant* until the human mind activates it by contrasting it

(1957), pp. 233-234). For Marx also, man is a being in which there is measure. While the animal is measured by its species, "man knows how to produce on the level of any species and to judge the product by the measure which is within him." (*Deutsche Ideologie*, cited by J. Y. CALVEZ, *La pensée de K. Marx*, Paris 1956, p. 395.) However, man measures and limits in such a way that he erases the limit itself, and the finite being becomes infinite (Calvez, p. 553).

[20] Perhaps this is what Teilhard de Chardin tried to bring out by referring to the "consciousness" of even the most material reality. One can judge on the validity of the controversial term (cf. C. D'ARMAGNAC, "Philosophie de la Nature et Méthode chez le P. Teilhard de Chardin," *Archives de Phil.*, I, 1957). There is a problem involved in any case. Perhaps, in this case, we must adopt a deliberately "analogical" concept of consciousness (cf. A. BAUCHAU, "Vers la synthèse de la vie," *NRT*, 4 (1958), esp. pp. 405-409, and 406, note 12).

[21] Cf. *La Pensée*, I, the title of chapter 1; pp. 17 ff.; and *Excursus* 7.

40

with its own duration and " measuring " it in turn. This temporal quality is the basis of everything else. Man is immersed in it because he is part of the universe. This is the *first actual dialectic* between the eternal God and His creation in which time proves to have a *dialectical relationship* with eternity. *Positively*, eternity establishes time as the actual course of the universe; *negatively*, time appears to contrast with eternity, as multiplicity contrasts with unity, succession with permanence, and non-being with being. In short, time, *enveloped* by eternity, is the unified progress of the Creator's plan. Eternity is expressed in time until finally time is dissolved in eternity.

And so the Creator's thought measures the actual course of the universe, and confers on the world's process of becoming its " due proportion and measure. " [22] This creative transcendent measure constitutes cosmic time. And it is expressed concretely in *signs* which are the various rhythms of the world : the sequence of days and nights, of months and seasons, of years and millennia; the biological periods of living things. Modern science gives us an astonishing view of these cosmic rhythms stretching into the infinite reaches of the past and the future. But more profoundly still, this measure is expressed by the very source of all rhythm, the primordial time we are trying to comprehend. To say that the world is created is to say that it does not contain within itself the cause of its existence; that it does not securely possess its existence in a complete and permanent way; that its motion is a breathless and ceaseless striving toward the Being who keeps it in existence. At every moment [23] the world receives its existence from the divine intellect and will. Every moment it drops into the past and arises from the future within the present. The moment is really the heartbeat of created things. It is a sign of their plenitude, since in it the Creator brings the world into existence.

[22] St. IRENAEUS, *Adv. Haer.*, IV, 38 (*PG* 7, 1107-1108).

[23] We use the word not in the sense of a limit between the past and the future but in the sense of a " present here and now. "

It is a sign of their finiteness, frailty, and transience, because in it existing things must be continuously renewed and maintained in existence. It is understandable that philosophers have emphasized now one and now the other aspect. [24] But the two aspects are interwoven. The world in its actual course through the process of becoming is continually measured by time through the instants which unalterably regulate its duration and its progress in existence. Since the world itself is not only an order but also a history, each moment is a visible sign of the continual genesis of the universe. All creatures, from man to the stars, come to experience birth, becoming, and growth — even through disappearance.

We must, therefore, affirm the " basically " temporal character of the universe and the existence of a " primordial time, " which measures its course in existence. Before the human mind conceives the unity of its three ek-stases and the full significance of time, time already exists *in some way*, [25] because there is this primordial, creative pulsation through which the world comes into existence *at every moment*. [26] The basis of time is the very nature of created things, which do not simply exist but rather *come into existence* in order to be fulfilled. Creatures are meant to appear, to grow, and to disappear. This is their course. Time is the result of this *required* journey through existence. It appears when this

[21] Philosophical views on the instant range from considering it as a simple abstract limit to viewing it as the presence of eternity. See the historical remarks in J. WAHL, *Traité de Métaphysique* (Paris : Payot, 1953), pp. 300 ff.; also the reflections of LAVELLE, *Du temps et de l'Éternité* (Paris : Aubier, 1945), pp. 144 ff., 238 ff., 423 ff.

[25] For St. Thomas time fully exists only by " the operation of the soul. " Yet, in answering an objection (unrelated to the soul or to time) he says : " signanter dicit philosophus quod tempus, non existente anima, est *utcumque ens*, i.e., *imperfecte*, " in IV *Phys.*, *lect.* 23 (conclusion).

[26] E. CONRAD-MARTIUS (who wrote the important book *Die Zeit*, Munich 1954) takes a position quite distant from every school of contemporary thought. In " Le Problème du Temps aujourd'hui et chez Aristote, " *Archives de Phil.* (Oct.-Dec., 1957), p. 485, she writes : " For Heidegger, *Dasein* refers only to man's essence and existence. Only man would possess

journey *begins*. When the *Creator* inaugurates the journey of creatures through existence, He inaugurates cosmic time. Time implies a gap between the creative act and the created being; indeed, it *has its origin* in this gap. Time *measures* the journey of creatures because it inaugurates it, spans it, and ends it. Time is the *necessary condition* for all becoming and the *de facto* condition for man's personal fulfillment. [27] On the other hand, time cannot exist for a pure being. He exists outside all forms of time because He exists outside all forms of development, becoming, and evolution. The journey of the stars, of life, of the psyche — all inaugurate a need for time and a specific kind of time, in the framework of created time.

Time and Eternity

The eternal God creates time, and *eternity establishes time*. Time starts and continues in *direct contact* with its transcendent source. Apart from this contact there is no time just as there is no existence. Undoubtedly, time can be viewed in its

---

a ' dasein ' in this original temporal sense. I think that this position (the common center of all existential positions, whatever their differences may be) which holds that man alone possesses a true temporal existence or rather, is himself the true essence of time, obscures or destroys the temporal essence and existence of the rest of the created world. A more profound ontological view reveals that man is not the only one to ek-siste. He is not the only one to possess an ek-static Dasein renewing itself every instant. In short, he is not the only one to possess an expressly temporal Dasein. Man is not the only one " existing " between the beginning and the end. The whole world does, and therefore man does too. The entire temporal world is traveling through existence, *its* very own existence, and , skipping ' from one here-and-now to another. The temporal Dasein is in fact an *ek-statikon* in Heidegger's sense, but the entire world is this *ek-statikon.* "

   [27] Thus, as St. Thomas reiterates, time is a " measure *by way of number*, " while eternity is a " measure by *way of unity.* "

43

horizontal development, in the successive relationships where past and future intersect in the present. But since time is the measure of the existential course of beings, it exists only in this course. Time presupposes the creative act which establishes the *course* and its *measure* simultaneously. Beings do not exist without the Creator's act; time does not exist without the act which establishes and unfolds it, in short, *without eternity*. Perhaps *the greatest* (yet the most obvious) *paradox* is that time *in its very succession always involves eternity*. Only this establishes and explains the complexity, the fecundity, and the forward progress of cosmic time.

As the whole Bible affirms, there is a *cosmic time* in God's eyes. In this time He measures the development and the fulfillment of His creation. The contingent, developing, complex world is completely contained in the pure, simple, indivisible act of the Creator. And time too with its development is completely contained in the simple indivisible plenitude of eternity. Eternity establishes it, measures the development of the world by it, and then recalls it to itself. At every moment, time coexists with pure immutable eternity. St. Peter Damian explained this with incomparable forcefulness in a famous text. " The omnipotent God encloses all ages in the treasury of His eternal Wisdom, so that nothing in the course of time can draw near to Him or pass far from Him. Subsisting in the summit of His unspeakable majesty, He takes in at a single glance all the realities existing in His presence. In His eyes, they never depart into the past or draw near from the future. He is the same for all eternity; He envelops everything that passes and embraces the entire course of time. And just as He contains all time immutably within Himself, so He also contains all places without space. " [28]

Before proceeding further, we can gain a great deal by eradicating any spatial connotation from two traditional expressions : eternity *envelops*, and *measures*, time. In saying

[28] *De divina omnipotentia*, c. VI (*PL* 145, 604 ff.). This text was familiar to the theologians of old.

that eternity *envelops* time, we mean that the eternal God envelops the temporal world as the *creative cause* [29] envelops its *effect*. Eternity is God's very being. The vast expanse of temporal succession is only the effect of the simple sovereign creative thought. And eternity is present to this succession as absolute plenitude concentrated in one permanent, indivisible instant. [30] The unlimited " segmentation " of time only affects created realities which are interconnected and interrelated by presence and succession. [31] Because they are the result of the creative thought, God knows them in their relationship by succession. He sees them all *in their proper existence*, appearing and disappearing at their proper time. And finally, He contemplates them all as a totality *present to Himself*. " All things which enter time are enveloped in God's stable, eternal presence — those in the past which no longer exist, those in the present which are existing, those in the future which do not yet exist. " [32] Hence He is always *related* to them *by presence* — *ordo praesentis ad praesens*. [33] In this sense, He knows things-in-time, apart from time — *temporalia intemporaliter cognoscit*. [34] But this " intemporality " is not an *abstraction* as compared with time. It simply means that " to understand it of God does not imply any kind of succession. It is His very being and He is completely permanent. He exists all at once and this is the essence

[29] Obviously we are using the word " causality " in the older (metaphysical, not scientific) sense meaning communication of being, generosity and ultimately love. On this point see J. M. LE BLOND, " L'Usage théologique de la notion de causalité, " *De la connaissance de Dieu* (Paris 1958), pp. 15-26.

[30] Cf. St. ANSELM, *de Concordia Praescientiae Dei cum lib. arbitrio*, c. V (*PL* 158, 513-515).

[31] St. THOMAS, *I Sent.*, d. 38, 9, 1, a. 5.

[32] St. AUGUSTINE, *Civ. Dei*, XI, 21. Cf. St. Thomas, *Ver.*, 3, 3, 1ᵐ (contra) : " In God's sight, time neither passes nor ceases to pass, because in His all embracing eternity He envelops the whole expanse of time. That is why He knows things past, present, and future in the same way. "

[33] *Ver.*, 2, 12, c.

[34] *I Sent.*, d. 38, a. 3, 3ᵐ.

of eternity. " [35] The " absence of time " in God is nothing else but the *very transcendence* of divine knowledge. [36]

In saying that eternity *measures* time, we are introducing the transcendence of divine power. This " measure " *does not depend on anything* — measurable realities, their proper movement, or any other measure. This " measure " *establishes and orders* the time through which everything in existence passes. And finally, this " measure " is not directly the " *proper measure* " of creatures themselves, but of the divine action from which they come about. [37] Hence, it is absolutely simple and immutable, just as is the creative act itself; and it is identical with this act. For God, *placing creatures in existence* is identical with *measuring* their existence through time. [38]

[35] I *CG*, 66, *amplius*. This admirable text goes on to say : " But the expanse of time is marked by the succession of before and after. Thus eternity is related to time as an *indivisible reality to a continuum*. By an indivisible reality we do not mean the end-point of a continuum which is not present in every part. (The instants of time are more like that.) We mean a reality outside the continuum which is present at every part of the continuum (i.e., at every determined point of the continuum). *In short, time does not pass beyond the process of movement and so eternity has nothing in common with it.*

" Furthermore, granting that the eternal Being does not cease to be, eternity is really present *(praesentialiter adest)* to time and every instant of time. The circle provides us with an example. A specified point of the circumference, indivisible though it may be, does not coexist with any other point of the circumference. For the continuity of the circumference stems from a series of positional relationships. The center of the circle, however, is inside the circumference and has a direct oppositional relationship with every point of the circumference. So too, the moments of time coexist with the eternal and are present to it, although they are related to each other as past and future. But things can coexist with eternity only because eternity itself has no succession.

" Thus, the divine mind sees the events of time as present to its eternity, even though these events themselves do not exist forever. "

[36] On the various scholastic positions one will find a careful treatment in P. DE FINANCE, " La Présence des choses à l'éternité d'après les Scolastiques " *Archives de Philosophie* (Jan. 1956), pp. 24 ff.

[37] On this whole subject cf. JOHN of St. THOMAS, *in* I^{am}, *disp*. IX, a. 2, 10, 17 (*Vivès*, II, pp. 75 ff.).

[38] To say " rem esse in tempore " is to say " mensurari esse ejus tempore. " St. THOMAS, in IV *Phys.*, lect. 20.

The creative measure brings about the existence of creatures, their motion and their duration. In an eternal present it *situates* them in the unfolding progress of the universe, which we cannot measure, but which is always perfectly circumscribed by God. This measure does not embrace them as passing fragments; it neither awaits their appearance nor recalls their passing. It *seizes* and *possesses* all beings in its all-embracing, immutable, indivisible *grasp* — from their appearance to their departure. And it determines their proper role and vocation according to the place and the duration granted them in time. [39]

Thus, the creative measure *establishes* the *inner measure* of creatures which constitutes their proper motion, rhythm and duration, and which is the heart and pulsation of their temporal existence. And this *measuring measure* makes possible all other measures, especially the measuring ability of the human mind. It allows the human mind *to participate in it* as a *measured measure*, to measure the course of created beings, and to open cosmic time on its own level. [40] When we say that God measures His creation, we mean that He sets a fixed finite time for it and confers on it *its total significance* as a means of progress and an instrument of salvation. We are simply voicing the mystery of the eternal God, the Creator and Savior. We are in no way accounting for the creative measuring operation which is God's very substance. [41] Nor are we explaining

[39] Because eternity coexists with a multitude of creatures and measures them, John of St. Thomas does not hesitate to say : " eternity itself is *virtually multiple* " (*in* I^{am}, X, *disp.*, IX, a. 3, note 33).

[40] To repeat, *the spirit is primary.* P. DUBARLE, noting the reality of the human mind" and the fantastic dimensions of the scientific universe, was perfectly justified in saying : " Undoubtedly, only by his mental activity is man linked integrally with the whole universe, not by his corporeal presence in it. " " Conscience chrétienne et Univers, " *Lumière et Vie*, 17 (Sept., 1954), p. 138.

[41] CAJETAN (*in* I^{am}, XIV, 13, note 24) in explaining that the first cause precontains in itself " the matter and mode of necessary and contingent causes, " states that this " precontaining " was : (1) strictly intrinsic to God; (2) perfectly simple; (3) but inexplicable because it is not formal (and able tobe an object of knowledge in the proper sense) but eminent (implying a dialectic process of negation and affirmation which signifies but does not represent).

time, the measure of beings, because the act which establishes this measure is the eternity of God Himself.

The Meaning of Cosmic Time

In the last analysis, the problem of cosmic time is always the problem of man. That is why the Christian view of cosmic time is so distinctively different from other views — such as the ycclic view of the Greeks and the Indians.

A. *The Greek and Indian Views*

It would be a grave injustice to reduce the subtle, complex Greek view of time to a cyclical notion although the Greeks were in fact almost obsessed with the myth of eternal return. [42] Plato brought about a philosophical revolution by gradually moving away from this notion, but the later Stoics and Neo-Platonists could not prevent its reappearance. In its purest form it is presented by such men as Anaximander as the solution of a complex physical and moral problem. By physical necessity, the extremely varied forms of the universe are involved in an unending cycle of appearance, evolution and disappearance. Caught in this rhythmic cycle, men live and die to be reborn with the universe itself and to relive their former life. The world has an eternal time-cycle *without any privileged moment*. And man has an existence which inevitably fades into nothingness only to begin again one day. This " intermittent eternity " was a source of hope in a period when individual and

[42] Cf. C. MUGLER, *Deux thèmes de la cosmologie grecque : devenir cyclique et pluralité des mondes* (Paris 1953). This work has inspired my treatment here. Also, J. MOREAU, *L'idée d'univers dans la pensée antique* (Turin 1953); M. ELIADE, *Myth of the Eternal Return* (New York : Pantheon, 1954); H. C. PUECH, " La Gnose et le Temps, " in *Eranos lahrbuch*, Bd XX (1951), pp. 60-76; J. TROUILLARD, " L'intelligibilité proclusienne, " in *La Phil. et ses problèmes* (Paris 1960),pp. 92-97.

social life had hardly any serious encounter with the elementary demands of justice. The Greeks' passionate attachment to life and joyous enlightenment was fulfilled by it. When its cosmological foundations are destroyed, the ancient myth survives because of its " moral aspects. " The progress of knowledge, conscience in the face of personal and social injustice, and Plato's world of ideas dealt it a fatal blow. Yet it reappears after Plato and Democritus.

Such a myth is directly opposed to the Christian concept of time. The eternity of the world is an illusion, because there is only one infinite time. And that of man is an even greater illusion, because it is the ephemeral appearance and reappearance of the same being. Cosmic time is *empty*, because it does not derive from absolute plenitude, and because it does not measure the real, new, progressive history of an advancing human race. It is *hopeless*, because man is entangled in the eternal cycle of the stars. He is continually starting over without ever reaching fulfillment. It is understandable that the religions groped for mysteries so that man might escape the fatalism of the stars. [43] In short, this time is not that of a *created world*. It is without beginning, without meaning, without purpose. It has no internal link with human liberty and salvation. It is a preposterous Absurdity — *Chronos* devouring his children.

For the Indians also, time is cyclic, but in a different way. [44] According to M. Éliade there are three levels. Individual time is an unending succession of unreal instants. Cosmic time is the eternal repetition of the same rhythmic processes (creation, destruction, re-creation) in an unending cycle — all that

---

[43] Cf. A. J. FESTUGIÈRE, *L'Idéal religieux des Grecs et l'Évangile* (Paris 1932), pp. 101 ff. and *id.*, *La Religion d'Hermès Trismégiste* (II, *Le Dieu cosmique*, Paris 1952).

[44] Cf. M. ELIADE, *Images and Symbols* (New York : Sheed, 1961) chap. II. Also the fine text of J. MONCHANIN, " Le Temps selon l'Hindouisme et le Christianisme, " *Dieu vivant*, Nr. 14, pp. 111 ff. The Indian concept of duration has just been carefully scrutinized by L. SILBURN in *Instant et Cause* (Paris 1955). On this topic see P. H. CORNELIS, " Le Discontinu dans la Pensée indienne, " *RSPT* (April, 1957), pp. 233-244.

representing *Maya*, the infinite unreal. Finally, there is the *intemporal instant*, before creation. It is outside time, outside flux, outside duration. It is a kind of eternal present. This " instant " is the source of everything else. Brahma reveals himself as time and eternity all at once, as time and free from time. The source of everything is both *Maya* and the Absolute Spirit, illusion and reality, time and eternity. Eternity does give meaning to time, and makes it a hierophany. But it does so only by *emptying* time of all meaning and making it *doubly illusory*. In relation to cosmic time, individual time and the world of history are only an illusory instant. And in relation to absolute reality, to the eternal present, cosmic time itself, together with its periods of startling duration, is only an illusion. The infinite universe appears and disappears from the body of Vishnu eternally, " like bubbles of soap. "

There is only one thing to do : *free onself from time and the illusion* it presents. Here, in contrast to the Greeks, awareness of the infernal cycle begets a *terror* which is the beginning of salvation. It drives the yogi to lengthy ascetisicm (ascesis) in the terrible technique. Through it he will be able to transcend individual time and enter cosmic time. Then, in a flash of illumination he will transcend time, space, and the universe and enter the eternal present. There, like Buddha, he can survey both kinds of time, cauterize the consequences of all his external acts, and be delivered.

Undoubtedly, there is spiritual boldness and grandeur in such a view. But it should be pointed out that it is opposed to the biblical view of time. For the Indians, time is certainly linked with human destiny. But its meaning is essentially ambiguous. On the one hand, *its intrinsic value* lies in the fact that it is *the prodigious obstacle*. (In the Bible, the only real obstacle is sin.) But compared with eternity, it is *completely valueless*. Eternity is not a plenitude from which time derives. It is an instantaneousness which establishes time by negating it, making it illusory and depriving it of all positive meaning. Furthermore, as Abbé Monchanin noted, this kind of time can be " *scanned.* " It is never " centered. " It can unfold

50

eternally, yet it is not fecund. When a long cycle of years disappears, everything disappears with it. Nothing grows, increases, or advances *in* time and history. " There is a complete break between being and becoming, between idea and history. " [45]

B. *The Christian Meaning of Cosmic Time*

We must analyze the true meaning of cosmic time as a dimension of the *created* world. Of course, its full Christian significance can only be realized and developed in Christ. But its essential meaning is revealed in creation. Cosmic time is not neutral. It has not only quantitative but also qualitative aspects. In short, like creation itself, cosmic time has more than one meaning.

First, time has a *natural meaning*. It has a place in the chain of secondary causes and in the natural finality of the universe. God gives time to each individual creature, and to that magnificent creature, the universe, so that *they may fulfill themselves*. He contemplates the world, and the world exists. But He contemplates it as an ordered whole — a *cosmos* — in which each being united with every other being is to reach its end. This " idea " through which God eternally contemplates *the ordering of things to their end* is what we call Divine Providence. [46] The latter establishes time as the *internal measure* of things moving toward their end in the cosmos. God actualizes [47] this simple, eternal, all-embracing " idea " by His immutable, eternal, creative act. [48] And this act not

---

[45] J. MONCHANIN, *op. cit.*, p. 116. Buddhism has known a spiritual drama analogous to that of the Greek spirit. Few things are more moving than the search for salvation through faith in Amida — which frees him from Karmân and from time. Cf. H. DE LUBAC, *Amida* (Paris 1955). There one can read, among a hundred others, the fine hymn of the " Pure Earth, " p. 216.

[46] Cf. *ST*, Iᵃ, 22, a. 1 and 3.

[47] It is the *executio ordinis* and the *gubernatio rerum*, Iᵃ, 103-105.

[48] *ST*, Iᵃ, 104, 1, 4ᵐ.

only *places* things in existence and *conserves* them [49] but also leads them to their proper end. [50] It apportions their end to them, orientates them towards it, and gives them the power to act. [51] St. Irenaeus expresses it magnificently : " The Lord of all things is without beginning and without end, truly and always absolutely identical with Himself. But all that comes from Him, that is, all that has been and is made, has had a beginning, has been begotten, and thus is inferior to Him. But everything endures and passes through the span of centuries in accordance with the will of God who made them. First He gives them existence. Then He maintains them in existence. . . All that has been made continues in existence for as long as God wishes it to exist and to endure. " [52]

Thus, " God gives time a purpose " [53] when He wills that it manifest His Power in some predestined way. He places creatures in time and time measures their striving for perfection, their ontological development, and the fulfillment of their purpose. The Bible is filled with this line of thought. There is a time for rain, a time for harvesting, a time for first-fruits, a time for child-birth. [54] God creates and arranges these times — *Creator temporum et ordinator.* [55] The past, the present, and the future are irreversibly ordered for the development of beings. Time is *the gift* which God gives to creatures that they may reach their fulfillment. If the world does evolve, mounting with slow magnificent steps towards life, consciousness, and thought, it does so *in* and *through* this *dynamic* gift.

[49] *Ibid.*, c.

[50] Man's case is unique and we shall return to it. Cf. I[a], 22, 2, 4; *Ver.*, 5, 5; I[a], 105, 3 and 4. " Only one kind of time envelops nature and man, the time of God's word, " NEHER, *op. cit.*, p. 134.

[51] I[a], 105, 5.

[52] *Adv. Haer.*, II, 34, 2 (*PG* 7, 835 B).

[53] *ST*, I[a], 46, 1, 6.

[54] Cf. VAN IMSCHOOT, *Théologie de l'Ancien Testament* (Paris 1955), I, pp. 105-107. Also C. TRESMONTANT, *Study of Hebrew Thought* (New York : Desclee, 1960) pp. 28-29.

[55] St. AUGUSTINE, *Civ. Dei*, XI, 6.

But this is only the *immediate natural* finality of beings. We must look deeper, because time has another aspect. It has a spiritual significance, because from its inception it is a salvation-period. God has created only one world and one time — the time of His eternal plan to create a nation of sons in Jesus Christ for His own glory. Above we noted that Israel's central thought was at first the Exodus and God the Savior. Only later did Israel discover that God the Savior was also God the Creator. By this very fact, *creation appears in the perspective of salvation*. It is the beginning of it, the first action. And the Bible continues to link these two aspects of the one God, these two major acts of His omnipotence and His mercy. [56]

In this priestly account (Gn 1), the divine Word inaugurates a world which reaches its peak in man made in the image and likeness of God. The world is a kind of cosmic temple, filled with the divine presence, and at its center is the privileged creature, man, who is, as it were, the priest of this primitive liturgy. [57] For Jeremias, the God of election is also the God of creation. The stability of creation is a *sign* and a *guarantee* of God's fidelity. " Thus saith the Lord : If my covenant with the day can be made void, and my covenant with the night, that there should not be day and night in their season : Also my covenant with David my servant may be made void... As the stars of heaven cannot be numbered, nor the sand of the sea be measured : so will I multiply the seed of David my servant " (Jer 33, 20-22). For Deutero-Isaias the one eternal God is Creator, Lord, and Savior : " I form the light and create darkness. I make peace and create evil. I, the Lord, that do all these things.... Let the earth be opened and bud

[56] For all this we make use of the article by G. LAMBERT *(op. cit.)* and the words of A. CHAVASSE : " The distinction between nature and the supernatural does not date from the Christian era. It goes back to the foundation of the world and *suffuses every part of creation* " (our emphasis). See the full text in " Du Peuple de Dieu à l'Église du Christ, " *Maison-Dieu*, pp. 32, 51-52.

[57] Cf. also T. MAERTENS, *Les sept jours* (S. André-lez-Bruges 1951), pp. 24 ff., 34 ff., 58 ff.

forth a saviour : and let justice spring up together. I the Lord have created him " (Is 45, 7-8).

Thus, Jahweh is the master of history because He is the Creator. His sole plan is to *create a universe* in which He can *form a nation of the saved.* And so, when St. Paul wishes to establish the relationship between *Jesus Christ as Man* and creation, he remains faithful to the Israelite approach by viewing creation through the covenant and considering it as fully accomplished in Jesus Christ. To him, the Adam of Genesis is a *figure* (Rom 5, 14) of *Him who is to come*, a *type* of the true Adam. God has *only one salvation-plan* which begins with the first Adam and is completed in the second Adam. God inaugurates *only one time* in the world, and from beginning to end it is a salvation-period. [58]

The non-spiritual world, therefore, exists *for man called* to a supernatural end. This is the final end of the created universe and its ultimate significance. Divine Providence is not just the divine " idea " which orders beings to their proper end. It is the " idea " of this ordering to their last end. The entire order of the universe is orientated to this end because God ponders, creates, and governs both the universe and time in the light of His *salvation-plan*. God *unfolds* cosmic time in the progressing universe and *brings it to the attention* of human consciousness. In the ordered succession of seasons and years [59] and in the free decisions of conscience, God reveals Himself and calls men to salvation. In the final analysis, cosmic time, as God views it, is a salvation-period. And St. Thomas does not hesitate to write : " In the movement of corporal beings, God seeks something else : to fulfill the number of the elect. " [60] The motion of the heavens — which the ancients considered divine and which even St. Thomas

[58] Cf. E. Jacob, *op. cit.*, pp. 213 ff.

[59] Act 14, 15-17.

[60] *De Pot.*, 13, 10, 3. Cf. 5, 5, c and 6, 11 m, 13 m. It is a classic statement of Christian thought. We find it already in St. Justin (I *Ap.*, 45) : " God, the Father of the world, must raise Christ to heaven after His Resurrection and keep Him there until His enemies, the demons, are smitten, until

regards as some kind of absolute [61] — finds its principal end in this " happy consummation. " For St. Thomas, every motion and every operation of creatures, of the cosmos and of the angels who serve the elect, is ordered to " the fulfillment of the ranks of the blessed "; when salvation is fully achieved, this motion will cease. [62]

Predestination as well as Providence is involved here. " The world will end when the number of the elect is fulfilled. This fulfillment accomplishes divine predestination. " [63] God

the number of the predestined is complete, the saints for whose sake He has preserved the world from the flames. " The theme derives from Jewish apocalyptic writings. The Kingdom will come when the world of the elect (the Jews) will be complete (cf. CULLMAN, *Christ et le Temps*, p. 113). That view is not found in the New Testament. Christian revelation works here too : all men (not just the Jews) are called to salvation. When the formula is taken up again, it has a completely different meaning (cf. H. I. MARROU, *L'Ambivalence du Temps de l'Histoire chez saint Augustin* [Paris 1950], pp. 22-23). The " number " of the elect is no longer a purely quantitative reality. It is a way of expressing the completion of the work of salvation. In Mt 15, 31-38, it is not a question of numbers but of spiritual discernment. On the " Book " (and the books) in which the names of the elect are inscribed, see J. DANIÉLOU, *Théologie du Judéo-Christianisme* (Paris 1958), pp. 151-164.

[61] We are all aware of the revolution wrought by modern science in this area. For classical science (contrary to Plato and Aristotle), space and time were ontological entities — absolute, infinite and independent of each other. In order to escape these " two infinite, eternal absurdities " Kant made them *a priori* forms of sensibility. But contemporary science no longer views them as independent absolutes. They are two " actors in the cosmic drama " (P. COUDERC). Space does not exist apart from time. " The measurement of space is a function of time " and " both are viewed as having a common origin. " That is why Sir James Jeans has adopted the phrase of St. Augustine : *Non in tempore, sed cum tempore, Deus fixit mundum.* On the problems of the philosophy of science, which are beyond the scope of this book, see the article (which we have quoted here) by JEAN ROHMER, " Astronomie et Philosophie, " *RevSR* (April 1956), pp. 113-114.

[62] *De Pot.*, 5, 5, 6m and 13m.

[63] *Ibid.*, 5, 6, c. This formulation is independent of any particular view of predestination. We shall see the problem again when we come across it in " its proper place, " in Jesus Christ.

wishes to transplant man from earth and time into eternal life. He orders him to this end and plants this call within him. He leads him from his temporal life to the Beatific Vision through a mysterious journey full of confusion, sorrow, and wonder. In the magnificent words of Irenaeus : [64] " There is only one God, who reads the heavens like a book, and renews the face of the earth. He made temporal realities so that man might bear the fruit of immortality through them. And from on high His goodness directs the things of eternity. " Cosmic time itself is a means of salvation for all men, an essential dimension of creation, a prerequisite for eternal salvation. In its final end and its ultimate significance it is the very time of salvation. This time *alone* reveals the word of God and is contained in God's eternal mind and will. This time alone enters the world from God's creative, redemptive will, and measures the complete development of the universe. It alone is the measure of the universe, measured in turn by the divine " idea. "

It is possible, then, to discern *the relationship between cosmic time and the salvation-period*. In one sense, cosmic time is the *basis* of all human time and of the salvation-period itself, since man is to reach fulfillment in this world within the bounds of cosmic time. The salvation-period is inserted in cosmic time, and cosmic time is its fundamental measure and its necessary prerequisite. But in a deeper sense, cosmic time is *enveloped* by the salvation-period, because it is measured by the creative idea in the light of the salvation-period which gives it its immanent purpose and its deepest meaning. In short, through the (truly real) *appearance* of things, cosmic time envelops and determines the salvation-period. But through the *very existence* of things, the salvation-period dominates and measures cosmic time. The time of the heavenly bodies alone can never determine a spiritual destiny. [65]

The salvation-period is as mysterious as salvation itself. It is one aspect of the salvation-mystery. Hence it is never directly

[64] *Adv. Haer.*, IV, 5, 1 (*PG* 7, 983 B).

[65] " The supernatural good of a single man is greater than the natural good of the entire universe " (*ST*, Iª IIªe, 113, 9, 2ᵐ).

expressed through cosmic time. In coming to fulfillment it dominates cosmic time. This is the basis of a history which faith alone can discover and fulfill. The time of faith and the time of human experience are linked by a *material coincidence*. But there is an *irreducible distinction*, a *time-lag*, between them. The salvation–period radically *transcends* cosmic time. This explains why a theological view of the universe cannot be linked to any scientific notion of space and time. Faith connects time with God as the measure of created beings in motion. This measure involves a beginning, a center, and an end. Time moves toward its center in Jesus Christ. But faith affirms all this solely on God's Word, considering it all as part of a strictly supernatural mystery.

This is enough to *exclude* any cosmological view of time, such as that of the Greeks and Indians which destroys time itself. But it *does not impose* any specific scientific theory. It is up to science to discover the forms of cosmic time proper to stars, men, and various forms of life. Science abstracts from the sum of human experience. The various sciences study different levels of reality and construe time accordingly. Using extremely complex measures which are not easily correlated, [66] they depict cosmic time as a series of (more or less closely connected) phenomena. But whether science pursues all the various time-cycles as it has been doing for a long time, or again considers, as Paul Couderc says, that the notion of an " oscillating universe " is " more attractive and dialectical " than " evolution in the strict sense " — the scientific notions do not come into direct contact with dogmas because they are on a different level and have a different meaning.

And so the believer as such does not measure the salvation-period by cosmic time. Instead, he affirms the sovereign

[66] Cf. F. MEYER, *Problématique de l'Évolution* (Paris : P.U.F., 1954) especially part 3, pp. 226 ff. In the light of the problem of time, he scrutinizes the connection between macroscopic causality and " directive reactions " (of the atomic or infra-atomic order) on the one hand, and between nuclear physics and biology on the other hand. See also F. HUANT, *Connaissance du Temps* (Paris 1950).

57

independence and *the control of the " years of grace "* over " cosmic years. " St. Irenaeus, with his typical vigor, said : " The Lord's year of grace is the time in which those who believe in Him are called by Him and made pleasing in His sight. It is the period of time between His coming and the end, when He plucks those who are saved, as if they were fruit. . . . It is very fitting that the time during which men are called and saved by the Lord is considered the Lord's year of grace which follows the day of retribution, the day of judgment. But this time is called not only a *year*, but also a *day* by the Prophet and St. Paul (Rom 8, 36). . . . ' The day ' does not signify a day of twelve hours but rather the entire period of time during which those who believe in Christ suffer and die for Him. So too, that year is *not a year of twelve months but rather the entire period of faith* during which men believe in the message they have heard, and are made agreeable to the Lord by being united with Him. " [67] The salvation-period is absolutely transcendent. It is never enveloped by cosmic measure but only by God's Word, God's Grace, and God's Sovereignty. It alone can give real meaning, spiritual meaning, to the budding universe, both magnificent and frightening, which modern science is revealing to us more and more. Thus, cosmic time does *not* have *cosmological* meaning. It has a *human* meaning. Its cosmological structure is maintained, but in the service of man. He is the real meaning of the cosmos. [68] But since anthropology does not resolve anything definitively, the meaning of cosmic time is *properly religious, Christological,* and *theological*. Finally, far from being a scientific implication or a philosophical necessity, temporal creation is a supernatural mystery — the first act in the history of salvation through Jesus Christ.

In order to specify the connection between cosmic time and eternity, we must say that time is linked to eternity for three

---

[67] *Adv. Haer.*, II, 22, 2 (*PG* 7, 781-782).

[68] For this reason St. Irenaeus said : Man receives " the beginning of his self-genesis. " *Adv. Haer.*, IV, 38, 1 (*PG* 7, 1105-1106).

reasons. First, it comes from eternity. The eternal idea fashions it. The eternal operation of creation, conservation, and Providence, gives it its reality and its dimensions. At every moment, it is rooted in an eternal act, and thus it accomplishes the eternal plan. The world is made for " the eternal happiness of the saints "; time is " determined " by that. It is a means of accomplishing the eternal plan of predestination. [69] And in the fulfillment of temporal creatures, it is a necessary condition which will disappear once their end is achieved. Finally, time itself is fulfilled in eternity. The world is made for the happiness of the elect, happiness which is a participation in God's eternity and communion with the Trinity through the Son. Like all the realities of this world, time will be fulfilled by disappearing into that which it has prepared : the merits of the saints and their eternal reward; their predestination henceforth accomplished for all eternity; and God's glory suffusing redeemed humanity forever. Thus, throughout its development time is rooted in eternity and finalized by it. And from moment to moment it is spanned by the eternal, creative, redemptive design. [70] Time does not exist apart from these connections with eternity. To understand time in its mysterious reality, one must comprehend the eternity which establishes it and opens it to its ends.

[69] In order to avoid a materialistic doctrine of predestination, one should read the precautions laid down by P. SERTILLANGES, *Saint Thomas d'Aquin* (Paris 1925), I, pp. 259-268.

[70] By affirming this we do not *deny* but rather *establish* the distinction between the natural and the supernatural. Natural finality and supernatural finality are radically distinct in themselves. But they involve each other as two aspects of the same *de facto* order. Supernatural finality demands a universe to transfigure, while natural finality anticipates and calls out for this transfiguration. Natural finality is ordered to supernatural finality. That is why there is only one order in the universe, a supernatural one, because of the divine intervention which actualizes it. Created time, then, has this twofold meaning and this twofold finality; but they are ordered to one another. If one considers the *ultimate meaning and full purpose* of the *temporal order*, cosmic time is salvation-time.

3

God and Human Time

God creates a universe orientated to its end and involved in a process of becoming. He measures this process by His creative intention, His Providence and His plan of predestination. And this measure is cosmic time as a whole — a transcendent, mysterious measure hidden in the bosom of God. Only the Father knows it, because His Omnipotence has determined it, and we are not permitted to know it here below (Acts 1, 7).

However, since time is rooted in eternity, a being *truly* possesses time only if it participates in this cosmic measure, only if somehow *it unites with the creative idea by a spiritual operation.* In other words, only a spiritual consciousness really possesses time. A tree develops in time. But it *does not* really possess time because it does not understand it, it does not have consciousness of it. It does not unite its past and future in its present, and it does not measure the rhythm of its development. Because it is only a *mens momentanea* it does not span seasons and years; the seasons and years succeed each other and are etched on it. It lives in time, but it does not live time because it lacks *the power to measure which makes time real.*

Man in Time

Let us remember that man exists in time *through his living body.* In this respect he is like other living beings. He appears one day and dies on another. His biological life hurtles him from birth to death, from one instant to the next. He is always beside himself. In Heidegger's sense of the term, he is an *ek-statikon.*

Furthermore, man recapitulates the obscure, lengthy rise of cosmic life. Countless millennia were needed to fashion him. Today scientists can unravel part of *the fantastic history which his body represents.* As Teilhard de Chardin once wrote : " The pentadactyl type dates from the Devonian period; triangular-shaped teeth and perhaps the developed brain go back to the Cretacean period; the fourth tubercle accessory to the upper molars appeared at the beginning of the Eocene period; his height was reached in the Miocene period; the chin appears only at the end of the Quaternary period. . . . Humanity as the apex of the Primates and *homo sapiens* as the apex of humanity are the product of a long process whose outline we are filling in today. " [1] Man " blossoms in the world as a fruit. "

Perhaps there is more to add. Perhaps *homo faber*, equipped with a " tool-making brain, " existed *before homo sapiens*, with his " reflective brain. " [2] The first already possessed what

[1] *La Paléontologie et l'apparition de l'Homme*, 1923. Reprinted in *Œuvres*, II, *L'apparition de l'homme*, p. 79.

[2] These views are presented by A. Leroi-Gourhan, " L'Illusion technologique, " *La Technique et l'Homme* (Paris 1960), pp. 65-74. If scientists reached agreement on such questions, the religious problem about man's origin would take on a different aspect.

paleontologists consider the characteristic attributes of man — "erect stance, small face, free usable hands"; "the tool-making stage" was reached immediately (Australo-Pithecanthropus) most likely about 600,000 years ago. But if "tool-making man had reached the end of his development, another type of man was beginning his evolution"; *homo sapiens* did not yet exist. The cranial structure still bore close resemblance to that of the Primates. When these traits disappeared and "the fossils have a cranial structure close to ours, " we already find religious and artistic manifestations of higher thought. And these fossils of *homo sapiens* go back 30,000 years before our time. A tool-making brain going back 600,000 years and a reflective brain going back 30,000 years — this is the history inscribed on our brain.

But we can observe directly the role of time in the formation of man. Not only must men pass from uterine life to birth and from infancy to old age through the well-known stages. For man *a slow process of maturation* is absolutely essential. The baby chimpanzee bears a striking resemblance to a human baby. But very quickly his forehead becomes slanted, his jaw protrudes toward his snout, and his behavior is canalized within three to seven years (at most). The human baby takes his time. [3] He must organize his fourteen billion brain cells and coordinate his nerves and his habits. As a result, man is still in a provisional state at the age of twenty. Time has preserved him.

And man *takes his time in coming to contemplate time*. It is no small paradox for the incarnate soul that the function of time is realized in time. The psychologists have attempted to observe this process in minute detail. [4] It takes many years to pass from the perception of time to a realization of it. "The child can have a temporal horizon, experience feelings of time and duration, before having an idea of time." [5] It only comes

[3] On all this cf. H. SEUNTJENS, " La Fonction temporelle dans le privilège humain, " *L'originalité biologique de l'homme* (Paris 1957), pp. 59-80.

[4] After the works of PIAGET, see P. FRAISSE, *Psychologie du Temps* (Paris 1957).

[5] *Op. cit.*, p. 147. See chap. 8 on " the notion of time. "

during adolescence. We need not emphasize the many experiences — corporal, spiritual, individual, and social — which
form a human being. Nor need we emphasize the contacts
with the universe, society, and various groups which are
necessary for mature development. They all lead us to *broach
the real problem* of human time.

Consciousness and Time

Man is meant to vitalize time because he is an *incarnate spirit*.
The human soul is created in time and eternity — *quasi in
horizonte existens aeternitatis et temporis*. [6] As the animating
principle of the body, it is linked to time. As a spiritual act,
it " depends on God, " as Ruysbroeck said; it transcends the
body, escaping the process of becoming and time. It is
measured by the duration proper to spirits. The ancients
carefully distinguished this duration from cosmic time and
called it *aevum*, [7] viewing it as a participation in eternity.

The paradoxical nature of the incarnate spirit is necessarily
revealed in its activity. All its spiritual operations — its
" I think " and " I will " — are affected. On the one hand,
its degree of perfection allows it to achieve a state of *actuality*
and *instantaneousness* in its operations. [8] Thus it transcends
the continuous time of the body through its spiritual motion;
and its operations have a plenitude which makes them
" fragments of eternity. " [9] But eternity means unity. These

[6] II *Contra Gent.*, 81.

[7] " The soul is measured by time insofar as its *esse* is united to the body;
but, insofar as it is a spiritual substance, it is measured by *aevum* " (*De Pot.*,
3, 10, 8. Cf. II *CG*, 68 and 81; III *CG*, 61).

[8] *ST*, Iª IIªᵉ, 113, 7, 4ᵐ and 5ᵐ; and 31, 2, 1ᵐ : " The acts of a free will
are *temporal only accidentally*, insofar as they are associated with corporeal
powers, insofar as the mind acquires knowledge through the senses, and the
will is affected by the passions. "

[9] J. MARITAIN, *Approaches to God* (New York : Harper, 1954) p. 77.

" fragments " find existence and meaning only in *connection with the unity* which is their foundation, from which they spring, and in which they reach fulfillment. Little by little they form the *unified continuity* and the spiritual duration proper to man. In this unity, permanence and becoming are inextricably linked, because the soul shares in the unity of eternity and imitates it. Its very being unifies its acts, giving them meaning and value. But, on the other hand, these operations are involved in time. Time is " connected " with them because they *involve* the activity of an animated body, the presence of material realities and the unfolding of a discursive activity. [10] The mystery of the incarnate spirit finds expression in a paradoxical linking of the temporal and the supra-temporal, to which we shall have to return.

Thus, an incarnate consciousness is a *consciousness in the world*. As Valéry said, " *In my combined activities I am body, mind, and world.* " Because consciousness goes beyond time, even while presupposing it, it can know, understand, and unify the universe. It can comprehend order, [11] that is, its purpose, its march through being, *and the time which measures it*. Although man is immersed in the cosmic, psychic, and biological activity of the universe, he does not merely *undergo* it like a star, a rose, or a dog; he knows it, lives it, and consciously

[10] St. THOMAS, *II Sent.*, d. 15, q. 1, a. 3; and I^a, 85, 4, 1^m : " The intellect is *above time* which measures the motion of corporeal things. But the numerous intelligible species cause a kind of *change in the operations of the intellect*, insofar as one operation precedes another. St. Augustine calls this change time when he says that God moves spiritual creatures through time " (cf. 5, 2^m). It is a kind of time because it *measures* the discrete spiritual operations of the soul (cf. *Quodlib.*, V, a. 5), but it is a discontinuous time. Number (measure) is *no longer quantitative* but an *abstract* principle of distinguishing and contrasting. Thus spiritual time directly measures instantaneous acts *as they really are*. It does not have to *abstract* them from a continuum. It implies a process of *formal succession* by distinct acts. These acts succeed one another but they do not continue one another. They derive their temporal value from the permanent unity of the act which produces them.

[11] Cf. III *CG*, 68.

65

measures it. Cosmic motion merely provides man with the starting point of his proper time. The *activity of the soul establishes the specific structure* of time by measuring motion. Time is a part of the realities which have their real foundation outside the soul, but only find their *full intelligibility* in the soul's activity. [12] The soul notes succession, [13] synthesizes it, and actualizes the *close-knit unity* of past, present, and future. Time is a *mixture* of the world and the soul. It is " subjectivity-objectivity, " [14] its objectivity coming from " the rhythm of phenomena united with the rhythm of consciousness. " [15] Time fully appears only *with consciousness*, because it alone can convert the future into the past through the present and *thus tabulate the march of the created universe.*

CONSCIOUSNESS TEMPORALIZED
AND PROVIDENT

This leads to *two* more conclusions which are equally important. The very fact that time is the living symbiosis of the soul and the world reminds us that consciousness is *not creative.* It is not the center of the world or time. It has only a partial hold on cosmic realities and time as God has made them. By this very fact the psyche is *limited* by cosmic realities, their opposition, and the rhythm of their various levels. There

[12] We know that St. Thomas viewed *universals*, such as humanity and truth, in this way (*I Sent.*, d. 19, q. 5, a. 2, sol).

[13] Regarding " this *measure by way of number* which is called time, " St. Thomas writes : " The *material* element of time (as it were), i.e., before and after, is based on motion; but the *formal* element is based on the measuring (numbering) operation of the soul. That is why the philosopher said that *if there were no souls, there would be no time* " (*I Sent.*, d. 19, a. 1). For a treatment of this last statement see *in* IV *Physic.*, *lect.* 23.

[14] F. ALQUIÉ, cited by DE WAELHENS, *Une Philosophie de l'Ambiguïté* (Louvain 1951), p. 303, note 3. Cf. J. F. LYOTARD, *La Phénoménologie* (Paris 1954) : " Time is *subjective* because it has a meaning, and it has a meaning because we are time.... But time is also *objective* because we do not create it by an act of the mind which is independent of it. Time, like the world, is always something given *already* " (p. 100).

[15] L. LAVELLE, *Du Temps et de l'Éternité*, p. 235.

is always a " world already there, " and the psyche must work with it. It does not invent days, months, and years. It does not cause the growth and the dissolution of the body. It does not even create the flood of images, emotions, and ideas which pass through it constantly and polarize it. It *is embodied* in all that and its " existence " is truly " kneaded from the same dough " [16] as the world itself. But the psyche does invent its own reaction to all this. It forms its reaction from within and *actualizes itself* in the universe.

But there is more to be said. Although man is not a creating psyche, neither is he hurtled through the world on a senseless journey. Like the Creator's thought, his *psyche* is also *provident*. God is Providence. He determines the proper end of creatures, allows them to move towards it, and guides them through time. Now men are spiritual creatures. God *wills* them *for their own sake*, as ends in themselves. And He wills that they be *their own providence*. [17] They are to freely determine their aims, choose their own means, discover His plan and fulfill it in obedience and love. [18] Man alone *inaugurates time for himself*. He is his own providence, because he must choose his distant end and fulfill it. But he can do it only through time. God inaugurates cosmic time that it may reach its end; but by His generosity man, too, inaugurates cosmic time for his own fulfillment. In an absolutely unique way, God *gives time to man*, more than to any other creature, so that " the wisdom of his own hands " may *freely* fashion *the means of his fulfillment*. How much respect God has for man — *cum reverentia disponis nos, Domine!* [19] Thus the psyche is *in time*, and this is a sign of its

[16] P. RICOEUR, *Philosophie de la Volonté*, I, p. 53.

[17] *De Ver.*, V, 5 and 7.

[18] M. BLONDEL has strongly emphasized this point; and G. BERGER had it in mind when, in 1957, he founded the " Centre international de Prospective. " This science does not aim to predict or to prophesy, but to construct. Berger has written : " Yesterday the goals of man were elementary ones, and the means at his disposal were few and frail. *Today there are abundant means, but we must discover and order the goals.* "

[19] Sap 12, 18, cited in *De Ver.*, V, 5, c.

dependence and its finiteness. The psyche is *provident*, and this is a sign of its grandeur and its liberty. But again, the source and the purpose of time are only explained by eternity. The human psyche has various *levels* of activity, according to its *intentions*. Hence man *discovers* and *lives* on varying levels of meaning, grandeur, richness, and genuineness in the fullness of time which God has established. It seems that we must distinguish at least two basic levels. Insofar as man is a psyche living in the world, he calls attention to time as a reality. He *structures* time. Insofar as man is a free psyche living in God's presence, he confers spiritual *meaning* on time.

The Structure of Human Time

As a *psyche living in the world*, man inaugurates cosmic time with all its levels. The psyche spotlights the reality of time by noting succession and thus constructing past and future through the present.

THE FIRST STEP

Let us take the most obvious example. [20] We perceive bodily motion only by grasping it in an interior operation which *gives unity* and temporal continuity to the successive stages of observed motions. The various stages succeed each other without being intermingled or confused, and each " stage " exists only *in relation to* the other stages. Thus, at each moment I *envelop* my present state in a space and time which include all my other states.

In short, time is *always* constituted and structured *by the present*. Man lives only in the present, yet " every present

[20] Cf. J. Maréchal, *Le Point de départ de la métaphysique*, cahier V, pp. 111-112. It is *the most glaring* example but scarcely the *clearest* one. Cf. Guitton, *Existence temporelle* (Paris 1950), p. 108.

is a point of time which evokes an awareness of all time-points. " [21] *In the present* I see the future as my own potentiality, and the past as my own accomplishment. In the present it is now living, the psyche measures the present lost and the present awaited, the present remembered and the present expected. And this *measurement* is time. We are always in the present; we never leave it. [22] St. Augustine said that, strictly speaking, there are not three times, but only one time : the present; but it is a present now of past things, now of present things, and now of future things. [23] The present is, then, the very ground of existence through which past and future are actualized and time is engendered. In short, time is only " a passing through different kinds of present. " [24] And so it is futile to try to picture time as a relationship *between different* successive *things*, events arranged *linearly* and arising irreversibly without past or future. [25] We can only understand time by focusing on the *same reality* as it *moves* from the future to the past, belonging to each in turn and obeying the *command* to actualize its potentialities to the fullest. This movement, this command, is time.

However, the psyche does *not first* measure time *in things*. Rather, it measures time *in itself* through its measuring activity

[21] M. MERLEAU-PONTY, *Phénoménologie de la Perception*, p. 83.

[22] RICOEUR, *Philosophie de la Volonté*, p. 143 : " We are always in today. It is always now. "

[23] See St. AUGUSTINE, 11, 20; *Confessions* (New York : Sheed & Ward, 1943), p. 276.

[24] LAVELLE, *op. cit.*, p. 221.

[25] *Ibid.*, pp. 143-145. Kant had already made the straight line " the external representation of time " so that " time is nothing for us except represented by a line. " These are the words of Jacques HAVET, *Kant et le Problème du Temps* (Paris 1947), pp. 67-71. He realizes that the Kantian system can " have real deep meaning " only if the idealistic concept of a passive, homogeneous time is joined to " a concept of a real time, the time stemming from a pure act (constituent or practical) of consciousness " (p. 225). GUYAU probably provides the most striking example of a deliberately spatialized concept of time. Cf. *La Genèse de l'idée de temps*, pp. 71-72, cited by G. GUSDORF, *Mémoire et Personne* (Paris 1953), II, p. 170.

— " *In te, anime meus, tempora metior.* " [26] The psyche arranges
its activities in a present which looks to the future and will soon
become the past.   And it does this arranging through its
psychism, [27] its own organized temporal parts, its " members
in time "; through its animated body, its organism in space
and time; and through the complex relations which its spatio-
temporal members have with the universe of space and time.
Man lives in time, because his measuring psyche opens him to
the world in a present which moves continually from the
future to the past.

TIME AS A DIMENSION OF EXISTENCE

This first step in structuring time is *spontaneous* and *necessary*,
because it outlines the existential course of created things.
It is a fundamental activity of a living psyche.   The psyche must
structure time because it is linked to the development and the
reciprocal relations not only of its own interior world but also of
the body and the world outside.   It *must* spotlight time because
time " wells up " from it. [28] This is a *level of time* more
profound than that of free acts.   It is a basic framework of
activity, a " fundamental situation " [29] of human existence.
Furthermore, this necessary temporality always stands out on
an *extremely complex temporal horizon* : astral time, involving
the periodic motion of the various stars; physiological time,
measured by the reversible rhythm of some organs and the
irreversible movement of tissues and fluids; sociological time,
inscribing on cosmic rhythms the cultural rhythms of labor
and festival, work and rest, and measuring time by clocks,
calendars, and social conventions.   *Through these surrounding
kinds of time* the psyche deploys its own time which always

[26] St. AUGUSTINE, *Conf.* XI, 36.

[27] Cf. STRASSER, *Le Problème de l'âme* (Louvain 1955), pp. 204 ff.

[28] MERLEAU-PONTY, *op. cit.*, p. 488.

[29] RICOEUR, *op. cit.*, pp. 50-51.

70

depends on its temporal " situation " and remains unique and intangible amid the most overwhelming circumstances. [30]

The *form* of this psyche could be characterized in various ways. Phenomenologically, it is protension, presentification and retention; psychologically, it is expectation, presence and memory; metaphysically, it is possibility, actualization and fulfillment. But this is a view of primitive time in its pure form and its pure development. And such a time does not exist except in certain pathological conditions. Time is always conditioned by an intention. It has content. Yet, *this need to structure time* makes us feel once again our dependence, our lack of being, our contingency, and our finiteness.

Although it is true that this structuring of time always occurs in the present, it does not follow that the present is only a point and a limit. The present has a *duration,* but this duration *is measured by the psyche.* [31] The psyche sets it, limits it and places it in relation to others. It runs before and behind it, inserting it in ever longer time-segments which are still linked together by a whole series of intentions and meanings. There is no time for man except *through the activity of the psyche* which establishes it in its relationship with the motion of the entire universe — the motion of things, beings, persons, and even the psyche itself.

But this duration is *not uniform.* It does not flow away in a vague continuity like the waters of a sluggish river. It is *structured.* It does not have only limits, a starting point and an end. It also has breaks, fresh starts, and varying levels of significance. It is shot through with " important moments. " Insofar as man is involved in cosmic becoming, these moments can be *forced* on him with all their weight. A mother's death, a prisoner's return, a business failure, a national catastrophe —

[30] The soul " is a spirit which forms itself and its self-awareness by establishing a relationship with the world and gaining control over the relationship which the world imposes on it. " J. M. POHIER, *Psychologies modernes et anthropologie chrétienne, RSPT,* 1960 (1), pp. 51 ff.

[31] Cf. the interesting analysis of elan and support by J. NOGUÉ in " Ordre et Durée, " *Revue Philos.* (July 1932).

all of these can end one time-period and begin another. They can *mark* a whole life and force a man to start a new kind of time. But, insofar as man writes his own history in the history of the cosmos, these significant moments can *spring from his own free action*. The choice of a career, marriage vows, faithfulness to a vocation, an act of vengeance or pardon — all of these undoubtedly begin a new period of time for man and introduce a new meaning and rhythm in his unfolding existence. Man *creates himself* and *his own time* by such decisions, which may take a lifetime to develop. These *interruptions* are an *essential* part of human time, [32] and they determine the basic rhythm of an individual's existence.

If the psyche *establishes* time, it does so *in order to develop itself* in two ways. First, it looks toward the future and its possibilities, realizes them in the present, and then integrates them into the past. It passes from possibility to accomplishment through the here and now. Secondly, because the psyche is a psyche in the world, it confronts the motion of other beings and compares its rhythm to theirs. Time is the direct *confrontation* and *measure* of these rhythms. For man, the time of things arises when the psyche measures it against its own time. The process of becoming (of things) and the duration (of the psyche) form time by their *interrelationship* which *the psyche has brought about*. Thus, " I do not pass mechanically through a time-continuum, rather *I make time a dimension of my existence.* " [33]

THE ROLE OF THE SPIRITUAL EGO

However, the psyche establishes time *in an act* which *transcends time*. Time is rooted in eternity. The psyche can structure time only if *something escapes time* and unifies past, present, and future. There must be something which *perceives* time,

[32] This is one theme of G. BACHELARD, *La Dialectique de la Durée* (Paris 1950).

[33] STRASSER, *op. cit.*, p. 215 (underlined in the text).

dominates and *measures* it, and thus structures it. This is the role of the *spiritual ego*. [34]

The spiritual ego cannot be depicted or imagined. It is not the familar self-image which we invent. It is the primordial source *from which* my being and my action *spring, my inexpressible center*, the living, subsistent, unifying principle of my existence. It can only be described as the point where the awareness of motion and self-presence converge.

This act *takes place continuously*. It is prolonged in the world through the body it animates. It gives the surrounding realities a share in its own actualization. *Time, too, is an instrument of its progressive actualization.* The spiritual ego is actualized by the animated body in limited time-segments, in the upheaval of important moments, and in a hierarchical series of temporal realities. Existence in time and actualization are one.

But, on the other hand, this spiritual being *always transcends* the finite circumstances in which it is involved. By making them present, it gives reality to the significant moments of its duration, links them in time, and integrates them into an ever expanding pattern of hierarchical time-sequences. It establishes the " *awareness of unity in diversity* " [35] which constitutes existence in time. Through it, in the words of Scheler, " the whole structure and plan of our life and person are present in each discrete moment. For each instant, each discrete point in time involves the living present, the past lived, and the future; and these experiences are collected in our perception, memory, and attention. " [36] The act in which the spirit *unfolds* time is also the act in which it *dominates* and *transcends* it. " Because the spirit in act creates time, it itself is not temporal.... The thought of time triumphs over time. " [37]

---

[34] Cf. STRASSER, *op. cit.*, étude 6 (which inspired our discussion). Also the refreshing text of A. VALENSIN, in *Balthazar* (Paris, n.d.), pp. 1-34.

[35] DE WAELHENS, *op. cit.*, p. 292.

[36] M. SCHELER in *Le Sens de la Souffrance*, p. 84.

[37] LAVELLE, *op. cit.*, pp. 72-73.

The necessary role of the supra-temporal *ego* in establishing and unfolding time should not surprise us. If time is rooted in eternity, if eternity is its transcendent cause, we must participate in eternity to inaugurate time. And the spiritual ego *is* this participation in eternity. Its activity is the activity of a spirit which is *not immersed* in matter and maintains its unity by remaining in direct contact with the Creator's Spirit. In man there is a *supra-temporal point* which inaugurates time. The psyche involves itself in time without losing its unity, because, in its living source, it goes beyond time and merges with the eternal act. I exist in time through my animated body. But I exist outside time through my spirit. Because my spirit shares in the eternal Spirit, time exists *in me* and *through me*.

Once again we encounter the *direct source* of time. Time — of the psyche and of the world — exists only for a spirit *rooted in eternity* and *vivified by it*. The embodied psyche inaugurates time only because it is open to eternity and can " imitate " the Creator's activity to some degree. Because its center *merges* with eternity, it *develops* in time without ever disappearing completely. [38]

Thus we see that there must be a *plenitude of spiritual activity* if *the genuine structure* of even the most " uncomplicated " kind of time is to be *strongly maintained*. On the level of cosmic existence, the psyche must organize the various time-levels. [39] At every moment it must establish and support the temporal structure with all its implications, in order to develop its " worldly " activity properly. The psyche must be alert and healthy. Its mind, its emotions, and its social relationships must be well balanced. If the *action* of the psyche *falters*, time *becomes tangled* and *slips away*. Nothing

[38] Only the poets can make us feel the truths which the mind expresses so feebly. The link between time and eternity is expressed most strikingly by Claudel in the *Cantate à Trois Voix* (in spite of its " rather allusive " quality). The *Trio* interweave time and eternity in a rhythmic music which is irresistible.

[39] Of course, the temporal function is slowly and arduously constructed in time. On its origin and growth, see the thesis of P. FRAISSE, *op. cit.*

remains but *shreds*, scattered fragments which come into conflict with each other in a terrible confusion. Time becomes pathological. [40]

The Meaning of Human Time

Man freely confers meaning and spiritual depth on time.

TIME AND LIBERTY

Time is given to a human being so that he may freely fulfill himself. For the individual, time is the means of freely perfecting himself by personal activity. It opens up this possibility and this personal obligation. It opens up his vocation. *In time* man *responds* to *eternity* and *must* make himself *eternal*. Time is the battleground of liberty and spiritual activity. It contains the great risk in human existence.

The meaning and the efficacy of *my time* depends on my liberty. Time is *ambivalent*. On the one hand, it is destructive. It throws everything, man included, back into the past, to absence and non-being. On the other hand, it is creative. It brings the future to realization, makes the past a rich synthesis, and perfects beings. But *my liberty determines which is to happen*. My liberty gives *my time* its spiritual, moral, or psychological *value*. If liberty is simply caught up in the passage of time and the weight of the past, the psyche renounces its task, dries up or disintegrates, and the being falls into nothingness. If liberty takes hold of its past and its future, the psyche grows, coordinates and spiritualizes itself, and the being perfects itself. Time is either absence or presence,

[40] So well studied by Minkowski (cf. " Le Temps en Psychopathologie, " *Recherches Philos.*, II, pp. 235 ff.; also, "Problème du Temps vu par un psychopathologue, " *Bulletin Soc. Française et Philos.* (Oct.-Dec. 1957). See also J. F. Cathalan, " Angoisse et Durée, " *Archives de Phil.*, XIX (Jan. & April 1956). We are well aware of Dostoevsky's extraordinary analysis of time and the epileptic (cf. e.g., *The Idiot*, part. 2, chap. 5).

emptiness or plenitude, bauble or treasure, despair or hope. But all this is determined not by *nature*, but by man's *liberty*.

Thus time is the *ever-present possibility* of *renewing* our existence and giving it fresh meaning. The past is valuable insofar as it has been integrated into our being and has become a part of us. The future is valuable insofar as it can be integrated into our being and can renew it. The present — in which we now live — is valuable because it can both anticipate and actualize the future and *take hold of our past to give it new meaning* and transform it into an entirely different future. Scheler points this out beautifully in *Repentir et Renaissance.* [41] Our liberty determines the whole meaning and value of our life. It can always reappraise our life, imbue it with new purpose, and transform it, by conferring a new meaning on it. In one sense, nothing is ever finished. Remorse, through the bankruptcy of our liberty, remains fixed on a terrible past; but repentance is the liberative activity of the psyche, an " effective intervention " in our past. It gives the past new meaning and value. It literally makes the penitent a new man. We are *really* the *free creators* of our *spiritual existence* because *through our present* we are *masters* of the *personal significance* of our life. But this " sense-giving " activity of the psyche is extremely complex. And so we must expand on it.

THE VARIOUS LEVELS OF MEANING

Man can give various meanings to the time he lives. The time-structuring activity of the psyche is never exercised in a vacuum. It always has content. That is why we have already indicated that the basic primordial structuring of time is *abstracted* and *extracted* from the *entire* structuring activity of consciousness. It is always influenced and utilized by a *personal intention*. This intention implies a connection between the psyche's activity and the world's process of becoming. Thus it can inaugurate within human time a *series of temporal*

---

[41] In *Sens de la Souffrance*, pp. 85 ff.

76

levels which are perfectly valid but only relative and incompiete, because they do not embody *explicitly* and *deliberately* the full meaning of time, the last end of man.

Human society with its sociological units, its collective rhythms and its socially transmitted and shared experiences, structures its own time. So does science, sharpening natural human perception and drawing data from phenomena rigorously tested. Its own techniques structure its time and affect or transform the rhythm of human life. Art too — creative or contemplative — has its own time. It penetrates deeply into the human universe and provides man with an extraordinary permanence and extra-temporal communion. The moral conscience introduces its own norms and values, subsuming and regulating the other rhythms of human action. Religious belief structures time through its personal absolute, its sacred universe, its connection with eternity, its personal and social implications. All these and many others indicate the *multi-dimensional structure* of human existence. [42] But the principal question remains. What is the *ultimate, definitive* meaning that man can and must give to time ? This is the fundamental, decisive choice for spiritual liberty.

THE FUNDAMENTAL CHOICE AND THE MEANING OF TIME

The unique gravity of the free act lies in the fact that its participation in eternity enables it to establish the *full meaning* of time by *linking* it with eternity or *disassociating* it from

---

[42] This point has been underlined clearly and forcefully by A. DONDEYNE in " L'historicité dans la Philosophie contemporaine, " *Rev. Phil. de Louvain*, (Feb.-Aug. 1956). He reminds us (as does HEIDEGGER, *Kant et le Problème de la Métaphysique*) that Kant had already made clear the various levels of the human being by his three questions (pp. 468 ff.) : (1) What *can I* know ? (2) What *must I* do ? (3) What *can I* hope for ? Man fulfills himself only after he passes beyond the plane of physical nature and the plane of reconciled human liberty to reach, by " metaphysical hope, " the synthesis of " faith in a holy, sovereign God. "

eternity. [43] It is *the* choice for human liberty and undoubtedly the deepest significance of human " historicity, " to use Jaspers' term. In his view, when man determines his place in history, " he surveys all the means at his disposal. For he is aware of one thing — *the eternal is determined in time.* " To emphasize the " importance of liberty developing in time, " Jaspers utilizes the notion of " historicity. " It is " man's *ability to effect and live the fusion of time and eternity.* " [44] In the last analysis, there are only two possibilities. Man may choose to make cosmic time his absolute and measure his life as if it were Existence itself, as if it were eternity. Or he may integrate cosmic time with the Absolute and measure his life *as it is measured by eternity*.

In the first instance, man makes cosmic time self-sufficient. It is linked only to itself and the world. Human destiny is encased in it. Thus man inaugurates *a time which extends to infinity*. He measures cosmic becoming only to be encased in it. He directs it only to be swept into it. He seeks total self-fulfillment in it because he seeks eternity concentrated in his use of time. But this makes him a prisoner of time. For time " gushes " from his psyche and he cannot stop it. And if he attempts to integrate the various levels of his time or his own duration, he is caught — ensnared — in the essential activity of his time-structuring psyche. And his spiritual *ego* — without which

[43] On this point see the interesting views of J. GUITTON, *Justification du Temps* (Paris 1944). Christian thought has always pointed out how man chooses to become temporal or eternal by directing himself towards temporal or eternal realities. Cf. St. THOMAS, 3 *CG*, 61, *Amplius*.

[44] K. JASPERS, " Letter to Bultmann, " *La Table Ronde* (Nov. 1956), p. 144. We can accept Jasper's formulations without adopting his punctualism. On the continuing dispute between the disciples of Bultmann and Jaspers, see X. TILLIETTE, " Jaspertiana, " *Archives de Philosophie* (April-June 1959), pp. 280-290. Regarding God's design in history NIE very justly remarks : " Such a design presupposes that *human time* is a time of *spiritual maturation*, in which the *goal* is somehow present in our *movement* towards it. Human time is viewed as the time of an organizing and unfolding liberty. *Eternity* is both *in* time and *at the end* of time. " — " Le sens de l'Histoire, " *RSR* (1958), p. 74.

there is no time — is reduced to a *vague meaningless process of synthesizing* these evanescent time-structuring efforts.

Cosmic time imposes on man its limits, its dissipation, and its endless succession. He is enslaved by it — whether it be astral time (and modern man often follows the superstition of the ancients), the time of civilization and " progress, " [45] or the time of an individual living according to reason, emotion, or pragmatic considerations. [46] When cosmic time, in any form, is viewed as *self-sufficient*, it becomes an illusion, a prison, a destructive instrument, a death-dealing time; and man himself becomes *a being marked for death*. In the inexorable journey of the future toward the past, death is always present. At every moment it casts its shadow and draws nearer. When this spiritual choice is made consciously and carried out, we are faced with a *spiritual time that is distorted*. It is spiritual, because it is established by the act of a spirit which has freely set itself against God. It is distorted, because it has been inaugurated by a refusal which has severed it from its source, eternity. For the philosopher, it is a time for death — a time

[45] On this point see Msgr. NÉDONCELLE, " L'Indigence spirituelle du devenir collectif et de son histoire, " *Recherches et Débats* (" Philosophie de l'Histoire "), (Oct. 1956), pp. 122-140.

[46] Rousseau lived and wrote vividly about such an emotional experience (cf. *Rêveries du Promeneur solitaire*, Ve Promenade). He also sought eternity in a privileged instant. (It does not matter here that later he changed his interpretation of this experience). He searched outside " the constant flux of things and the uncertainties of a long life " and found " perfect happiness " in " reverie, " the simple *feeling of existence* itself, the state in which the soul finds a solid resting-place to *gather up its being* without having to recall the past or straddle the future; *where time means nothing* and the present subsists without duration, succession or any feeling of privation, without pleasure or pain, desire or fear; where the *feeling of our existence alone* suffuses everything. " Here he wrote the well-known phrase : " What does one enjoy in such a state ? *Nothing outside oneself*, nothing except oneself and one's very existence. As long as this state lasts, *man is self-sufficient, even as God*. " The case of Proust is so obvious that it does not need comment. On this problem in literature see G. POULET, *Études sur le Temps Humain* (Paris 1949). And one genre of the contemporary novel seeks to study this specific point.

for man who is " too much " in the world. For the believer, it is the time of sin, condemnation, and the progressive destruction of being.

THE TRAGEDY OF DISTORTED TIME

Distorted time can be marked by *all sorts of symptoms* — boredom, disgust, despair. Man abandons himself to sterile repetition and nausea, and slips toward the " black pit. " It is a time of fierce lust, when man wants to enjoy each instant as an atom of eternity. But it escapes him always. Or it is a time for savage domination. Man wants to harness the world and control it for his purpose. But time is always too short. It is a time of brutish or sinful revolt. Man disintegrates in the inexorable rhythm of the passing days. In any case, it is always cosmic time, because that is the only time we have. But its purpose has been distorted by *a rejection of God and His time*, cosmic time *as* the time of salvation through Jesus Christ.

By this radical choice man can integrate the individual time-structures, but the result is *negative*. He deprives them of their fundamental value and their real meaning. He has voluntarily separated them from eternity which alone can introduce them to the plenitude of existence and time. These time-levels are relative, but man can make them absolute. They are incomplete and conditional. When man chooses to make them definitive, infinite, and eternal, *they collapse*. As long as this destructive choice remains fixed, the time-structures of society, science, art, ethics, and even religion, are *corroded from within*. They are burdened with promises which cannot be kept.

From this viewpoint, original sin is the *distortion* of time. It is a part of the psyche as God sees it, and therefore, it is a part of the psyche as it exists in the world. It is the *privation* of meaning and value at the heart of human existence. It affects the whole human psyche insofar as it is involved in a supernatural history where man has been called and has fallen.

80

It affects the psyche insofar as it is separated from the time of salvation and eternity, because it is *separated from Jesus Christ* through whom the salvation-history is inaugurated. Original sin involves the psyche in the *tainted measure of a universe* without God and against God. Because this measure is connatural to fallen man, it envelops him, drags him down, and orientates him toward sin and nothingness. If the human psyche is not detached from this cursed world by faith and baptism, if it willfully rejects Christ's saving grace (and here there is a real divine mystery), it is submerged in " vanity, " empty pleasure, misery and senselessness. There it lives and there it is lost. This is the essence of sin. Man chooses to consider himself the master of his God-given time and the measurer of temporal existence. He rejects his true existence and his real end. *To set time against eternity* is to empty it of its profound meaning and substance, to make it an instrument of *annihilation*. [47]

But man is not made for this foolishness. His vocation is *to give meaning to cosmic time* by welcoming it, through faith, *as the time of salvation*. Because the salvation-period is rooted in Jesus Christ, man can fulfill his vocation in time and eternity only through Him. This is the heart of our present study — Jesus Christ and Time. Time is the necessary prerequisite if man is to perfect himself. In time man is born, grows, chooses, and either succeeds or fails for all eternity. Man only uses time. Time is opened and closed *for him, not by him*. He does not know the *personal measure* of his own existence. [48] Time passes and he is either lost or saved. All this indicates that there is a *tragic* element about existence in time. Only Christ's grace can support it and transform it through the virtue which truly belongs in time — Hope.

---

[47] St. Augustine strongly emphasized this aspect of time. Several essential themes can be found in L. Boros, " Les catégories de la Temporalité chez saint Augustin, " *Arch. de Phil.* (July 1958), pp. 324 ff.

[48] Man may *want* to be the sovereign measurer of his own existence and to end it himself. This is the most radical choice of self-deification and revolt and the most extreme perversion of the meaning of time. This alternative is the essence of Dostoevsky's *The Possessed*.

II

Christ and Time

4

The Word and Time

By creation, God inaugurates the time of salvation for the world, but the world does not know it. When God reveals His plan, man becomes aware of salvation-time, but only in an obscure, limited, human way. The mystery of time attains its full stature and meaning only when it is grasped in its totality by a human mind. God accomplishes this through Jesus Christ; but only because Christ is the Word Incarnate. Therefore, we must first attempt to understand the relationship between creation and the Word.

The Word as Creator

God created everything by His Word, which is His inner speech, His own thought. This doctrine is presented clearly in the New Testament and is normally applied to Christ Himself. Here are a few texts.

St. Paul, [1] whose thought is concrete and does not allude to " natures " in Christ, fixes his gaze on this unique Being, Christ made flesh and glorified, the Lord " made of a woman, " (Gal 4, 4) who is always the Son of God Himself (Rom 8, 32). God the Father is the Creator, but through His Son, Jesus Christ : " There is but one God, the Father, *of whom* are all things, and we *unto* him; and one Lord Jesus Christ, *by whom* are all things, and we *by him* " (1 Cor 8, 6). The Epistle to the Colossians clarifies and expands this theme : " Who is the image of the invisible God, the firstborn of every creature ? For *in him* were all things created in heaven and on earth, visible and invisible, whether thrones, or dominations, or principalities, or powers : all things were created *by him* and *in him* " (Col 1, 15-17). The Epistle to the Hebrews [2] affirms that " God hath spoken to us by his Son... *by whom* also he made the world; who is the brightness of his glory, and the figure of his substance, upholding all things by the word of his power " (Heb 1, 2-3). Finally, the Prologue of St. John's Gospel reveals the role of the Word as such : " All things were made by him : and without him was made nothing that was made. In him was life, and the life was the light of men... He was in the world, and the world was made by him " (Jn 1, 3-4.10). [3]

The liturgy underlines Christ's role as creator in magnificent strokes. In the Credo the faithful chant : " the one Lord Jesus Christ, born of the Father before all ages, " and, " through whom all things were made. " The Canon ends with the

---

[1] On St. Paul's view of Christ as Creator see, among others, L. CERFAUX, *Christ in the Theology of St. Paul* (New York : Herder & Herder, 1959); A. FEUILLET, " L'Église Plérôme du Christ (in Eph 1, 23), " *NRT* (May 1956), pp. 463-470; P. BENOIT, " Corps, Tête et Plérôme dans les Épîtres de la captivité, " *RB* (Jan. 1956), pp. 5 ff. (" Christ is the *eikôn* in whom, by whom, and for whom all things have been created, " p. 34.)

[2] Cf. C. SPICQ, *Épître aux Hébreux* (Études Bibliques), II, pp. 9-10.

[3] Cf. the reflections of P. BOISMARD, *Le Prologue de saint Jean* (Paris : Cerf, 1953). " Everything that exists came by and in the Word, " and " in the Word all created things acquire life " (23).

86

solemn proclamation : " Christ, our Lord, through whom You create all good things. " The Advent liturgy invokes Jesus as Creator and Redeemer :

> *Creator alme siderum*
> *Aeterna lux credentium*
> *Jesu Redemptor omnium.*

One has only to open the Breviary to Matins to read, in the Lenten hymn :

> Christ, King and Creator of all the ages;

in the hymn of the Passion :

> When the fullness of sacred time had come,
> The Son, the Creator of the world, was sent from His Father's side;

and in the hymn for Paschaltime :

> Eternal King of the elect, Creator of all things,
> Workman since the foundation of the world,
> You who imprinted the trace of your visage on Adam.

and in the blessing of the paschal candle we say :

> Christ, yesterday and today!
> The Beginning and the End, the alpha and the omega!
> His are the centuries and the ages,
> To Him be glory and sovereignty
> Forever and ever! Amen.

Let us consider Time in the light of this fact : through His Word God conceives of and creates Time. The Word is the eternal utterance through which the Father apprehends Himself and subsequently conceives of and creates the world. [4] The Word expresses the Father directly and perfectly, and by that

---

[4] *De Ver.*, IV, 4-8; *ST*, I[a], 34, 3c.

very fact He expresses and actualizes the creatures conceived by the Father. He is, as St. Paul affirms, " the creative and re-creative *eikôn.* " [5] All creatures, therefore, exist first in the Word. [6] Because the Father produces all creatures through His eternal Word, they find their " image " in that unique Word; and this image is the source of their intelligibility, [7] their existence, and their activity. In this sense [8] they have a more real existence in the Word than in themselves, since their image in the Word is the cause of their reality and their operations. [9] To express the same idea in Johannine terms, creatures are " life " and " light " in the Word, since their eternal image is the source of their existence and their intelligibility.

Consequently, every movement of creatures toward their end, every motion of the universe toward its final end, every measure of this movement, every moment of time, is present, expressed and actualized in the Word, the perfect image of the Father and of His thought. Since time is a constitutive dimension of the universe, *God creates time and gives it to the world through His Word.* Even more, He creates the universe and time for His Word, because the Word " does not proceed from Him as if ordered to an end, but rather as the end of all things. " [10] The world is merely a multiple and continuous

---

[5] P. BENOIT, *op. cit.,* p. 20.

[6] God ponders creatures (*Ver.,* 3, 2) through His essence and sees them as so many frail imitations of His essence. The " idea " of a creature, therefore, is the divine essence insofar as the creature is related to it. Because these relationships are numerous there are many " ideas "; but since God " utters " them in the Word which expresses Himself perfectly, there is only one Word, perfectly simple and infinitely rich, which expresses the Father and the totality of creative " ideas. " Thus, *creatura in Deo est creatrix essentia.* (Cf. St. Thomas explaining St. Augustine, *in Joann.,* I, lect. 3, note 3.)

[7] *Pot.,* 3, 15, c.

[8] *Ver.,* 4, 6.

[9] *Ver.,* 4, 8, c.

[10] *Pot.,* 3, 15, c.

refraction of this unique Word, and time is only the means by which the universe, created by and for the Word, is realized. For these two reasons, cosmic time is completely enveloped in the eternal Word, in the transcendent simplicity and eternity of the Father's Word. If cosmic time has both a natural and a supernatural meaning, its full meaning is expressed in the Word and completely actualized by the Word. Thus time is completely ordered to manifest and to actualize the riches of the creative thought expressed in His Word. The Word is the source, the center, and the end of the created universe; He is the Unique Word, " by whom all things subsist, " [11] and from whom spring these " divine words " called creatures. Cosmic time belongs to the Word, because by means of time the Word-Image imbues all the " words " uttered in their proper turn with the richness of the divine thought. And in time the Word-Creator unites under His sovereignty the infinite multiplicity of a creation which is still in the process of becoming.

The Incarnation as a Fulfillment

The entrance of a man into the world is always a fulfillment because he develops at a given point in the history of human generations. It is an upheaval because he appears as an individual being who will never be seen again. It is a source of activity because his being is expressed and fulfilled in actions. [12] Since the Word willed to become a real man, we find these three characteristics in the Incarnation; but they are transformed and assume an infinite dimension because this man is really God.

[11] Col 1, 17. Cf. FEUILLET, op. cit., pp. 469-470. (The phrase goes back to Wisdom and through it to the Stoics and Plato.)

[12] Fulfillment underlines the continuity involved; upheaval underlines the discontinuity. Human activity contains these two characteristics : a constant meaning in the process of becoming, and sudden unforeseen but inevitable eruptions.

89

The subsequent pages are devoted to the implications of this fact.

God wills the Incarnation in the time of His eternal Word; *then, He recapitulates all things, and time itself, in the Incarnate Word, Our Lord Jesus Christ.* The Incarnation is, as the elders said, " the miracle of miracles, " in which all of God's wonderful works are brought to fulfillment. There is no *necessary* link between creation by the Word and fulfillment of this creation in the Word Incarnate. Between these two realities there is a gap which divine love freely chose to cross. When the Word becomes flesh, a center of human existence becomes, in a strict sense, the center of existence for the universe itself and the center of time. But it is inconceivable that the Word would appear in a world which did not expect Him and which was not prepared for His coming. So God *in human fashion* provided a lengthy preparation for the awesome coming of His Son. Notice that the entire time of the Old Testament is a time of preparation for Christ.

A. If we consider this period in terms of Christ, [13] it will appear to us as *dotted* by *meaningful moments*, " appointed times, " *kairoi.* The continuity of the salvation-period is regulated by divine interventions which mark the progress of the divine plan and the temporal stages of this progess. The " Mirabilia " of God are periodic irruptions which are always unforeseen and unique. They are new creative moments in the one continuous salvation-period. That period, like ours, is a period of human time; but it is a period whose meaning and worth are properly divine. It is the time of God

[13] Here we are concerned with the *total meaning* of this time. An exegesis of time as viewed in the Old Testament would do us little good. Undoubtedly it would show that the Hebrews saw a different meaning from ours in the present, past, and future (cf. G. Pidoux, " A propos de la notion biblique du temps, " *Rev. de Théol. et de Phil.* (1952, II), pp. 120-125); that there are not one, but several notions of time in the Old Testament; that the time of the patriarchs is not the time of the prophets and that the latter is not the time of the sapiential writers. There are some interesting suggestions in A. Neher, *L'essence du Prophétisme* (Paris : P.U.F., 1955), passim.

the Savior. We can trace the principal stages of this development.

Creation, as we have seen, is the first act of salvation; it culminates in Adam. But Adam is a type and a foreshadowing of Christ; he is the first Adam announcing the Second. Original sin marks the breaking of the first covenant, but not the end of the salvation-period. The tragic story of the fall closes with a mysterious promise. The deluge is at once the first judgment and the first renewal of the Covenant through a pledge of cosmic order; it is also the proclamation of judgment by water, which will be baptism, and of a perfect covenant in Jesus Christ, the true Noe. With Abraham God inaugurates the Promise in the strict sense, the definitive covenant, which man accepts on Faith and which God seals with a promise. Thus Abraham is the father of those who believe, and his seed is Christ, through whom all the redeemed have life (Gal 3, 16). Moses is the friend of God through whom Jahweh reveals Himself, renews the Covenant, establishes His people, rules them by the law, and is involved with them in history; this first mediator is a distant type of the mediator who is to come. Instead of ending with Moses, the line of mediators continues at every stage, through David and his dynasty, the prophets, and then the priests. And they continue to become a closer type of the Messias. In this complex messianic line, two antithetical figures appear. One, more terrestrial and humiliated than any other, is the *Servant* of Jahweh who saves the world by his sacrifice; the other, more celestial and transcendent than any other, is the mysterious *Son of Man* (Dn 7, 13-14) coming on the clouds of heaven and receiving power, glory, and dominion for ever. Undoubtedly the two types have both an individual and a collective sense. Israel and her leader are inextricably linked in these types. But, in the end, it is always God who saves, purifies and transfigures His people by His omnipotent activity. Moreover, in the midst of this unfolding plan, despite the untiring efforts of the prophets, there must be the Exile — the terrible punishment, the profound rupture, the great transformation through which God " roots up and destroys, " " plants and builds, " and forms His people with a purified faith that is more radical and more universal. Then, " after the exile, the Old Testament faith is orientated toward a greater, more unifying theme, the coming of God, which can be considered as a shadowy approach to the Incarnation. " [14]

It seems that the conception of a time-span marked out and determined by the approach of " He who is to come, " gradually grows in Jewish consciousness. For example, G. Vermès has shown that for the Essenes the passage of time implied different forms in the observance of the Mosaic Law. *Each period* has *its norm* which must guide the religious observance of every man : revelation, knowledge, and spiritual activity are to some extent linked with the period. The period is the divine measure of fidelity and obedience, of the new exodus and entrance into the covenant, in short, of the progressive formation of God's people. In the Rule of the Community we read that the " instructor " of the believers " fulfills the will of God *as it is revealed in every age.* He teaches the known learning and the *precepts of each age.* He discerns and judges the sons of Sadoq according to their spirit, so that they may persevere *among the elect of their age* in accordance with His will; he apportions true knowledge and justice to those who choose the way according to their spirit and *the norm of the age ;* and thus he introduces them to wisdom. " [15]

B. However, as St. Irenaeus said, in the midst of these " meaningful moments " and historical stages, we must single out *a deeper* inner *fulfillment* concerned with their conception of God Himself. The God of the Old Testament is the One God, the Jealous God, in comparison with whom there is no other. " Hear, O Israel, the Lord our God is one Lord " (Dt 6, 4). The protected Jewish faith proclaims this oneness more and more during inevitable and dangerous crises (which we shall not recall here). But alongside these notions of God's

---

[14] A. GELIN, " Messianisme, " *DBS*, col. 1206.

[15] *Rule*, 9, 12-16. Cited by G. VERMÈS in *Moïse, homme de l'Alliance* (Paris 1957), pp. 75-78 (the italics are the author's).

absolute oneness and simplicity, there gradually develops the notion of His inner richness. [16]

God possesses *a Spirit*, the *ruah of Jahweh*. It is a strange, indefinable Power. It is cosmic like the terrestrial wind; biological, like the breath of life; psychic, like an ecstatic force or a superhuman energy; spiritual, like prophetic inspiration; divine, like the power which transforms, purifies, and converts hearts, filling men with holiness, and like the greatest messianic gift (which the Messias himself possesses in all its fullness), which revives the waiting people and leads them to transform the earth. The *ruah* fills the entire universe. But everywhere it accomplishes the will of God. In the last analysis it is " God Himself in His activity " (Jacob). God also possesses *a Word*. It too is a sovereign Power. It is Word, Law, and Action which signifies, orders, and accomplishes. It creates the universe and regulates the sudden appearances of its creatures. It " establishes history and renders it intelligible " (Robert). It decrees and fulfills; it bestows historical unity and design on the most disparate and distant events; it reveals the projects, the plans, and the secrets of God; it organizes the chosen people and orders them by laws; it passes judgment and at times destroys; it is a blessing — but when man rejects it, it is a curse; it summons men unceasingly to respond, to communicate, to " believe. " This Word, which is at the source of creation and of salvation-history, will be brought to fulfillment in the Incarnate Word. And finally, God has a mysterious hidden *Wisdom*. It is known by Him alone and it does not dwell here below. It is intrinsic to God Himself as His firstborn Son begotten before the ages; it is present

---

[16] We can only hint at these themes. For a fuller treatment see : on the Spirit, J. GUILLET, *Biblical Themes*, chap. VII; VAN IMSCHOOT (resuming his earlier studies) *Théologie de l'Ancien Testament*, I, pp. 183-200, and the article " Pneuma, " (Baumgärtel) in *TWNT ;* on the Word, the articles " Légô, " and " Logos, " *TWNT*, 4, pp. 69 ff.; " Logos, " *DBS* (Robert), and E. JACOB, *Theology of the Old Testament* (New York : Harper, 1958), pp. 127 ff.; on Wisdom, A. ROBERT, " Les Attaches littéraires bibliques de Prov 1-9, " *RB* (1934-1935), and A. M. DUBARLE, *Les Sages d'Israël* (Paris 1946).

to creation as the Artist who delights in it; it is present to men as a teacher, both severe and kind, who creates, calls, and reproaches so that they may follow His call which provides divine nourishment and promises happiness. It is present to God as " the effusion of His glory, " and " the reflection of His eternal light. " These three are distinct but they intertwine, fuse, and separate again and again like the themes of a great symphony. On the one hand, they reveal some intrinsic aspect of the divine mystery and of God's infinite richness. On the other hand, they reveal the *progress* of Israel's *thought*, [17] which is difficult to define at any given point, but which is ordered toward a mysterious ineffable plenitude of superabundant life. Only Christ reveals it explicitly and makes the preceding stages intelligible. Here the time of Israel appears as a time of *revelation* and a time of *preparation* for the final Revelation. From this point of view it is eschatological; its orientation, its openness, and its pregnant character announce the fullness and the End of time.

C. Finally, the Old Testament period seems to have *an extremely meaningful structure*. Each stage resumes and makes explicit the same basic plan; each stage confirms and enriches it anew; each stage resumes all the others in order to advance them further, even when the living are not fully aware of it or do not fully understand it. Thus, the salvation-period is ordered, developed, and enriched; it climbs gradually toward the point of fullness and " concentration " that is Jesus Christ; and *this* " drift, " which is at once *immanent and directive, insures its continuity*. Man always lives in the present, a present which depends upon the past and looks toward the future. But the present of the chosen people, which God opens up by His creative love and places in the forefront of Israel's consciousness,

---

[17] That is why we do not like the use of the term " personification " in this question. Personification is a literary device which treats abstractions as living realities. But Old Testament thoughts on these qualities of God are direct, concrete, and vital. Besides, a real poet does not write " personifications, " he just writes poetry. Later, scribes try to analyze it at their desks, and disciples " make the personifications. "

is a present dependent at every stage and moment upon the Promise and the Covenant, " the election in Abraham and through Moses. " [18] It is a present of the Promise-to-be-realized, a present straining toward its fulfillment, toward the day of " He who is to come. "

Concretely, this present is the *Covenant* between God and His people. Here the important point is that the Covenant itself is realized in an atmosphere of extraordinary, mysterious *mutual knowledge*, [19] in the biblical sense of this word. Jahweh " knows " His children : " You only have I known of all the families of the earth " (Am 3, 2); they, in turn, " know " Jahweh. They recognize Him, listen to Him, and give themselves to Him in obedience and love : — " I will say to that which was not my people : Thou art my people. And they shall say : Thou art my God " (Os 2, 24). The salvation-period opens up in this present, and is founded entirely on the Word of God (which is both Word and Action) and the Love of God that it reveals. Thus, this period is *a present in which an endless dialogue* [20] between God and man begins, stops, and is taken up again. It is a present in which man must respond by faith. It is a present which unfolds the salvation-period in its three dimensions. And, finally, because this Covenant is the shadow of the new and eternal Covenant, this period of time is a present of hope in Jesus Christ, as the Epistle to the Hebrews explains magnificently : " All these died according to faith, not having received the promises, but beholding them afar off, and saluting them " (11, 13). Israel is the people of hope, the race of those " who before hoped in Christ " (Eph 1, 12).

It is apparent, however, that this present, glowing in the consciousness of Israel and lived so intensely, does not originate

[18] As Rowley says, cited by JACOB, *op. cit.*, p. 167.

[19] " In essence, the Covenant is based on God's preliminary knowledge of men, to which is added man's knowledge of God. " A. FEUILLET, *op. cit.*, p. 178, c, f; VAN IMSCHOOT, *op. cit.*, pp. 255 ff.; and M. E. BOISMARD, " La connaissance dans l'Alliance nouvelle d'après la première lettre de saint Jean, " *Revue Biblique* (1949), pp. 365-391.

[20] It is one of the major themes in the previously cited book of A. NEHER.

in the consciousness of Israel. It finds its *unique, eternal, ever-active source* in the will of God. He forms His People that He may fashion His Son, and at every moment he gives unity to the course of time. This present is revealed in the Judaic consciousness only in that moment when man responds to God by faith, and thus links himself at once to the past and future unfolding of the promise. It is a *moment* which lies *beyond time* and is *supported by eternity*. No spatial comparison can give us an idea of this kind of time. Its existence rests on faith, on a call and a response, on the meeting of grace and liberty. At each and every moment it hangs vertically on the eternal, merciful, Dominion of God. To represent this time linearly would obviously be a mistake; it would be an implicit denial of its " vertical " (direct) dependence upon the divine and of *the grip which eternity has on it.* For it is eternity which establishes this time and unfolds it in history, or rather, in the consciousness of men who live this history.

From this point of view, the biblical notion of the *remnant* acquires an astonishing meaning. It originated in a terrible atmosphere. In the eyes of Amos, the shepherd, the remnant was " two legs and the tip of an ear " snatched from the mouth of a lion. It became the focus of Israel's hopes, the exiles, the " saints " who returned to the homeland, the small flock of the faithful, the " poor " of Jahweh. They were a community of minds and hearts united by faith, the commandments, and the liturgy. In them pulsed the time of salvation. They were to " hasten the days of the Messias. " [21] In the end, it is all completed in one mind, the Virgin Mary's, which is linked to all the others. In this humble girl all Israel is concentrated. In her the chosen people are " personalized " and begin to take possession of the promises made to their Father Abraham. [22] " Behold you will conceive and bear a Son. " The salvation-

---

[21] " Remnant of Israel, of Jacob, or of Joseph, little Remnant, holy Remnant — these are formulas peculiar to the prophets which epitomize the sorrowful and wondrous destiny of the chosen people. " R. DE VAUX, " Le ' Reste ' d'Israël d'après les Prophètes, " *RB* (1933), p. 526.

[22] R. LAURENTIN, *Structure et théologie de Luc 1-2* (Paris 1957), pp. 82 ff.

period culminates in a maternity, because at that moment a woman becomes the mother of God. Humility, poverty, anonymity : what is one maternity among countless others? But this one is unique, because it inaugurates the New Creation. It is the *hapax* of God among men, and in a twinkling we are directed to another aspect of the mystery of the Incarnation.

The Incarnation as a Breakthrough

Besides being a wondrous fulfillment, the Incarnation is the most astounding breakthrough in the history of mankind. God Himself inhabits a woman's womb, assumes a body like ours, and appears in our midst as one of us; henceforth, the universe finds its source not only *in God* but also *in a man who is God*. [23] Nothing could be a direct preparation for this event, because nothing precontained it as its immanent end. Throughout the salvation-period the paths of Christ, His coming and His dwelling-place, were prepared. But time did not prepare for what transcends time itself and suddenly appears in time. With Christ something absolutely new appears, a new beginning, *a complete renewal of temporal creation*, founded not only on God but also on God-incarnate.

Because the Word becomes man, He assumes an existence in time with all the relations which determine and limit it. He truly breaks into the universe. But because this man is the eternal Word, He at once becomes, even in His earthly existence, Him in whom " it hath well pleased the Father, that all fullness should dwell " (Col 1, 19), the fullness of divinity, the fullness

---

[23] As we know, the Incarnation, viewed as a " shattering breakthrough " into history by God, is the mythical concept par excellence for Bultmann. We shall return to this problem. But our treatment up to this point should indicate that nothing is less mythical than this breakthrough unless one views every divine revelation in history as a " myth. " On the varied meanings of the word myth in Bultmann's work, see L. MALEVEZ, *Christian Message and Myth* (Westminster, Md. : Newman, 1960) pp. 68 ff.

of the universe, the fullness of time itself. [24] He becomes the one in whom all things are born, nurtured, and fulfilled, the one who is the source, the center and the end of cosmic time in its totality. He is the Eternal One, personally involved in the process of becoming, who in His very humanity establishes, imaugurates, and measures time. It is the *ephapax* of Christ which makes Him the *Absolute Hapax*. *Only once* was He sent; *only once* did He appear. *Only once* was He born; *only once* did He die and rise. *Only once* did He mount the heavens to the right hand of God in order to intercede for us. *Only once* is He the Savior of the world, the head of the Church, the Alpha and the Omega. We just said that the Virgin Mary was the flower of Israel in whom the Lord Jesus was to ripen and come forth. Now we must add that she also shares in this " once. " The Immaculate Conception, the virginal conception and birth of Christ, are " signs, " conditions and fruits of the appearance of the Word in the womb of the Virgin and time.

Thus we affirm *the most scandalous mystery* of our faith; the coexistence in a single being of divinity and humanity, of infinity and finiteness, of eternity and time. But we must do more than affirm it. Before we undertake a detailed analysis, we must extract the overall significance of this " day of Christ, " which is, in contrast to the " day of eternity, " *the day of His Incarnation and His humanity*. [25] We cannot say positively what the entrance of the Eternal into time is; but we can underline the absolute paradox involved.

Only once, the Word as *Creator* enters His creation, enters the process of becoming and time as a man by means of His soul and His body,

Tempus implens corporis.

But the absolutely transcendent being becomes an immanent human being to ensure that transcendence will be present in a

[24] BENOIT, " Corps, Tête et Plérôme dans les Épîtres de la Captivité, " *RB* (Jan. 1956), pp. 31-40.

[25] St. THOMAS, *in Joann.*, chap. VIII, lect. 8, note 7. Cf. St. LEO THE GREAT, epistle 31, 2 (*PL* 54, 792) : by the Incarnation " the Creator of time is born in time, and He who made all is begotten in the midst of all. "

unique way in immanence itself. The Word is made flesh to give the world existence, meaning, and value through His humanity. *Creative power now pulses through Christ's humanity.* By bringing His own humanity into existence as the source of mediation between God and the universe, the Word establishes the existence of the entire universe. Because the Eternity which established time is literally present and active in Jesus Christ, the Eternal personally creates the temporal world and makes time the measure of all existential movement, through His humanity which exists in time and His thought which created time. The *time of the world*, now and forever, in every part and in its totality, *is rooted, established, and measured by Jesus Christ.*

Only once does the Word as *Image* enter the universe of distant images, His creatures, who " represent, " as an ordered whole, the Father's wisdom. [26] But if the Word appears in the world as one particular image in the midst of others, He also comes as the *eternal, uncreated Type* of all the created images of God's glistening creation. He is the living idea which actualizes all created beings, the one and only source of the world's intelligibility. And this idea is *concentrated* in Jesus Christ, *expressed* through Him and *projected* by Him. Insofar as time is measured by the divine idea and is necessary if the world is to have meaning, it finds its vital source in the human psyche of Jesus Christ. He is the meaning of the universe.

The Word as *Redeemer* enters sinful humanity only once as a man among other men, lost in the countless throng. But He is the God-Man, the Man who embodies all men. And He enters the world to re-create what sin has de-created, [27] and to restore fallen creatures to the unity, purity, and holiness that God has destined for them. *Once* in time the Eternal personally accomplishes His unique plan for redemption and divinization, through His humanity. It is not a " divinized " humanity, but a humanity which has become the humanity of God Himself.

---

[26] " The world as a whole is but a representation of divine wisdom, conceived in the Father's mind, " St. THOMAS, *in Joann.*, chap. I, lect. 5, note 1.

[27] I borrow this *word* from Simone Weil, who gives it a different meaning.

From it springs the time of hope and salvation for all, which will last until the end of time itself.

The entrance of the Eternal into time means that *the Eternal has assumed time*. Time has been re-created and given its most important role. It opens the salvation-period for all men. Time has been assumed, transfigured, and consecrated in Jesus Christ, who is the *unique meeting point of time and the Eternal*, of the Creator and His creation. Only once, the Infinite takes on the finite, and everything is consummated. The appearance of the Incarnate Word is, therefore, *the preeminently eschatological event*. When the Eternal enters time, the " first days " are over and the " last days " have begun. The Covenant is sealed forever. Now it is no longer between God and men, but between God and the God-Man, who represents God to men, and men before God. All the possible events of the salvation-history, including the Parousia, unfold through this unique event. All the complex and indefinable temporal relations of the Christian universe are enveloped in this mystery, *the infinite concentrated in a moment* yet *spanning the whole expanse of time*. Essentially, *eschatology is Jesus Christ Himself*. In Him the whole mystery of salvation is fulfilled, because He is the " Savior of the world, " " yesterday, and today; and the same for ever " (Heb 13, 8). Thus existence, its meaning, and the world's salvation pass through humanity, specifically, through Jesus Christ's *psyche*.

Since this " only once " of the Incarnation is the sudden eruption of the Eternal into time, it *also fulfills the " only once "* of eternal predestination. The Father " chose us in him before the foundation of the world, that we should be holy and unspotted in his sight in charity. Who hath predestinated us unto the adoption of children through Jesus Christ unto himself " (Eph 1, 4-5). The " before the foundation of the world " of which St. Paul and the whole Bible speak, is God's eternal present which establishes the temporal existence of the universe and coexists with Him. Hence this eternal act does not " determine " human existence *from without*, as if it were inserted into time. Rather, it *directly* establishes each instant

100

of human existence, *by opening it to its vocation and liberty.* God thinks and wills [28] a humanity which is to pass through Jesus Christ from earth to heaven, from a sinful life to a life redeemed, from the life of " saving grace " to the life of the Blessed Trinity. The " idea " which effects this transfiguration is predestination itself. It is completely fulfilled in and by Jesus Christ and it in turn envelops *both* Christ and those who are to be saved. This is the deepest level of time. Time is always the intersection of eternity and becoming, and the Incarnation reveals that *this intersection takes place in the mystery of a Being* who is both divine and human. Through this " Same " who is both God and man, time is found in the heart of a Being, in a psyche, *at the crossing-point of the Eternal and human existence.* The time of all human psyches can be borne in the unique psyche of Jesus Christ.

The Incarnation as a Point of Attraction

Because predestination integrates everything, it involves maturation in time, order, and progress. It is, therefore, " from all eternity, the divine predestination of what is to be fulfilled in time, through grace. " [29]   The focal point of this fulfillment is the *hapax* of the Incarnation, " the work of grace in time whereby a man is truly God and God is truly a man " *(ib.).* Christ is the proper and natural Son of God in whom all men become God's adopted sons. The perfect image of the Father is realized and manifested through Christ's humanity. Now men can share in this image during the course of time. " God has ordered our salvation in advance by deciding in eternity that it will be accomplished in time through Jesus Christ. " [30]   Predestination has a temporal dimension, because it involves the temporal Incarnation of the Word. It establishes

[28] *ST*, IIIᵃ, 26, 1-4.
[29] IIIᵃ, 24, 1, c.
[30] IIIᵃ, 24, 4, c.

101

the temporal conditions, structures and processes [31] which prepare the Incarnation. Christ is predestined to be *the Head of all men throughout cosmic time.* [32]

But, to repeat, this does not destroy human liberty. It establishes it — for two reasons. First, it is an eternal divine act *which cannot be measured* by its effects. It is not equivalent to the highest effects it produces — " thinking " and " choosing. " It is above them all, creating them and establishing an order which gives liberty and free choice to men. [33] Furthermore, the real result of this divine act is Jesus Christ, Savior of the world, i.e., He who radically *raises up* created liberty, and comes to *recover* it from captivity by transforming it through grace. *The predestination of Christ must be viewed as the effective redemption of human liberty in time.*

The Incarnation of Christ makes Him the *head of a body* which is *essentially temporal* at its origin. It is temporal because it is coextensive with humanity itself in its growth through time, and is composed of all men existing from the beginning to the end of the world. The first men, *from the first moment of their existence*, were able to be saved by faith, [34] no matter what *the conscious form* of their adherence had been. Faith is the spiritual act which envelops and transcends cosmic time, and through which man approaches the salvation-period centered in Christ. [35] Until the Word becomes incarnate, this center is

[31] " Eternal predestination embraces not only the events of time, but also the way and the order in which they are to occur, " III[a], 24, 4, c.

[32] III[a], 8, 3, c.

[33] This has been clearly expressed by J. MARITAIN, *Existence and the Existent*, chap. IV (New York : Doubleday, 1957).

[34] Cf. J. DANIÉLOU, *Holy Pagans of the Old Testament* (New York : Longmans, Green, 1957).

[35] Cf. *ST*, III[a], 42, 6, c : " The link which faith establishes (with Christ's passion) is forged by an act of the soul. . . . There is nothing preventing a reality *later in time* from *moving* something *before it exists in reality*, because the act of the soul precedes; for a goal which is realized later in time can move an agent insofar as he sees and desires it. "

102

not visibly realized in history. But *because of the Creator's intention*, Christ is already the *"focal point"* of all cosmic motion. He is present in the salvation-period as its immanent meaning and its organizing plenitude — the one who accomplishes its purpose. The center is present from the first day *by His power of attraction*. By following this gracegiven moment of faith, men living before Christ were saved by Him.

After Christ's Incarnation, Death, and Resurrection, " the eternal Redemption is accomplished, " and all humanity is called to glory in Jesus Christ. But individuals living in time find themselves in *very different relationships* to the salvation-period. Some have heard and rejected the Lord's clear call. They are " in them that perish " (2 Cor 2, 15); they are already judged. They have transformed the time of salvation into a time of condemnation. But *there is still time*. Nothing is yet decided, because Christ is still at work, and men can be converted. They are still summoned by the powerful, inde-structible call — " God indeed was in Christ, reconciling the world to himself " (2 Cor 5, 19). The man " on the road to perdition, " can always become, through Christ, a man " on the road to salvation. " There are also some who are gradually drawing nearer to Christ. For them the present is a steady progress from the time of sin to the time of salvation. Some part gradually from the Lord because they have lost charity. For them the present is an ever-continuing diminution of the salvation-period. Some love God with their whole heart and soul, and draw near the core of the salvation-period. They experience its full temporal plenitude, but must still reach its absolute plenitude, which transcends time.

All these people go through time in Christ's Body. [36] Their time is *distinct yet unified* in Him. His grace gives all His members access to the salvation-period, and solidifies them more and more in His eternity. Their multiplicity is a quality proper to psyches approaching more or less rapidly toward

[36] Those who freely choose not to join His Body are still linked to it by their act of refusal.

Christ's salvation-period. All these individual existences in time form the growth-period of Christ's Body. This time-period, composed of countless individual time-periods, remains a mystery because it is the very achievement of salvation. It is *totally assumed into the mediating psyche* of Christ the Lord, who establishes and restores all these individual time-periods to Himself, unifying them and making them eternal. However, all this is really the fulfillment of the eternal plan of predestination. It is " the Father who attracts " all men to Christ, and saves them in time through the resurrected Christ. He inaugurates the salvation-period through the Savior. In " the day " of grace until the end of time, He inaugurates the process of birth, growth, and maturation in Christ, which leads us into His Eternity.

The salvation-period is not a dis-incarnate or " de-historicized " time. It is the *intrinsic measure* and the *essential meaning* of *cosmic time*. Since man has inaugurated in the world the time of sin, against God's will, he has changed the present meaning of cosmic time. He has made it a time of separation and condemnation. The time between birth and death now leads to eternal death. Therefore, every level of cosmic time must be " redeemed. " Its true meaning must be restored so that it may again be a means of salvation. The Incarnate Word accomplishes this. Christ *recapitulates cosmic time* as a whole *in His incarnate psyche.* [37] He restores the meaning which God gave it, and makes it a means of salvation once more. He enters the world of time and sin, donning a " body " like ours. He sacrifices Himself and rises to *re-create* cosmic time. Now it is enkindled in His own psyche as the day of grace. He reunites the center and the source of cosmic time *as* the time of salvation. In Him it finds its *unique point* of reference to the cosmos and its absolute *summit in history*.

[37] St. Thomas thought (*Pot.*, 5, 6, c and 4m) that the end of the world had been revealed only to the Man-Christ, because it is connected to the fulfillment of predestination accomplished in Him. In other words, Christ alone bears the totality of cosmic time and salvation-time *in His human psyche, as a gift from God.*

Furthermore, Christ's redemptive power is poured out through His resurrected body to men involved in time through their body. He establishes contact with sinners through the sacraments. In them Christ's transcendent, glorified body detached from time, unites with men's earthly bodies immersed in time. Time, then, in all its complexity, is *immersed in the Christian transformation* and becomes *a dimension of Christian existence*. It disappears when the Body is complete and cosmic time is properly achieved.

Jesus Christ saves time from sin, from the Prince of this world and the Powers which use it for their own ends. He makes it His time, *the Father's* time, the time of predestination and salvation. As long as men remain sinners, they are still in the *time of sin*. But Christ is present in the world. So *this* time disintegrates as it is penetrated, broken up and transformed by the time of salvation. Insofar as men unite themselves to Christ by faith, they enter the *time* of salvation. They *recognize in Jesus a man in the plenitude of time*, the man who has re-inserted cosmic time into God's eternal idea and into eternity, the man who has " redeemed " it, re-created it. By faith men share in the mystery of Christ and are inserted into His eternal present. They anchor themselves in the mystery of His death and resurrection, and struggle toward the mystery of His Parousia.

Faith is thus *a principle of creative interpretation*. It gives cosmic time a new dimension, its true dimension, and reaches the deepest level of created time. But even more importantly, faith is *a principle of ontological transformation*. Man can open himself to the time of grace because through faith he can reach the very core of *his own psyche* and the deepest meaning of *his own spiritual being*. *The Christian is able to transform cosmic time, because his own soul has been transformed.* Reuniting with Christ's creative intention, he establishes, *in principle* at least, the unity of his psyche and the world, [38] because he has been reunited with God through Christ. He joins the real time which

---

[38] Later we shall add the necessary restrictions on this statement.

105

God has willed, and which Christ has established and communicated.   Through grace, he enters into communion with Jesus Christ's life and eternity.   Here the time-structuring psyche acquires its true depth, because it transcends itself through faith and love and participates in Eternal Life through Jesus Christ.

5

Christ's Psyche* and Time

Christ's Mission in Time

At the appointed time the Word is made flesh. Henceforth
" He is perfectly divine and perfectly human, true God and true
man, with a rational soul and a body. " [1] The Word takes a
human nature into the unity of His divine Person. He becomes

* In rendering the author's word " conscience " as psyche, I have
no intention of introducing the debate over soul and psyche. It merely
seems to convey what it meant better than such words as — conscience,
consciousness, mind, etc. — Translator's note.

[1] Chalcedon, *DB*, 148. The psyche of Christ is a central problem
in contemporary theological thought. For a detailed treatment and an
historical purview see the interesting treatment of J. TERNUS, " Das Seelen
und Bewustseinsleben Jesus, " *Das Konzil von Chalkedon* (Würzburg
1951-1953), III, pp. 81-237.

a living human being and embarks on man's earthly journey. He inserts Himself into human time. For Him, existence in time and the Incarnation are one. " He who exists before time, begins to exist in time. " [2] The Word makes His human soul a principle of spiritual activity [3] in the most perfect sense. Like us, Christ enters the world through His animated body. It opens Him to time as it does all human beings. Through His spatio-temporal organism (His body) and His temporal organism (His psyche), the principle of spiritual activity (His soul) establishes and unfolds a human time. In it, as in every human psyche, the past and future are linked through the present.

But there are extraordinary difficulties in approaching Christ's human psyche from a theological viewpoint. [4] The Synoptic Gospels clearly indicate some traits of this psyche. But there is the danger of personifying it as if it were a self-sufficient reality instead of the human psyche of God's Son. In Christ there are not *two* thinking *subjects*, a man who thinks (in a human way) the same thing God thinks (in His divine way). In the prologue which outlines the themes of his Gospel, St. John provides us with another type of interpretation. The Word is made flesh, and the eternal Idea is expressed through a human psyche. Therefore, it is the Word which is contemplated through His human psyche, not the reverse. This union remains a " veiled " mystery for us, but it does not degrade Christ's human psyche. Instead, God enriches and expands the humanity He assumes.

[2] St. Leo the Great, *DB*, 144.

[3] Cf. III^a, 17, 2, 4^m.

[4] Usually we shall refer simply to the psyche of Christ. This is not just for the sake of brevity. One could refer, perhaps, to the " divine psyche " of Christ. But strictly speaking, we cannot attribute a psyche to God (who is perfect act), nor to angels (who intuitively know their essence and their operations), but only to men, who have knowledge insofar as they are in act and whose self-intuition is reduced to simple self-awareness, the most primitive level of intellectual intuition. (On this, cf. J. Maréchal, *Le Point de départ de la métaphysique*, V, pp. 239-241.)

Perhaps, then, we should investigate Christ's human existence from *the viewpoint of His mission*. [5] Here the relationship between the Father and the Son, and between time and eternity, are interconnected. For the Incarnation derives its meaning and purpose from the Father's will. For the Son, it is the mission He has received from His Father : *Eo missum quo factum*, said St. Augustine and St. Thomas. This mission establishes, frames, and directs Christ's human existence.

" But when the fullness of the time was come, God sent his Son, ' made ' of a woman, ' made ' under the law : that he might redeem them who were under the law : that we might receive the adoption of sons " (Gal 4, 4-5). This mission, willed by the Father, involves Christ's human existence, His journey through it, and His time which is the measure of this journey. Its purpose is to glorify God by saving mankind. And this is to be accomplished through Christ's human life. He gives glory to the Father and salvation to men through His inner dispositions of love, obedience, and sacrifice, and through the redemptive activities which express these dispositions — revelation, pardon and sanctification of souls, death and resurrection. But the *form* of this mission is *His existence in time*. The eternal plan of redemption is accomplished in time.

This decisive epiphany, the Incarnation, has been prepared by God during a long period of time. In his Gospel, St. John outlines the anticipatory manifestations of this " glory " in the Old Testament. [6] But the fullness of time is inaugurated when God's Son is born of a woman. God measures time by the mission, and dots this epiphany with " significant moments " —

[5] On this point we are indebted to H. URS VON BALTHASAR, *A Theology of History* (New York : Sheed, 1963).

[6] One can start from the beginning and work up to Christ as we did above. Or one can start with Christ and work back toward the past, regarding it in the light of Christ. St. John does this regarding Abraham (8, 56), Isaias (12, 41) and Zachary (19, 37). Cf. D. MOLLAT, "Saint Jean," *BJ*, p. 17.

Christ's birth, His baptism and preaching, the ascent to Jerusalem, the Passion, Resurrection, and Ascension. All this is a prelude to the final epiphany, the Parousia. *The Father* officially *inaugurates the salvation-time in and through Christ*, who becomes its source and center.

Christ, in turn, personally accomplishes the Father's plan. *This reciprocal activity is essential for the Divine Persons.* The Father communicates His being to the Son, and makes the Word a perfect expression of His own thought. The Son in turn gives Himself entirely to the Father in an act of perfect love from which the Holy Spirit springs (as from a single principle). *And the Incarnate Son continues the activity of the Eternal Son.* In His psyche, He responds to the Father joyously and lovingly. This response inaugurates the salvation-time for Him and through Him.

There are two dimensions to this response. On the one hand, it *accepts* the Father's will and *opens* the mission. Christ says Yes : " Yea, Father, for so it hath seemed good in thy sight " (Lk 10, 21). Through His response, He becomes the recapitulation-point of the redeemed universe and cosmic time. All God's promises, His plan of salvation, and salvation-time itself, are really Christ's response to the Father (2 Cor 1, 20). In His Son, His unique Word, the Father pronounces His eternal yes. And the Incarnate Son takes the pronouncement to men, makes it His own, and expresses it through His love and adoration. In Christ's human psyche it assumes its full redemptive dimensions. It envelops the entire mission — its source (God's will), its object (mankind), all the activities which will fulfill it, and time itself which conditions it and measures it from within.

On the other hand, this response is also *a fulfillment.* Christ is not content to say yes. He fulfills this yes in His human life, obeying His Father's will, " I do always the things that please him " (Jn 8, 29). Through this redemptive activity which culminates in His death and Resurrection, Christ becomes the focal point of the universe created and redeemed, of humanity called and saved, and of salvation-time unfolding

110

through history. This interior, supra-temporal yes insures the unity, the plenitude, and the true value of salvation-time. Christ's time is the means through which the Father gives all men access to His life, to the day of grace, and to salvation.

Christ's Time-Structuring Intentions

Christ's existence in time is close-knit and extremely complex, because it is completely determined by His mission. In a sense radically different from Heidegger's, [7] Christ's time is a " time for, " *a time-for-the-mission*. It exists for the mission, it is the means of accomplishing it, and it passes through various levels of planning which have a more and more mysterious link with eternity. There are certain decisive moments — *kairoi* — in Christ's life. In St. Luke's Gospel there are four " moments " which are clearly interconnected : the Baptism and the first preaching of the Gospel (3, 1—9, 5), the ascent to Jerusalem (9, 5—19, 27), the royal entrance and the Passion (19, 28—23, 56), the Resurrection (24, 1-31). This sketchy account certainly symbolizes a spiritual journey. [8] We must study *the structure* of this mission-time. It is complex because various time-structuring plans are involved; yet it is unified because it is a single offering to the Father. And we must begin with Christ's Baptism, the first period treated in the Gospels.

A.   Christ's time is *a time-for-service*. After His Baptism and the temptations in the desert, " Jesus came into Galilee,

---

[7] For Heidegger, the " time for " (already described by Aristotle) is the common time of everyday life filled by practical preoccupations. It is always associated with a point in space and measured by " nature's clock, " the sun. It is the " public time of the world. " Cf. DE WAELHENS, *La philosophie de M. Heidegger*, pp. 210 ff.; also J. WAHL, *Traité de métaphysique*, pp. 292-293. For us, the " time for " of Christ is not only the " authentic time " but also the necessary condition for any authentic temporal existence.

[8] On this point cf. CONZELMANN, *Die Mitte der Zeit* (Tübingen 1954) with the remarks of X. LÉON-DUFOUR, *RSR* (1958), pp. 242-248.

preaching the gospel of the kingdom of God, and saying : The time is accomplished " (Mk 1, 14-15). The material content of this service is *the Word*. But, like the Hebrew word *Dâbar*, this implies both words and deeds. It is a revelation which brings to fulfillment the promises and expectations of the Old Testament. It is completed by the revelation of the mystery of the Father, Son, and Holy Spirit, and by a communication of Their life. The person who believes and accepts it is " saved " and " passes from death to life. " It is a prophetic Word, revealing the secrets of the future and what is necessary for the growth of the Kingdom. It entrusts the growth process and its maturation to the Holy Spirit, the Father's Promise realized in Jesus Christ. It is also a judicial Word. Even though Christ has been sent to save, not to judge (Jn 3, 17), His presence and His call force the decisive choice. He pulls men from comfortable neutrality and drives them to say yes or no. And this is judgment because " He that believeth in him is not judged, " but " he that doth not believe, is already judged " (Jn 3, 18). The Word announces and realizes the end of time. Christ's " deeds " involve service to His " human brothers. " With humility and friendliness, the Good Master serves His disciples, the humble, the little ones, the multitude, and the great. Some of His deeds are miracles, wondrous signs which inscribe God's infinite mercy on the universe and on human misery, and reveal the presence of God in Jesus Christ. And finally, His work involves the formation of His disciples, the gradual training which prepares them for their mission and establishes the keystone of the infant Church.

The form and rhythm of this task establish a specifically human kind of temporal existence — a *time for work*. The work involved is the redemptive mission itself, with its finite and infinite aspects. On the one hand, Christ remains *locked in the limits of space and time*. He is sent to the Jews, to the land of Israel, and He refuses to leave this point in space : " I was not sent but to the sheep that are lost of the house of Israel " (Mt 15, 24). He is fettered by time with all its possibilities, and

112

must submit to the rhythm of days and nights, seasons and liturgical feasts. His days are numbered, His " hour " draws near and the " night, " during which no man can work, approaches inexorably. But this typically human existence is joined to a supra-temporal point which throbs in Christ's psyche. His messianic consciousness — to which we shall return — transcends all limits, even though it is immersed in them. It dominates the temporal existence it has established. It ponders the future and predicts it. It contemplates the Father — the eternal God — and reveals Him to His own.

Furthermore, Christ's task, which is inserted into a specific space and time, centers *on an equally specific spatio-temporal milieu*. It centers on the Jews who surround Him, and the apostles whom He has chosen, " that twelve should be with him " (Mk 3, 14). What an extraordinary limitation! His work is limited to a small group of people, enemies and friends, gathered around Him for a few moments. Yet, through them Jesus Christ sees and influences all men for all time. He offers His life as a ransom " for many " (Mk 10, 45); He gives His blood as drink, but this blood is shed " for many " (Mk 14, 24). He dies " not only for the nation, but to gather together in one the children of God, that were dispersed " (Jn 11, 52). The whole expanse of cosmic time is involved in this universal task. When a woman pours precious ointment on the feet of Jesus in the house of Simon the leper, He gives the act universal dimensions. " Amen I say to you, wheresoever this gospel shall be preached in the whole world, that also which she hath done shall be told for a memory of her " (Mt 26, 13). And when Christ prays for His apostles and their successors, He prays for all the faithful throughout time : " Not for them only do I pray, but for them also who through their word shall believe in me " (Jn 17, 20). Such is the first time-structuring intention in Christ's psyche.

B. The second is no less mysterious and is the most dramatic. Christ's time — from beginning to end — is *a time for death*, the supreme act of service. Death is a reality for all

113

men. St. Augustine reminds his flock of it constantly. And Heidegger has reminded us of it in such forceful terms that modern man can scarcely forget it. But Christ's case is still unique. He has been sent to die. " The Son of man also is not come to be ministered unto : but to minister and to give his life a redemption for many " (Mk 10, 45). He has taken " the form of a servant " to become " obedient unto death, even the death of the cross " (Phil 2, 8). He is the servant of Jahweh who must be burdened with our sorrows, transfixed by our sins, and who " delivered his soul unto death " (Is 53, 12). He is the " Lamb of God . . . who taketh away the sin of the world " (Jn 1, 29) by His sacrifice.

The act of dying is, therefore, the fulfillment of His mission. And so *Christ anticipates it* as man cannot. We do not experience the pangs of death until we begin to cross its threshold. Such is the case in certain grave illnesses, dire forebodings, extreme danger, and mystic experience. [9] With Christ it is entirely different. He knows what death means. From the beginning of His public life — at the Baptism and the Theophany at the Jordan [10] — Christ is on a road which leads to death. He knows He must die soon, and He also knows what kind of death it will be. This is the testimony He renders to His Father — fidelity to His mission — which forges and tightens the vise of death upon Him. On three different occasions, He solemnly announces His Passion, crucifixion [11] and death. He forbids those who were privileged to see His Transfiguration to speak of His Glory " until He be risen from the dead, " because the Scribes " will make Him suffer " as they did John the Baptist (Mt 17, 9-12). He knows that in order to glorify the Father's name and to be glorified by Him, in order to draw all men to Himself, He must fall into the ground and die like the good grain. Or, to be more exact, He

---

[9] Cf. the strange case of *Râmana Maharsi* cited by O. LACOMBE, *Études Carmélitaines* (Oct. 1937), pp. 173-175.

[10] At least implicitly, and, according to many exegetes, explicitly.

[11] At least in Mt 20, 19 as far as the Synoptic Gospels are concerned.

114

must " be lifted up from the earth " on the Cross (Jn 12, 23-33). In short, He knows that this death is " His hour. " [12] It has been fixed by the Father. He has no right to anticipate it (thence His mysterious disappearance s) nor to delay it. He can only accomplish it " according to the time " (Rom 5, 6).

And yet, without turning back, He chooses to offer up this death in magnificent and complete liberty. He chooses it because it is the Father's will which fulfills the Scriptures, saves the world, and opens up the new world of glory. He accomplishes the " commandment... received of my Father " (Jn 10, 18) and will drink " the chalice which my Father hath given me " (Jn 18, 11). But His obedience is so perfectly identified with love that it is also perfect freedom : " No man taketh it away from me : but I lay it down of myself " (Jn 10, 18). Finally, He chooses His death, and gradually enters the developments leading to this moment. Death begins to envelop Him. He feels it in the looks and words of His enemies. Several times He must flee because they want to kill Him before His hour. He gradually becomes more troubled in the depths of His soul over the actual approach of death and begs to be delivered from it (Jn 12, 27). Under the symbols of bread and wine, [13] He offers His sacrificed body and His spilt blood (Lk 22, 19-20). He offers Himself as a sacrifice in order to sanctify His own in truth (Jn 17, 19). He feels death itself in His body and soul during the agony and accomplishes it on the Cross through torture, dereliction, and abandonment. " It is consummated " (Jn 19, 30). He ends His life there consciously, willingly, and supremely.

There has never been such a concrete example of a time for death. Only the Incarnate Word could have lived it. This time for death involves clear foreknowledge, an absolutely generous offering, real human anguish, and a direct realization of its redemptive value. It is a life-giving time, because in

[12] We shall discuss this " hour " in St. John at a later point.

[13] This would be especially significant if it were accepted that Jesus celebrated the Last Supper on Tuesday evening.

this death the prophecies are fulfilled, the eternal *agape* is manifested, and the source of the world's salvation is revealed,

Terra, pontus, astra, mundus
Quo lavantur flumine. [14]

And finally, it is suffused with the certain knowledge of the Resurrection, which is inaugurated, merited, and anticipated in the exaltation of the Cross. " He began to teach them that the Son of man must... be killed *and* after three days rise again " (Mk 8, 31). The time for death is necessarily a time for life. This is the temporal aspect of the paschal mystery. Instead of suppressing the time for death, it deepens and develops it so that it appears at the very core of the redemptive mystery.

C. Christ's time, therefore, is also *a time for Resurrection.* This is the result of a life of service. The Resurrection is a real implication of death. Conversely, Christ's death is never *an end in itself*. It is always *suffused* with the Resurrection. The mission given by the Father is to die in order to rise. The Resurrection is not an extrinsic addition to His death. It is not simply the result of death. It is an intrinsic part of His death because it is its intrinsic, hidden meaning. That is why St. John always views the Cross as the beginning of Christ's exaltation. The time for death is the time for resurrection. Christ must rise — to become the Son of God in the fullest sense, [15] to accomplish the whole salvation-mystery and the Promise of the Spirit, to give His Church the sign to which it must bear witness forever (Acts 2, 32-36), to announce in Himself the final resurrection of the faithful (1 Cor 15, 12-28; Jn 6, 53-58). It is such an essential part of the Christian mystery that Christ anticipates it in His Transfiguration, announces it every time He mentions His Passion, and speaks of it obscurely elsewhere as well. [16] The Resurrection is the full glorification of Christ, His definitive entrance into God's world.

[14] *Hymn of Lauds* for Passiontide.
[15] Cf. D. DUPONT, " Filius Meus es Tu, " *RSR*, 4 (1948), pp. 522 ff.
[16] Especially in St. John : 6, 63; 10, 18; 16, 16-23.

116

Through it the eternal Mediator takes firm control of humanity and the universe. Hence all human time, insofar as it is a salvation-time, is apprehended in the Resurrection. The connection between death and Resurrection involves and actualizes the mystery of Redemption. And so it forms a kind of time which we cannot conceive of. It is incomprehensible and inexpressible. We can only link it to its eternal source in Jesus Christ. It is *a time leading to the non-temporal*, and to an eternalization which belongs to the Incarnate Eternal alone. The time for Resurrection plunges Christ into Eternity and is, therefore, the time for the Parousia. Christ rises to save humanity, to fashion His Body and complete it on the last day, to establish the Kingdom and deliver it to the Father, to prepare His bride for her glorious entry into the eternal Nuptials. [17] Hence, only the Parousia definitively fulfills the temporal existence of Christ.

D. Finally, Christ's time is a *time for God's glory*. [18] This is the deepest purpose in Christ's soul. It establishes all the others, because it is the ultimate meaning of His mission. It is the loftiest purpose, because it looks to that point in eternity where this soul meets the Father face to face in mutual love and perfects His earthly existence by uniting it with eternity. The Word is a pure relation to the Father. Through His human nature this relation is translated into the ebb and flow of mutual love which makes this eternal union complete. His living relation to the Father, which makes Christ what He is, is expressed primarily by prayer — adoration, praise, thanksgiving, petition. It is the natural impulse in Christ's soul, His source of joy and perpetual youthfulness. [19] And it is perpetuated by

[17] We encounter this problem again when we consider the time of Christ in the Church.

[18] We use this word in the sense implied today. The synoptic writers show Christ living for the " will, " the " good pleasure, " the " plan " of His Father. St. John focuses on the *doxa*. Later we shall examine these two " treatments " of the " mystery of Christ. "

[19] This has been admirably pointed out by Père DE GRANDMAISON, *Jesus Christ* (New York : Sheed, 1961) pp. 196 ff.

the joyous or sorrow-laden fulfillment of His Father's will. Christ always does the things that please His Father. It is achieved by the redeemed, who give glory to God also. Christ exults in the Holy Spirit after His disciples' first mission. The essence of the prayer for unity (Jn 17) is the Father's glory. Even the Son's glory given to Him by the Father, which gives Him the " Name which is above all names " and makes every knee bend before Him, is still " in the glory of God the Father " (Phil 2, 11). This impulse to glorify the Father radiates from the very center of Christ's soul and suffuses His whole life and being. It gives His life its deepest meaning and unifies the other facets of His temporal existence by directing them toward Him who is their source and their end.

The Unity of Christ's Temporal Existence

These four intentions make up the richness and complexity of the temporal existence of *Christus viator*. They cannot be diminished, separated or confused. We cannot grasp their unifying principle in itself, but we can *approach that extra-temporal point* from which all four of them spring to fulfill the temporal mission received from the Father in the eternal act of Procession. " I have come from the Father, I have been sent. I was born and entered the world. I said: Behold, God, here I am to do Thy will. " This is the essence of Christ's temporal existence, and it projects us toward that mysterious point which gives unity to Christ's human psyche.

A. This point is *at the apex of Christ's human soul*. The human soul is related to the body as its " form. " It makes a body " its own " body, its point of insertion into the world. The temporal nature of the body gives a beginning to the soul and imposes certain restrictions on it. On the other hand, the human soul is turned toward God. It is a spirit in God's image and is destined to enter into personal communion with God. The human soul, with its double orientation, is completely linked to the body in its development. It will attain

118

its proper spirituality only when the body permits it, when its higher intelligence is completely formed, its nerves properly coordinated, and its " corporal education " completed.

Christ's soul is in a similar yet different situation. [20] It is in a *similar* situation insofar as it is the form of a body. It gradually attains self-awareness by controlling its biological organism and its nervous apparatus and by performing all types of activities — physical, mental, and psychic. Like other human souls, it acquires knowledge day by day. From His mother Christ will learn how to act and to communicate with others. From her He " will learn about " God Himself. Only after thirty years have passed will He act as Christ. But Christ's soul is not just linked to His body and to God the Creator. *Its very existence* is *linked to the Person of the Word of God.* The Word assumes this soul and gives it His existence and His " personality. " Christ's soul belongs to the Person of the Word, who is expressed through it, saves men through it, and gives glory to God. Since it is the soul of the Word, it escapes the *purely* existential condition of other human souls. It does not escape their *natural* condition. Together with its body it forms a human nature like ours. But it does escape their *personal* condition. Christ's soul is not the principle of subsistence. It is not the immediate source of His personality. This comes from the Person of the Word. As the soul of the Word, it has " more, " not " less, " than other souls. In Christ's soul, the knowledge proper to every human soul becomes unique awareness of God's own intuition. This is the " more " as expressed in His psyche.

In this respect Christ's soul has a unique existence before God. From the first moment of its existence it is the soul of the Word of God. And so it is not in potency, not involved in any becoming or in any series of *material* circumstances. In this *one* respect, the soul of the God-Man *necessarily* escapes the existential condition of other human souls. From the very

[20] Cf. a similar line of thought in M. J. NICOLAS, " Théologie dogmatique, " *RT*, 1 (1957), p. 102.

first it exists outside the mere human condition, outside the darkness of ignorance. It exists in God's brightness. Hence it realizes that it is the soul of the Word. It knows the One who makes it what it is. It knows the Father who begets and sends His Son. It says : " Here I am, Lord, to do Thy will. " Christ's soul exists in the sight of God, sinless and blessed. It is completely transparent to itself (as a spirit), because it is transparent to God. [21]

Christ's soul, like other souls, is *subject* to its bodily condition. But, unlike other souls, it *transcends* this condition because it is assumed by a divine Person and endowed with a " divine condition. " The Absolute Spirit assumes a created spirit to unite it to His person. He divinizes it completely. He could keep it in its bodily condition but insteads He joins it to Himself and brings it into His own brightness — the very brightness of God. He makes it a soul which is open to the vision of God at its very core. It attains its final end and is sinless. However we must remember the dogmatic implications. Between the soul of the Word and the Word Himself, there is an ontological gap which cannot be spanned. It is the gap between the created and the uncreated, the finite and the

[21] We could reach the same conclusion by beginning at the other end. It is the Word who is made flesh, who expresses Himself, knows, and acts through His body and soul. But a soul is not a material thing; it is a spirit, an entity which *in se* implies self-awareness. So the Word has only one means of knowing Himself through His human soul : *this soul knows itself to be the soul of the Word*, the soul of the Son, a living relationship with the Father. We can say that the Word is joined to a human body which is not yet mature and must develop naturally. We can also say that His soul, as the form of His body, follows the natural process by which His body, His knowledge, and His activity develops. (This is all part of the *Kenosis* which we shall discuss later.) But we cannot say that the Word is joined to a soul which is so completely immersed in its corporeal environment that it is unaware of God. This is one major difference between Christ's soul and the soul of Mary. Her soul is perfectly holy because it was preserved from original sin; but it is completely human and totally subject to the natural laws of human development. On this problem cf. J. GALOT, " La psychologie du Christ, " *NRT* (1958), pp. 351 ff., and *id.* " Science et conscience de Jésus, " *ibid.* (1960), pp. 113 ff.

infinite. [22] However, this gap is *spanned in reality* by the fact that the created and the uncreated are indissolubly united in the Person of the Incarnate Word. The consequences for our problem are immediate and extremely important. We can now pinpoint the mysterious source from which springs the unity of Christ's time-structuring psyche.

B. We can catch a glimpse of this mysterious source by analyzing the famous *Logion* of St. Matthew. [23] " All things are delivered to me by my Father. And no one knoweth the Son, but the Father : neither doth any one know the Father, but the Son and he to whom it shall please the Son to reveal him " (Mt 11, 27). This text results from three biblical currents — the prophetic, the apocalyptic and the sapiential. [24] Its richness surpasses them all. It is presented in connection with the work of the Kingdom of God, the work of Christ, His " mission. " But it connects all this with a transcendent mystery and succinctly affirms three major facts. First, no one can penetrate the mysterious world of the Father and the Son. Everyone is excluded from it. Secondly, the Father and the Son see each other in the plenitude of mutual knowledge. [25] There is a reciprocal relation between them. Thirdly, this transcendent reciprocity can be disclosed to men by the Son's

[22] There is also a distance connected to " the economy of the Kenosis, " which we shall treat later.

[23] We have selected the Logion but the entire Gospel of St. John treats the same mystery — Christ as hidden and revealed, incarnate and transcendent. Cf. J. GIBLET, " La Sainte Trinité dans l'Évangile de saint Jean, " *LV*, 29 (Sept. 1956).

[24] For an exegesis of this text and a list of sources, cf. A. FEUILLET, " Jésus et la Sagesse divine d'après les Évangiles synoptiques, " *RB* (April 1955), pp. 161-196; L. CERFAUX, " Les sources scripturaires de Matt 11, 25-30, " *Ephem. Theol. Lovan.* (1954), pp. 740-756 and (1955), pp. 331-342. Also by the same author, " Le Logion johannique, " *L'Évangile de Jean* (Paris 1958).

[25] " The characteristic note of John's *Logion* is that the Father and the Son are part *of one mystery* which man can know only from Revelation " (FEUILLET, *op. cit.*, p. 181, note 1.)

121

revelation. [26]   There is a communication.   This profound text has several implications for our study.   It reveals a mystery which cannot be known by human means but can be communicated by Revelation.   The one who reveals this mystery is present to the Father through an eternal reciprocity, [27] and present to men through the words of Revelation.   And finally, the one who speaks is the man Jesus Christ.   This human being is equally at home in the Father's world and in the world of men.   He is the *intersection* of God and men, time and eternity.   The psyche expressed through His words is a human psyche.   But it expresses the Divine mystery.   And it can do this because it receives it willingly, contemplates it, and reveals it to whom it wishes.

Now we can try to understand this affirmation and the situation responsible for it.   As we already saw, there is a mysterious spiritual point at the apex of the human soul.   Here occur the acts of thinking and willing, judging and deciding, affirming and loving — the acts which open man to Being.   Here the spirit attains self-awareness, because it is present to itself in a mysterious way, as a source of activity outside physical and mental realities, outside time.   Christ cannot have this kind of self-awareness, because He is not a human person, a human "ego."   At the summit of His human soul, there

[26] This theme is emphasized in the sapiential writings of the Old Testament.   Cf. Dt 30, 11-14 and the notes of CAZELLES, *BJ*, p. 117, a, b. Cazelles considers it one of the probable sources for the theology of the Word expressed in St. John's prologue.

[27] I cannot understand those exegetes who want to make the *logion* a purely "functional" statement about the mission and the Kingdom. The rationalists focused on this text precisely because they saw it as a "Johannine" way of expressing a direct relationship with God.   Regarding the distinction between the "functional" and the "metaphysical," we must ask what significance it has.   As J. GIBLET says (apropos of St. John): "Such a distinction arises in a mentality alien to the tradition of the Bible and to St. John.   For him, both aspects are grasped simultaneously.   Christ's salvific power comes from the fact that He is the Son of God who became man and worked among men" (*LV*, Sept. 1956, pp. 29, 97).   The problem has recently been clarified by L. MALEVEZ, "Nouveau Testament et Théologie fonctionnelle," *RSR*, 1-2 (1960), pp. 258 ff.

122

is a point where He opens Himself immediately, freely, and completely, not just to Being, but to God His Father. [28] Here, as man, He becomes aware of what He is, the only Son of God, who receives His being from the Father and returns it to Him in an eternal communication of love and glory. He realizes that He knows the Father in His relation of total dependence and has been given a mission to reveal this mystery to the world. He is the one who can say : " Before Abraham was made, I am " (Jn 8, 58), and apropos of the Father, " I and the Father are one " (Jn 10, 30).

In men this spiritual point is on the border between time and eternity. It is supra-temporal and can, therefore, inaugurate time. In Christ this point is *the living and enduring juncture of time and Eternity*. It exists only in the act of thinking, willing, and loving which completely accepts the mission, the message, and the action of the Father and which, therefore, inaugurates all the temporal implications of the redemptive mission. This act transcends the time it inaugurates. It participates in eternity in a unique manner. Even though it takes place *in* a human psyche, it *springs from an eternal subject*. At this supreme point, Christ is present to His Father. He knows Him and, through Him, the realities of His mission. And so, this point, too, begets time, because in it the Father communicates His mission in time, so that, in His human psyche, *Christ knows what the Father wants Him to know for the fulfillment of His mission*. From this point Christ's human time springs, measured by that knowledge, that Vision which,

---

[28] We are not saying that Christ must have the Beatific Vision in order to have self-awareness. But He cannot be aware of Himself without being aware of His Father *at the same time*. One can say that these are the subjective and objective aspects of Christ's knowledge. But these words are rather inexact. Self-awareness, even for Christ, does not focus on an object. It is really the subject's transparency to himself. But to what extent can we say that the vision of the Father is of the objective order ? This " vision " precludes any representation and refers to the " Subject " who makes Christ Himself a " Subject. " In speaking of this mystery we must set aside such inadequate terms.

insofar as it is communicated in time, is measured in turn by the mission from His Father.

This point of communion with the Father — this immediate vision of the Father — is not in time. It could not be, of course, because it exists in the loftiest part of the spirit. It is the acme of the God-Man's soul where eternal Life is received and possessed beyond time, motion, and temporal succession. But it is not a separated point suspended over time, a reality cut off from the temporal universe. It is, on the contrary, the living source of full redemptive life and of salvific time. Christ's vision is not, primarily, a " commanding point, " [29] which is to define the mission and its redemptive work. It is, primarily, a reception-point, where Christ possesses eternal life as a gift from His Father (see Jn 5, 26), and where He comes and goes to the Father in acts of love and adoration. That is why it becomes the source of the entire mission-time and redemptive activity.

C. This point explains one of the most mysterious aspects of Christ's temporal existence — His possession of the future. Christ is a prophet. It is one of His principal messianic functions. But He is not like the prophets who preceded Him and announced His coming. [30] At certain times the Jewish prophets heard of God's plans in an obscure, limited, fragmentary way. God spoke through them " at sundry times and in divers manners " (Heb 1, 1). It is very different with Christ. [31] In Him God has " spoken to us by his Son " (Heb 1, 2). With Him the fullness of time has come, and everything is to be accomplished *within* this fullness. In the eternalized point of

[29] Von Balthasar, *op. cit.*

[30] He is *the* great prophet expected by the Jews. Cf. *TWNT*, " Logos, " 4, pp. 114-115, and Cullmann, *Christologie du N. T.*, " Jesus the Prophet, " pp. 18 ff. Eng. trans. *Christology of the New Testament* (Philadelphia : Westminster, 1959).

[31] A. Neher, (*Essence du Prophétisme*, pp. 55-56) distinguishes the Hebrew prophet (waiting for an event) from the Christian prophet (waiting for the Parousia). If there is a school of Christian prophets, it finds its source and its fulfillment in Christ Himself.

124

His psyche, Christ learns of the events which form His mission, and of the time which measures its progress. In this respect *the mission received* from His Father becomes *His personal task.* It is not a task which is measured by some fleeting, limited aspect of the mission. It is the entire mission itself, because it is the anticipated realization of it in the vision which establishes and measures it.

This explains Christ's prophecies concerning the Kingdom or the Church. The Kingdom is already present — in Christ. It is still to come — again, in Christ. If Christ the individual is the seed of this Kingdom, Christ, the universal man, the Son of Man, the Second Adam, is the unique source of the Kingdom. *He is the Kingdom.* When Christ becomes aware *of all His individual dimensions*, He also becomes aware *of all the dimensions of the Kingdom* — past, present, and future. And He announces what He sees. He sees the Kingdom being organized by the leaders to whom He has entrusted His message, His people, and His own body. He sees the Kingdom growing in time from a mustard seed into a huge tree — through silence or words shouted from the housetops, through the apostolic work of the Twelve and their disciples, through the direct encounters between good and bad people, through suffering and persecution. He sees the indestructible permanence of the Church and the apostolic office of Simon renamed Peter. He sees the final perfection of the Kingdom and the Church, when the Angels will come to separate the wheat from the chaff and to gather the harvest, when the Son of Man will appear on His glorious throne to judge the just and the wicked. A psyche which expresses itself in such a manner is equally at home in the present or the future. Or, to be more exact, it is a psyche in which the future is present and unveiled [32] in some mysterious way. Unless we want to minimize the importance of these prophecies and posit more miracles to account for Christ's

[32] Of course, Christ's psyche transcends the limits of space and time. In revealing the " secrets " (of the past, present and future) He utilizes His divine power and reveals it to men. (Cf. St. THOMAS, *in Joann.*, I, lect. 15, note 8, lect. 16, note 4.)

possession of the future, we must see in Christ the fullness of prophetic light corresponding to the fullness of time. And we must base this awareness on His complete communion with His Father's mind and will. In short, we must consider it a necessary, wondrous *gift* from the Father, and *an essential part* of Christ insofar as He has a mission. [33] Only the man who is the center of time could possess such knowledge of time. Only He who is eternal, whose soul has a unique participation in eternity, could dominate time in this way.

Furthermore, since this awareness is a gift, we must look for its source in the mysterious point we are trying to fathom, in *the redemptive oblation* which Christ makes of Himself to the Father : " When he cometh into the world he saith. . . Behold I come. . . that I should do thy will " (Heb 10, 5. 7). This is the unifying principle of Christ's time. Although the text does not make explicit reference to a temporal relationship, it seems correct to equate the Incarnation with the redemptive oblation. [34] Just as the Incarnation and His mission must be equated — *eo missum quo factum* — so we must equate His Mission and His awareness of the Mission. The Incarnation itself begins " the oblation of the body of Jesus Christ once " (Heb 10, 10). We encounter once more the *ephapax* of Christ's coming. But now it is on the level of knowledge and love. Christ's oblation is based on a divine kind of " awareness, " which is perfectly

[33] We have alluded to the synoptic texts. In dealing with St. John we would have to go further. Note the remark of LÉON-DUFOUR; " Actualité de l'Évangile, " *NRT*, 5 (1954), p. 454 : " By virtue of His messianic psyche, Jesus does not envision His contemporaries of Palestine alone — His message makes *all men of all times* His contemporaries, those who have not seen but have believed (20, 29). " On Mk 14, 62, showing that Christ realizes He is the eternal high-priest and not a temporary one, cf. CULLMANN, *Christologie du Nouveau Testament*, p. 79. Eng. trans. *Christology of the New Testament* (Philadelphia : Westminter, 1959).

[34] The early Christians did not hesitate to say this. St. Irenaeus, for example, commenting on the *Logion* of Matthew explained that the Son had revealed the Father from all eternity, not just from the Incarnation : " it is affirmed in a general way *(communiter)* throughout time " (*Adv. Haer.*, 4, 6, 990 B). Cf. SPICQ, *Épître aux Hébreux*, II, pp. 304-305.

simple, unconnected to any corporeal image and (as such) strictly incommunicable to a human psyche. It is a knowledge based on eternity, and therefore on unity. This awareness, and the oblation involved, *establish* all the rest, because they inaugurate in Christ the mission itself and the time of the mission. In Christ there is only one act of oblation, [35] and it is measured by eternity. It begins with Christ's existence and never ceases. It establishes and unifies all Christ's actions which bring it to gradual fulfillment. Finally, it is accomplished on the Cross and blossoms into Glory. This point is not eternity. It is *the eternalized point in Christ's soul*, in which all His time-structuring intentions are united. These intentions differ greatly, because their different objects give them different content. They are realized and emphasized differently in the situations of Christ's life. Thus they are discontinuous in

---

[35] The text of *Mediator Dei* is well known : " No sooner, in fact, ' is the Word made flesh ' than He shows Himself to the world vested with a priestly office, making to the Eternal Father an act of submission which will continue uninterruptedly as long as He lives (Aeterno Patri seipsum subjiciens *quod quidem per totum vitae cursum intermittit* unquam). ' When He cometh into the world He saith... behold I come... to do Thy will. ' This act He was to consummate admirably in the bloody Sacrifice of the Cross " (*On the Sacred Liturgy*, New York: America Press, 1948, p. 18, note 17). Cf. *Mystici Corporis*. Many theologians consider this doctrine to be *proxima fidei*. In any case, the " Beatific Vision " of *Christus viator* is a deep mystery for several reasons : (1) it is not all-consuming and affects only God; (2) it does not confer beatitude and so it does not confer its effect on every human being. (K. RAHNER has suggested that it be called *visio immediata*); (3) it does not involve a difference between the extremes of presence or absence. Rather it is a question of varying degrees of illumination; (4) it seems to be controlled by an external factor, the mission. Thus, it is not the immediate encounter of the Risen Christ with His Father. But it does put Christ *in His Father's presence in a unique and absolutely transcendent way*, because it is the vision of the Son's soul and implies that He is aware that He is the Son. Hence the remark of Père J. GUILLET regarding the theophany at the Jordan when Christ was baptized : " The Bible does not say that Jesus saw the Father with His human eyes, but that the heavens opened and He saw the Spirit descending on Him. The Spirit brings the Father to Him. *In the Spirit He encounters the Father directly...* " " Baptême et Esprit, " *LV*, 26 (March 1956). (*Baptême et Nouveau Testament*, I, pp. 95-96.)

time. But all of them are evoked, animated, and directed by the unique oblation " made only once. " They are unified by this eternalized point, this unique offering, which is expressed partially in them on the temporal level and will be completely fulfilled in the eternal intercession at the Father's right hand.

Conclusion : Time and Eternity in Christ

This eternalized point exists only through the personal eternity of the Word of God. All Christ's redemptive intentions and their unifying principle itself, in short, Christ's whole temporal existence, must be directly connected to the eternity of the Word Incarnate. This explains why the relations between time and eternity in Christ are extremely complex. To the extent that His humanity is a manifestation and an expression of His divinity, so His temporal existence is a manifestation and an expression of His eternity. And the Father sets, determines, and fulfills this measure. No one has ever seen God. But His only Son became incarnate and dwelt amongst us. *He entered our space and time*, and thus revealed His Father to us.

In the unity of the Incarnate Son there is both a *connection* and an *opposition* between humanity and divinity, time and eternity. More precisely it is between that by which He is *One with the Father*, not only God like Him and eternal like Him, but also one single God with Him — and that by which He is *the visible expression of the Father*, i.e., the created, human, temporal, historic manifestation of the Father. There is opposition in this very unity, because, in the unity of the person, humanity and divinity are irreducible to each other, and not to be confounded, and because the mystery of Christ has a double edge in its very essence. His *human* existence is an expression of eternity but at the same time His *bodily* existence veils that eternity. This is the limit which this created manifestation sets on His uncreated existence. Only the Resurrection will erase this limit by erasing the visible manifestation in our world. But the connection is as strong as the opposition. His whole human

128

existence is meant to express His divinity; the whole *meaning* of His temporality is to express His eternity; and the whole *purpose* of the Incarnation is to communicate Christ's divinity and eternity.

Thus, Christ's whole human existence is real only insofar as it is assumed in His eternity to bring about the substantial living presence of eternity in time, *of the Eternal Himself in human time.* Christ's temporal existence reveals and communicates eternity, because it is rooted in it and springs from it at every moment. *In time,* Christ is the Being who *transcends* time but is *really expressed* through time. His temporal existence is rooted in His mission. And His mission is rooted in the act of eternal Procession. In this respect His mission itself is a manifestation. But because Christ's temporal existence is inaugurated by His acceptance of the mission, the mission measures His appearance in time, His time-structuring psyche, His temporal activity — in short, His whole time.

Hence all Christ's actions partake of this duality assumed into His unity. The Eternal is active in human time and all His actions are inserted into human temporality. But they are not absorbed by it. They transcend it every time, because they are always rooted in the eternity of His subsistent Person. They all have this twofold dimension because they are performed by an *eternal Person* through a *temporal ego.* Each " moment " of man's temporal existence emerges beyond time, because it is activated by a spiritual, supra-temporal " ego. " And each " moment " of Christ's historical existence is suffused with the eternal reality of the Son. Each moment springs from His eternity and expresses it. Each moment is the emergence of an eternal presence into time, *a temporal epiphany of the eternal God.* And they, in turn, are measured by the mission which establishes Christ's temporal existence, and gives it its structure and content, its amplitude and limit, its meaning and value. Christ's activity in time is enveloped in an incomprehensible mystery which is expressed through it. This mystery establishes and limits His temporal activity, which is a created manifestation of an uncreated Being.

6

The Phases of Christ's Temporal Existence

Christ's time is always rooted in His Mission. It is engendered in Him through His acceptance and fulfillment of this mission. Its structure is a constant, so we do not have to come back to it. But the mission is carried out *on three* extremely different *levels*, which involve three different kinds of temporal existence. Christ's humanity is an expression of His divinity, just as His temporal existence is an expression of His eternity. But these expressions of His divinity and eternity are of different kinds. So we must now study them.

Bultmann's View

This brings us face to face with the well-known radical interpretation of Bultmann. There are profound ideas in

Bultmann's theological synthesis. [1] He prevents us from relaxing in a superficial interpretation of New Testament texts, which are always so mysterious when one attempts to " understand " them. Bultmann is a rationalist, and so the mystery of a pre-existent *and* Incarnate Son is challenged. Bultmann has a somewhat Heideggerian view, and so he divides the human world into two parts, one part being the existential " decision " *(Entscheidung)* of the other. And finally his view is a Lutheran one. Only faith — the decision itself — gives reality to human existence and the Christian message and enables us to understand them.

Bultmann has *a very specific concept of time*. One might say it is " the keystone of the whole edifice. " [2] There is a radical cleavage between two types of time. One is an impersonal time, composed of measurable successive fragments (before — after). In it we find marked the phenomena of the natural sciences and various historical facts — in short, everything outside the existential sphere *(ungeschichtlich)*. The other is an existential time, a momentary instant without any duration, the " now " in which a decision is made. This *purely qualitative* kind of time is the time of human existence, and especially the time of existence in Jesus Christ. Both are characterized by existential decisions which establish them — in an instant.

---

[1] We need not repeat the work so well done by others. For an interpretation of Bultmann's work as a whole see the already classic treatments of L. MALEVEZ, *Christian Message and Myth* (Westminster, Md. : Newman, 1960) and R. MARLÉ, *Bultmann et l'interprétation du Nouveau Testament* (Paris 1956).

[2] The expression comes from J. N. WALTY. In a " Bulletin de Théologie protestante, " *RSPT* (April 1958), pp. 364 ff., he introduces two important German works : H. OTT, *Geschichte und Heilsgeschichte in der Theologie Rudolf Bultmanns* (Tübingen 1955) and J. KOERNER, *Eschatologie und Geschichte* (Hamburg 1957). We follow WALTY's presentation. Add also BULTMANN's *History and Eschatology* (New York : Harper, 1962). Père BENOIT has justifiably remarked that there is an *exegesis* of Bultmann to discuss; cf. *Exégèse et Théologie* (Paris 1961), I, p. 92. But our remarks here are concerned with the more general problem of a *theological interpretation* on which Bultmann has taken an explicit stand.

The " now " of this decision is never a fixed definable point in the flow of phenomena. It cannot be objectively pinpointed. The instant of decision is always " beyond time. "

This notion of time structures Bultmann's theological views. Once he has reduced real human time to a pure instant of decision, he attacks the Incarnation itself. A pre-existent God becomes man and redeems us by His death and Resurrection! This is the myth of myths, and Bultmann strives to demythologize it. The only source of salvation is the pure divine action which is necessarily " beyond time " [3] *(jenseits der Zeit)*, but is manifested in Jesus Christ. It cannot be submerged in deeds, beings, or " history. " A " salvation-history " is a contradiction. [4] The same holds true for Christ. Divine action can affect and challenge us only in the form of God's Message. And Jesus Christ is the example of this. To be sure, He did die on the Cross under Pontius Pilate. But this historical fact, His death, is of no importance. It is the " tragic end of a great man. " But it is also an existential decision in which God's eternal action is expressed. Jesus Christ is really the Message of God, [5] and thus His death affects me, challenges me, and forces me to make the decisive choice — either to let myself be crucified with Him, or not. [6] From this viewpoint the Resurrection — which is obviously not an historical fact — signifies that the Cross is a victory over death. It is manifested in the Church's Message and forces me to make a choice. The Cross and the Resurrection are *the* eschatological events, and they are simultaneously " in time and beyond time. " [7]

The Christian's real time is the " now " in which he encounters God's Message in Jesus Christ. It is the pure

---

[3] Cf. L. MALEVEZ, *op. cit.*, p. 91.

[4] It is one of Bultmann's chief complaints against Cullmann, who would have written only a " Christian philosophy of history. " (Cf. WALTY, *op. cit.*, p. 367, note 44.)

[5] L. MALEVEZ, *op. cit.*, p. 112.

[6] R. MARLÉ, *op. cit.*, p. 153.

[7] *Ibid.*, p. 154. We cannot see then how the *eschatological* event can be in time.

instant in which God's decision and man's decision confront each other through the Message, the time of " existential shock " *(Anstoss)* outside time. [8] God holds our time in His hands. He meets us everywhere. But we encounter Him only when He is revealed through His message. It is the message which makes the instant intelligible and supremely discriminative for us. Man must respond to this decision with another decision. He must respond to this " moment " with another " moment, " the moment of faith. This moment is necessarily eschatological because it sees the Message as *the* eschatological event, which transports it into an eschatological existence. Here *presence and transcendence* are one. And for Bultmann this is indicated most clearly in the eschatological message of St. John, where the " last hour " is already present, the " resurrection of the dead " already accomplished, and " judgment " already pronounced. In short, historical time is completely eliminated for the sake of the existential decision; Christ's person is completely eliminated for the sake of God's Message. Only the eternal action of God remains, encountering men through the Message in the time of decision. And it is always outside time.

Bultmann's view, undoubtedly, reveals a profound awareness of the transcendence of divine action and of the inability of " empirical " history to grasp the deep significance of Christ. It indicates a keen appreciation of the permanent actuality of the salvific event. But we must challenge his philosophical and theological point of departure. No existential decision exists as a pure instant cut off from human time. Every authentic decision involves a spiritual, psychic, and cosmic duration. It is actualized at a supra-temporal point in the human psyche, only because it inaugurates and establishes a new time for this psyche.

The existence of Christ in time is to be understood as a human duration inaugurated and prolonged by the eternalized point in His psyche. And His " hour " is indivisible, not because the Cross and the Resurrection are telescoped, but

<hr>

[8] Cf. MALEVEZ, *op. cit., passim.*

134

because His acts involve only one meaning, one purpose, and one presence — the presence of the saving-God-in-Jesus Christ. The Cross is *the unique intersection of time and eternity in Christ's body and soul.* Through it God reconciles us to Himself. And through this exposed (Rom 3, 25) and lifted up (Jn 3, 14-15) human being, the Cross is the unique intersection of time and eternity *in the entire history of the universe.* The Resurrection is not a well-understood fact like the Cross. It is not, as Bultmann thinks, just the " return of a dead man to earthly life. " It is the real completion of the redemptive mystery, the Father's glorifying response to the Son's oblation, the sovereign entrance of the Word Incarnate into His Father's glory and into His own glory. And in accordance with God's will, this redemptive mystery is also the great eschatological sign, the fulfillment of the great prophecy, and the great testimony of faith through Christ's appearances, through the outpouring of the Spirit, and through the apostolic Kerygma. We might say, as Bultmann does, that the Resurrection is the meaning of the Cross. But we do not mean the same thing. For him, the Resurrection is *simply* a *meaning* proclaimed by the message of the Cross, which men discover and " actualize " through this same message. For us, on the contrary, God the Savior thinks and wills the Resurrection as the *real fulfillment of the meaning* of the Cross. It is the seed of the new creation. And the Apostles believe, preach, and convert, because they have witnessed this new creation. They have eaten and drunk with the Resurrected Lord.

But there is a deeper gap between Bultmann and us. The Incarnation itself is at stake. Bultmann's thought is prejudiced because he rejects outrightly the Incarnate Word as such, the God-Man, the eternal God who is Mary's Son. He rejects Christ, who was called the Creator and Lord by St. Paul, and who was pictured by St. John as the incarnate Logos, living in glory from His first manifestation. Bultmann tries to discover the unity of the salvation-event in the message, the meaning, and the decision of a pure instant. But this unity is a *Being*, a *real Existent*, the *Word Incarnate*. Christ Himself unifies

Revelation, its words and deeds, eschatological time, and all time. Christ, with His humanity and divinity, is the Presence on which everything is established, through which everything unfolds, and in which everything is fulfilled. Christ is the living personal principle of Redemption in all its aspects. He is the principle of those aspects which exist in human time — the Message, the Body, Grace. And He is the principle of those aspects which perfect human time — the Resurrection and the final judgment. Redemption in all its aspects has human and supernatural reality because it is rooted in *the personal eternity of the Risen Son.* He is before God pleading for us in an eternal now (Heb 9, 24) and is, therefore, present in every moment of our time to establish it and unite it to Himself. Everything finds its unity and subsistence in Him : *omnia in ipso constant.* We must, therefore, study the temporal nature of Christ's " history. "

The Time of Pilgrimage

From Bethlehem to the Cross Christ's temporal existence is a *real human* one, a " fleshly " existence as opposed to His " spiritual " existence after the Resurrection. It veils eternity, even while it reveals it to some extent. Here we encounter the mystery of the eternal Son's humility, His *Kenosis.* [9] Christ takes a human nature like ours, a humble human state, which is realized in an incredibly mysterious humiliation. It is a state which is not consonant with the glory of the Word Incarnate, but is similar to the state of sinful man. His humble humanity veils His divinity, and involves a truly human existence which veils eternity.

At this stage Christ is seen and believed " according to the flesh. " He is a man like other men — *habitu inventus ut homo* —, the son of Mary, the son of a carpenter. In His human form the eternal Son is revealed indirectly, partially, sketchily —

[9] On this point see the extensive study of P. HENRY, " Kénose, " *DBS.*

through signs granted by God. It is brought about at first through the mysterious and secret radiance of the life, words, and attitudes of Jesus. Then it is brought about through the sudden and repeated burst of miracles which indicate God's presence, God's finger working through Christ. But these wonders are always signs which must be interpreted. And the need for interpretation involves the possibility of scandal and refusal, because there is a striking contrast between the wonder of the sign and the humility of the man, between the eternity revealed in a flash and the ordinary human temporality of the Galilean prophet. Finally, Christ's human existence conditions the gradual realization of His redemptive mission. Each of Christ's " mysteries " must be situated properly in this process of gradual realization. Each must be studied as an effective manifestation of the redemptive plan, linked to all the other manifestations. We could not attempt such an analysis here. It would be premature. We must emphasize a more essential fact. The temporal existence of *Christus viator* is a constant. But it has *two poles*, and either one can be emphasized. The Synoptic Gospels treat one. St. John treats the other. Only the two combined can give us a complete view of Christ in time.

The Synoptics

The Synoptic Gospels emphasize the Son's humanity and His humility, the temporal nature of His Kenosis. But they also insert eternity into the Kenosis itself. And in two important mysterious events, the Transfiguration and the Agony, they reveal the full dimensions, the two extreme poles of Christ's temporal existence.

Only once, before the Passion and because of it, does *eternity break openly into time* — in the Transfiguration. [10] Christ's splendor, the presence of Moses and Elias, the cloud, the Father's words — all this is a breakthrough of Christ's glory. *Eternity reveals its presence in time.* This is an amazing

[10] Mt 17, 1-9.

theophany because it does not hurtle us beyond the dimensions of time. Instead, it implants the presence of eternity and its manifestation in time. In one respect, the Transfiguration fulfills and completes the past. [11] Only Moses and Elias had climbed the peak of Sinai to contemplate God's glory. Moses was granted this favor to seal the Covenant; Elias, to restore it. At the Transfiguration, the three privileged witnesses " saw his glory " (Lk 9, 32) in which the Ancient Covenant is completed and the New Covenant inaugurated. The Fathers were not mistaken in thinking that the Word of God was revealed gradually throughout the Old Testament. For the theophanies of old lead to this extraordinary " manifestation " of a man in whom the resplendent glory of God resides, because He is the only Son of God. In another respect, the scene on Thabor anticipates Christ's Resurrection and exaltation. His body radiates glory and the Father gives Him His royal title, " beloved Son. " The New Covenant is ratified. But this is a unique, limited, conditional anticipation. His disciples are to tell no one before the proper time — " till the Son of Man be risen from the dead " (Mt 17, 9). This " significant moment " shows us in singular fashion the *complexity of Christ's present.* Eternity is seen to be involved in time because it is the source of time's meaning and value, and because it is present, concentrated, in the man Jesus Christ. Every current moment of a man's life is a focal point of interrelationships. Hence Christ's moment of transfiguration, which completes the past and inaugurates the future, is directly (vertically) joined to eternity, which unifies it and gives it meaning and value.

The mystery of the Agony is the opposite extreme. It reveals *the most typically human* kind of temporal existence, that of a crushed soul whose body is resigned to a vanishing life (Mk 14, 32-42). It is the state of abandonment. Jesus is alone, terribly alone as He faces the test. He cannot bear His isolation. He needs others. He takes three disciples, the three who should have been prepared and fortified by the Transfiguration.

---

[11] Cf. E. BOISMARD in *Élie le Prophète,* I (Paris 1956), pp. 124-126.

Christ needs others to be present and to share His agony. He needs their physical presence — " Stay here! " — and their spiritual presence — " Watch! " And to break the vise of abandonment, He returns three times and begs them to watch with Him. It is the temporal existence of a being-destined-for-death. Christ is hemmed in by the nearness of death. His whole being is dragged down by fear. He is beside Himself with nausea and distress at the thought of dying. He is stretched out, His face flat on the ground, bathed in a bloody sweat. The inexorable temporal process of death has begun. Finally, Christ sees His dereliction in all its depth. No longer is He the one who dwells in glory, the one who does the Father's Will determinedly, spiritedly, and tenderly. Now it seems that the heavens have closed. His Father has disappeared. The mission is faltering and His death has lost its meaning. At this moment His spontaneous thought is : " Father, if it is possible, let this chalice pass from Me. " He repeats it once, twice, three times — who knows how many times ? This is the most tragically human kind of temporal existence. And it is marked by a characteristic phenomenon, repetition. Christ, overwhelmed, attempts to face His destiny. Like the man who is about to die, He catches a breath, stops, breathes again. [12] The Transfiguration was a moment of exaltation, a revelation of eternity. The Agony is a moment of prostration and submersion in the lowest depths of human existence.

But our analysis is not complete. For it does not shed light on *the connection* between these two constrasting mysteries. It does not clarify the unique kind of temporal existence which they both share, the tension between time and eternity which profoundly unifies them. In the Transfiguration where Christ's eternity and His glory are revealed, the Passion is also present, signified by several facts. The scene occurs in the context of prophecies concerning the Passion. Christ gives the three

[12] We must add here Heb 5, 7 ff. Cf. C. Spicq, *in h.l.* and O. Cullmann, *Christology of the New Testament* (Philadelphia : Westminster, 1959).

apostles a sign to " keep " at the time of His Agony. He speaks
to Moses and Elias about His " decease " (Lk 9, 31). He
forbids His disciples to reveal this secret before " He shall be
risen from the dead " (Mk 9, 9). The Transfiguration implies
an overshadowing annihilation. It is a preparation for His
" hour. "

Conversely, in the Agony where Christ's humiliation is
revealed, there are several reflections of His glory. Only the
three apostles are taken with Him. Thus, there is *continuity*
between the meaning of the Transfiguration and the meaning
of the Agony. Furthermore, the terror which Christ feels
is infinitely more than a human sentiment. It is connected to a
death for the " ransom of the world " and the " remission of
sins. " It shows Christ rejected by His own and immersed in
the sins of men. He has " become sin for us. " But one really
comes to understand sin only through God. And Christ is
overwhelmed by a realization of sin which springs from the
eternalized point of His psyche. The night into which He is
hurtled is a sign — an obscure, consuming sign of light. Finally,
the eternalized point where Christ's soul communes with the
Father is revealed in two utterances. It is revealed in the
suppliant cry, " Abba, Father, " where we see the mutual
tenderness of Father and Son, and it is revealed in the decision
of absolute fidelity, " Not what I will, but what thou wilt "
(Mk 14, 36), — which is followed soon after by the lively words,
" Rise up! Let us go! " In the midst of His communion with
sinners, in the very throes of sin, He is still aware of His
communion with eternity. " The angel " in Luke's account
indicates this continuing mutual relationship. Indeed, this
very tension explains the horror of the agony. [13] But there is
more to be said. These two mysteries cannot be separated
from their context. The Gospels reveal the same integrated
duality. Christ's glory is enveloped in humiliation, even in

[13] On this hidden presence of eternity, we have usually quoted St. Mark.
However, we should at least add : Mk 14, 49 and 61-62. If we were focusing
on St. Luke alone, who is quite close to St. John on this point, there are
many other texts which could be cited.

the miracles, and yet eternity pierces through His fleshly existence.

St. John's Gospel

Once anyone has come to appreciate the tension between time and eternity in Christ, the interior linking of glory and humiliation, and the permanent presence of eternity and glory in the most humiliating kind of human existence, he can never forget it. If he has personally encountered this mystery, he can write the whole history of Jesus from the viewpoint of His " glory. " This is precisely what St. John does. [14] His Gospel centers around two " moments, " Christ's public life (1-12) and His *hour* (12 ff,) which completes and fulfills this public life. In St. John's Gospel, this " hour " is the key to an understanding of Christ's existence in time.

For St. John, Christ's hour embraces His Passion, Death, Resurrection and Ascension, and the outpouring of the Holy Spirit. In one respect it involves a series of temporal events, linked to the Jewish feasts. They are marked by precise details of time and place. In short, they are implanted in our history by the Father, and Christ does not anticipate them. But on the other hand, Christ's " hour " is an " indivisible event " (Bussche), a mystery enveloping time, because it is rooted in the eternalized point of Christ's psyche. St. John dares to do what no one else had done. For the synoptic writers, Christ's glory is realized primarily in the Parousia. For Paul, it is the Resurrection. For John, it is already realized in the Cross itself. He identifies the crucifixion with the exaltation, because on the Cross Christ completes His Father's work, draws all men to Himself, and begins to pour out the Holy Spirit in the stream of living water coming from His

[14] On this point cf. in *L'Évangile de Jean* (Paris 1958) the articles of H. VAN DEN BUSSCHE ("Structure de Jean I-XII ") and W. GROSSOUW (" La Glorification du Christ dans le quatrième Évangile "). Add also VAN DEN BUSSCHE, " L'attente de la grande Révélation dans le quatrième Évangile, " *NRT* (1953), pp. 1009-1019 and A. GEORGE, " L'Heure de Jean XVII, " *RB* (1954), pp. 392-397.

pierced side. *John does not telescope the facts*, confusing the act of dying with the act of rising. But *he does reveal their deeper unity*. He indicates their identical meaning and purpose, and connects it to the divinity of the Incarnate Son, the unique, supra-temporal point which is the source of His *doxa*. That is why the sacerdotal prayer (17) " is situated in the present and the future, in time and eternity. " [15]

Using Christ's hour as the focal point, John *extends* the process of glorification to Christ's whole life. His analysis of Christ's life presupposes the fulfillment of the hour, the Son's return to the Father and the outpouring of the Spirit on His disciples to teach them from within, to " remind " them of Christ's words, and to help them " reach the whole truth. " John casts the eye of faith on Christ's life and transfigures it by revealing the Mystery of Jesus. This " transfiguration " is neither an arbitrary metamorphosis nor an added signification. It identifies and reveals the Incarnate Logos in all His glory from His Incarnation and His first miracles. The Transfiguration in the synoptic manner has no place in St. John's Gospel, [16] because glory radiates from within Christ and envelops Him from the very beginning. There is no place for the Agony either. John alludes to Christ's troubled soul and to His prayer, " Father, save me from this hour " (12, 27). But this prayer is immediately followed by the words, " But for this cause I came unto this hour. Father, glorify thy name " (12, 27-28). And a voice from heaven is heard. The sketchy treatment of the Agony is concluded by a hint of the Transfiguration.

Glory *suffuses* Christ's earthly life *in two respects*. First, the glory of the Incarnate Logos is only a participation in His eternal pre-existent glory. One who has read John's prologue can scarcely give any other interpretation to Christ's prayer

---

[15] A. GEORGE, *op. cit.*, p. 394.

[16] Cf. W. GROSSOUW citing C. H. DODD : there is no room " for a visible, transitory metamorphosis, because all the acts of the Incarnate Christ are suffused with the *doxa*, which faith alone can glimpse " (*op. cit.*, p. 137).

(17, 5): " And now glorify thou me, O Father, with thyself, with the glory which I had, before the world was, with thee. " [17] Christ's Hour proceeds from this glory, manifesting it and completing it. On the other hand, Christ's glory is prolonged in the Church. For the time of the Church depends on Christ's Hour and fulfills its purpose. And it is connected to His original glory as well as His final glory, to its source in eternity as well as its consummation in the Parousia.

Even if the *three* Synoptic Gospels could be considered *one* account, it would still be impossible to make their chronological history coincide with St. John's account. But their interpretations and their message do *converge and complement* each other. The Synoptic Gospels show us a man in whom God is gradually revealed, a human existence suffused with eternity, and different events to emphasize these two dimensions. From beginning to end, St. John shows us the Incarnate Son of God, who is imbued with glory and eternity. But the synoptic history is incomprehensible apart from the Risen Christ; [18] and the radiant glory of the Fourth Gospel is the glory of the Logos made flesh, whom John himself has seen and touched. Time and eternity are always the two inseparable, constituent,

[17] The text is uncertain and the exegetes are divided. Père MOLLAT (*BJ*, 175, a), for example, understands it as " either the glory which Jesus possessed in His divine pre-existence, or rather the glory which the Father reserved for Him from all eternity. " We think that, whatever the precise nuance is, it is the same reality and the two affirmations are inseparable. If it is the eternal glory of the Logos, Jesus does not need the glory which He has never lost. Rather, this *doxa* must be fully communicated to the *sarx* which He has taken on and which He is going to sacrifice. If it is the glory " reserved for Him " by the Father, it is still divine glory which is being communicated. (John knows no other kind — outside the banal sense of the word.) Since " everything of Yours is Mine, " this glory is the glory of the only begotten Son. We always find ourselves up against the mystery of the Incarnate Logos where time and eternity are inextricably linked. (Cf. the accurate and significant remarks of W. GROSSOUW, *op. cit.*, pp. 137, 140, 142, and VAN DEN BUSSCHE, *Le discours d'adieu de Jésus*, pp. 154-155.)

[18] See, for example, the statements of W. MARXSEN, *Der Evangelist Marcus*, 1956 (cited by X. LÉON-DUFOUR, *RSR* [1958], pp. 240-241).

irreducible dimensions of Christ's historical mystery. In the Synoptic Gospels, the Lord's human existence is always centered between glory and annihilation. In St. John's Gospel, it is centered in a fraternal, strong human being who is seen and touched every day. Now we must note the true characteristics of Christ's temporal journey.

True Characteristics of the Temporal Journey

Eternity in Exile

We have emphasized, as the Gospels do, the presence of eternity as the source of Christ's time. But this does not mean that the point of divine glory, communion, and vision in Christ's soul destroys His normal human psyche. As long as " the economy of exinanition " lasts, [19] this eternalized point is " exiled, " separated from the normal human activities of Christ's soul. The Son's eternal glory does not sparkle in His body and soul. His communion with the Father does not put His body and soul in the state of beatitude. His beatific vision does not affect His knowledge on the human level. This should not surprise us. Christ's beatific vision contemplates things in God through the divine essence. It is knowledge by way of simple unity, concentrated at the apex of His spirit. Its content *of itself* cannot enter the area of human knowlege where reasoning and intuition are always at work, constantly reorganizing the fruits of their complex activity. It cannot be the content of human judgment, which must synthesize the raw material of concepts before formulating them. Christ's human mind can learn only those things which the Father deems *necessary for the mission.* The mission determines this just as it makes Christ what He is and determines the glory, the knowledge, and the activity proper to the poor, humbled, suffering Servant destined for death. The point of glory in

[19] The fine phrase of DE LA TAILLE, cf. *The Mystery of Faith* (New York: Sheed, 1940) Vol. I, p. 241, note 6.

Christ is, first and foremost, *the point where* His human soul *is attached to His person.* At this point a human soul is embodied in the Word and made the personal soul of the Word. Everything else derives from this point in accordance with the demands of the mission. Christ does not know the hour of judgment; [20] He is overwhelmed by the Agony; He falls under the weight of the Cross; He lets out a cry of distress on the Cross. It is all part of the same plan. It is the *humiliation* of the Son, but it is really the humiliation of the *Beloved Son* imbued with " the glory as it were of the only begotten of the Father " (Jn 1, 14).

This mysterious coexistence, in which the various levels of the soul are separate, is not a contradiction or a gratuitous formulation. We see examples of it in the Gospels and in the experiences of the great mystics. J. Huby did well to advert to them, [21] because the mystics share in the Cross of Christ and in His glory in a unique and wonderful way. Their spiritual experiences indicate that the soul has different levels. Its depth (or height) is not attained in ordinary experience. God can separate these different levels and activate them simultaneously. One soul can experience at the same time light and darkness, joy and sorrow, the most wonderful communion with God and the most unspeakable abandonment. God can keep light, joy, and communion at one level of the soul and prevent it from spreading to the other levels. There are countless examples. We shall quote the words of Marie of the Incarnation, an Ursuline nun, whose mystical experiences were quite extraordinary. She was " about seven years old " when

[20] Mk 13, 32. Whatever be the correct interpretation of this very primitive and difficult text, cf. the remark of Msgr. CERFAUX, " The events of the last days are part of the secrets with which the eschatological prophecies are concerned. It seems strange and improper that the Son does not know the exact date. For normally He knows all other secrets and He can reveal them. " (" Le Logion Johannique, " *L'Évangile de Jean*, p. 150). Cf. A. MICHEL, " Intuitive (vision), " *DTC*.

[21] J. HUBY, *Saint Marc* (Coll. *Verbum Salutis* 3, pp. 382 ff.). He cites a fine text of St. Thérèse (*Autobiography*, chap. 20).

she was introduced into the mystical life, but this particular experience occurred when she was nearly sixty-five. She remarks that " the purity of divine love is awesome, penetrating and inexorable. It is the implacable foe of the spirit of nature. " Only the Spirit of God can effect such a purification. Then she says : " When and as He wills it, it is a purgation more piercing than lightning. . . In this purgation, one still sees the sacred Incarnate Word. But formerly He was the divine Lover who consumed the soul in His divine embrace. Now He crucifies the soul, piercing it everywhere and wrenching it from the spirit — *except at its deepest point, in which God is enthroned, and which seems to be an abyss and a separated place.* I can find no other words to express this state.

" The soul and the spirit are divided by the cross and suffused with its piercing effects. But these effects never touch the *deepest part of the soul, which seems to be a separate entity,* even though the soul itself is a simple substance without parts. Sometimes God, the Master of the soul's depth, seems to hide Himself and leave it gradually. It then seems to be a pure vacuum, and the suffering is unbearable. This gives rise to the despairing thoughts which would hurtle body and soul into hell. " [22]

These words indicate to us the distinct levels of the soul, the depth which underlies them, and the power of God's omnipotent love to separate them. Consequently, we should not be astonished to find glory and painful humiliation coexisting in Jesus Christ. This is *the* mystery which explains the others, and thus is explained itself.

The Complexity of Christ's Fleshly Existence

Christ lives a real human existence in time. He " grows " physically, mentally, and spiritually — " in wisdom, and age, and grace with God and men. " [23] He has a true human

[22] Text in Dom JAMET, *Le Témoignage de Marie de l'Incarnation* (Paris 1932), pp. 227-228. (Our italics.)

[23] Lk 2, 52.

146

time-span, nurturing, developing, and perfecting His human nature. Through His body and soul, He " actualizes " what was only potential before. And He can do this only because His body and soul are involved in a temporal progression, and are influenced by the world of nature and men. The eternalized point of Christ's psyche, in which He knows and loves the Father in a strictly divine way, does not prevent Him from living a normal human life. In fact, this point establishes His human existence, *because it too exists only for and through His mission.* It is " in exile, " because Christ as a human being must attain the fullness of knowedge. He must render full testimony and service. He must endure the full agony and abandonment of His Passion and death. Only thus can He merit to open the portals of the Resurrection (Lk 24, 46). Only thus can He become eternal and, through the eternalized point in His psyche, acquire the fullness of power which the Father has ordained for Him in time and eternity.

It is in this framework that we must explain *Christ's development during His mission.* Consider the events in St. Luke's Gospel. Christ as a boy converses with the doctors of the law; He is baptized in the Jordan and tempted in the desert; He preaches for the first time; He goes up to Jerusalem, a journey of deep redemptive significance; He attempts to gather in the faithless Jews as a hen gathers her chicks; He is hailed as king with branches of palm; He suffers the Agony and gives final testimony before the high priest. All these events are *stages of growing self-awareness, involvements in strictly human realities,* where the fate of a human being is affected by the love of the Father and the love or hate of men, and where the eternal plan is accomplished each time in Jesus Christ. These experiences which Christ must undergo spring from the eternalized point in His psyche. They are unified there in a strictly divine way. There they are potentialities which are yet to be actualized, divine plans which are yet to be realized, projects and discoveries which Christ will accomplish in human history and human time. It is significant that the Epistle to the Hebrews (5, 7-10) cites the sad human elements in Christ's sacrifice — His prayers, pleas, and tearful cry — and then summarizes the whole mystery in this phrase : " Whereas indeed he was the Son of God, he learned obedience by the things which he suffered. " Christ experiences fraternally human suffering through His body and blood (Heb 2, 11-18). This is the apprenticeship through which He accomplishes the Redemption and reveals the mutual ties of love — the Father's love for His sinful children, and redeemed humanity's love for the Father.

In Christ's temporal existence before the Resurrection, *eternity is enveloped by time.* It is the time of Redemption in the strict sense. It is completed by His death, because this completes His mission and ends His " fleshly " temporal existence. His temporal existence is *a means* of Revelation *and a proof* of it. The sensible perception of the man Jesus Christ is the normal means of perceiving spiritually the Lord Jesus Christ. But by its very nature it involves the risk of restricting Christ to a temporal existence and obscuring the impression He has made on those around Him. At this point faith must struggle to pierce through flesh and time in order to glimpse eternity. Because it is a difficult struggle enmeshed in time, the Apostles' faith at this stage is obscure, rudimentary, and unsteady. It matures only after many fluctuations between affirmation and denial, doubt and belief. It is not perfected until Christ has risen and the Spirit is sent, until He has been snatched forever from His humiliating fleshly existence and all is consummated.

The Resurrection and Temporal Existence

The Resurrection is a complete mystery rooted in the Father's omnipotence. It is *affirmed*, but *never fully explained*. The Risen Christ, the glorious Christ, has never been seen by human eyes as He really is. Even Paul Himself saw only the brightness of His glory and heard His voice.

He did not see His face. The Risen Christ "manifests" Himself, but in a veiled way. His temporal existence during the forty days after the Resurrection is marked by " appearances. " This whole period is difficult to analyze, but we must attempt it. [24]

Mystery of Christ's Presence

We must start with the discovery of the empty tomb (Mk 16, 1-11, Jn 20, 1-10). Christ's body has disappeared. The fleshly link between Christ and our space and time has been broken. It is a sign that Christ has entered a new state and has escaped these earthly dimensions. The Gospels express this fact in a *negative* way. After the Resurrection, [25] Christ is no longer in our world as He was before. He is at the Father's right hand. Even though He still manifests Himself, His presence and His temporal existence are of an entirely new order.

In St. Mark's Gospel (16, 6-7), the young man clothed in white garments says : " You seek Jesus of Nazareth, who was crucified. He is risen : he is not here. Behold the place where they laid him. But go, tell his disciples and Peter that he goeth before you into Galilee. There you shall see him, as he told you. " This message is couched in terms of time and space. But it indicates that the Risen Christ has escaped these dimensions forever, that He will be present in space and time in an entirely new way as He promised. In St. Luke's Gospel (24, 5-6), the two men in shining garments say : " Why seek you the living with the dead ? (Where else would He be ?) He is not here. " But if not here, where ? " He is risen. " This reply contains no reference to space and time. Christ has entered a new mystery. He is at the right hand of God. " Remember how He spoke to you when He was still in Galilee. " There is still continuity in this break with the past.

---

[24] For the exegesis of texts, cf. J. SCHMITT, *Jésus Ressuscité dans la Prédication apostolique.* For a philosophical study of the problem, cf. J. GUITTON, *The Problem of Jesus* (London : Burns, 1955), pp. 126 ff.

[25] Cf. P. BENOIT, " L'Ascension, " *RB* (1949), pp. 195 ff.

The Resurrection is a part of God's message, a prophecy come true. It is a part of God's plan, the fulfillment of His will. The same Christ who was dead is living once more in glory. [26] But now His glory is freed from all terrestrial limitations. What then will His presence be like?

The Gospels show us a Christ who appears and disappears *suddenly*. He is no longer in time and space, appearing and disappearing at specific moments. He does not come from one place and go to another place. He appears at only one occasion at a time. His sporadic appearances indicate that He is present " elsewhere " — at the Father's right hand, which is beyond time and space. [27] His former kind of presence and temporal existence has ended. He is no longer corporally in our world, our time, our space as He was before. His presence is now a " spiritual " one hidden from human touch and perception. His body is no longer a " fleshly " one like ours. It is no longer *here in any part* of our time and space at all.

When Christ appears now, His presence is *the appearance of a strict mystery*. Someone is present in time who has already escaped time and space. He is now in another world, so much so that He is not recognized at first by Magdalen, by the Apostles in the Upper Room, or by the disciples on the road to Emmaus. Each time He must give them a sign before they recognize Him — a personal word to Magdalen, a familiar action for the travelers of Emmaus, a meal and a touch for the Apostles in the Upper Room, a miracle for the fishermen. The extra-ordinary fact is that there is no reminder of the Transfiguration. Christ does not appear in all His glory. Each time He appears " in another shape " (Mk 16, 12). He who can no longer be seen by human eyes, makes Himself mysteriously visible, to give testimony and to seal His mission before disappearing until the end of time.

[26] So says the Apocalypse : " I am the First and the Last, and alive, and was dead. And behold I am living for ever and ever " (1, 17-18).

[27] For St. Thomas (*ST*, III^a, 55, 6, c) this is a manifestation of Christ's glory.

His appearances are so astonishing, so other-worldly, that the Apostles are seized with a holy fear until they recognize Him. After the miraculous catch of fish, Christ says to His own : " Come and dine. And none of them who were at meat, durst ask him : Who art thou ? Knowing that it was the Lord " (Jn 21, 12). It is He and yet it is not He. He is the same and yet He is different. To recognize Him they must have a miraculous sign. It is John who understands it and tells Peter and the others : " It is the Lord. " Christ's unique kind of presence is an absolutely unique manifestation. He is in a " time " free of all cosmic and bodily connections. As Jean Guitton wrote, [28] " this vision was not simple human perception. " Each apparition is a pure epiphany, joyous and ebullient as the gift of grace, tenuous and fleeting as the memory of one gone, mysterious and frightening as the unknown.

Reality of the Presence

In spite of all this, the Lord *really* does enter the time of His disciples. The Eternal One, the Man at the right hand of God, is truly their fellow-traveler through the successive moments of their temporal existence.

Christ is really present in time. In fact *He finds new ways of inserting Himself* in human time. His disciples see Him, touch Him (Lk 24, 39), hear Him, and speak with Him. He eats real food with them. He walks with the disciples on the road to Emmaus, talks to them, and enters the inn with them. Whatever the real nature of His mysterious presence may be, He is involved in the temporal existence of His disciples. The appearances of the Risen Lord are appearances of the humble, fraternal Servant. Jesus eats with His own; He explains the Scriptures and condescends to their weakness — *Put your finger here, Thomas !* He prepares a meal for them (Jn 21, 9-25). He is still the " Good Master, " gentle and humble. All this links His present existence to His past one. There are familiar traces in this new, mysterious existence.

[28] *The Problem of Jesus*, p. 210.

Christ's new kind of presence is also more real insofar as it *reveals more*. Now His temporal existence unveils eternity. Its sporadic nature reveals more than did His strictly human existence during the Kenosis. During the forty days He does not live in successive moments of time. He lives in " significant instants " where His presence, independent of temporal succession, gives meaning and value to man's temporal existence because it reflects the mysterious Being who is its source. First He was not present, then He is, and then He is no longer present. At each moment of His presence, the Lord of time, the Eternal One, breaks through into time.

These moments are *more significant than ever*. Each of these " presents " in all its complexity fulfills the past and anticipates the future. Christ had proclaimed that He was the fulfillment of the prophecies [29] and the theophanies in the Old Testament. [30] Now He shows that the past has been fulfilled in His own flesh. The Passion is etched on His body : " See my hands and feet, that it is I myself. Handle, and see : for a spirit hath not flesh and bones, as you see me to have. And when he had said this, He shewed them his hands and feet " (Lk 24, 39-40). He also shows that the Promise has been fulfilled in Him, and He explains it to His disciples. On the road to Emmaus, " beginning at Moses and all the prophets, he expounded to them in all the scriptures the things that were concerning him " (Lk 24, 27). He tells the apostles : " These are the words which I spoke to you while I was yet with you, that all things must needs be fulfilled which are written in the law of Moses and in the prophets and in the psalms, concerning me. Then he opened their understanding, that they might understand the scriptures " (Lk 24, 44). At the same time, He reveals the future and establishes it. He predicts the coming events; pardon for repentant sinners " in his name, unto all nations, beginning at Jerusalem " (Lk 24, 47); their testimony in Palestine and " to the uttermost part of the earth " (Acts 1,

[29] Regarding Moses, for example, Jn 5, 45-47.

[30] Cf. Jn 1, 51 (Jacob); 5, 26-27 (Daniel); 8, 56 (Abraham); 12, 41 (Isaias).

8); their universal mission, " Going therefore, teach ye all nations " (Mt 28, 19); the gift of " the power of the Holy Ghost " (Acts 1, 8) for all that work. The future is formed in the only Present which has ever existed with the plenitude of eternity.

In this " present " *the time of the wayfaring Church is founded.* Christ's appearances are the basis for the testimony which the Church must render concerning His Resurrection. They are the foundation of the Church. Hence the Apostles replace Judas by choosing one who has " companied with us, all the time that the Lord Jesus came in and went out among us, beginning from the baptism of John, until the day wherein he was taken up from us " (Acts 1, 21-22). They are all " witnesses preordained by God, " who " did eat and drink with him, after he arose again from the dead " (Acts 10, 41). Christ's actions during the forty days inaugurate the temporal existence of the Church's mission and her sacraments. His appearances to the Apostles as a group[31] are recorded near the end of the Gospels. They sum up the meaning of the Resurrection. The Apostles are sent by Christ, even as He has been sent by the Father. After they receive the Holy Spirit, they are to preach the Word, call men to repentance, baptize them, confer the Spirit, and pardon their sins. And Peter's mission as the universal pastor is confirmed. Through these " meaningful " acts, Christ reveals and carries out the full implications of the ancient Promise. They also prove Him to be what He was from all eternity — the personal center of salvation-time.

This new presence and this fulfillment are *eschatological.* Here is the deepest dimension of their mystery. This mysterious time is the crucial moment. It *places all the other* moments in some relationship with itself and gives them *their ultimate meaning.* They either anticipate this moment, prolong it, or complete it. Christ now reveals what He knew in eternity from the Father because He has definitively accomplished it. And this act completes His temporal mission. The forty days

[31] Mt 28, 16-20; and Lk 24, 36-49; so close to Jn 20, 19-29.

and all the other moments linked to them reveal the meaning of time itself and its purpose. Time is rooted in its sovereign center, because it is assumed into the personal eternity of the crucified and Risen Christ, the Lord of time, of man, and of the world.

This " moment " of the Risen Christ, therefore, is both a *fulfillment and* a *promise.* It inaugurates a new time, the definitive salvation-time which will last for centuries. It prefigures and prepares the ultimate fulfillment — the glorious Parousia. Christ's epiphany during the forty days is eschatological because *anticipation and fulfillment intersect in it.* The Synoptic Gospels give only hints of the anticipatory aspect. But St. Paul has clearly elucidated it. In the First Epistle to the Corinthians (15, 1 ff.), he affirms three truths. First, there is the historical mystery of the Resurrection, confirmed by the testimony of Scripture and the Church (15, 1-10). Secondly, there is a necessary connection between Christ's Resurrection and the resurrection of Christians. Both stand or fall together, and all Christianity with them (15, 12-19). Thirdly, they are interconnected because mankind stems from two sources, Adam and Christ. The former brought physical and spiritual death; the latter brought Resurrection and life. Christ is " the first fruits of them that sleep " (15, 20). In other words, through Him and in Him the dead are planted for the resurrection-harvest, and in the face of death, the last enemy, God " hath given us the victory through our Lord Jesus Christ " (15, 57). In a later epistle St. Paul makes a closer connection between the Risen Christ and the faithful, asserting that Christ will transform our lowly bodies into glorious images of His own body through God's omnipotence : " But our conversation is in heaven : from whence also we look for the Saviour, our Lord Jesus Christ, who will reform the body of our lowness, made like to the body of his glory, according to the operation whereby also he is able to subdue all things unto himself " (Phil 3, 20-21).

St. John's treatment is less extensive and not so precise. But it is more vigorous. When Peter has been confirmed in his pastoral office, he points to " the disciple whom Jesus loved, "

154

and asks : " Lord, what about him ? " Jesus replies : " So I will have him to remain till I come, what is it to thee ? " (21, 22). He simply affirms the fact of His own return. John has already given two important indications of this. First, the Son has received all power from the Father (5, 21-29). He has been given two privileges — to have life in Himself, and to judge mankind. The hour is coming when the Son of God will summon the dead. They will rise from their tombs and eternal judgment will be passed on them. " They that have done good things shall come forth unto the resurrection of life : but they that have done evil, unto the resurrection of judgment " (5, 29). But there is more to be said. Christ can utter the summons to resurrection because He is the master of life and death. He has received life and possesses it in such a way that He is its living fountainhead. No one can take it from Him. Death can touch Him only if He freely wills it. And His free will can restore eternal life to Him. This is the profound insight of St. John. Earlier tradition shows the Father raising Christ from the dead. But John, who clearly emphasized the absolute dependence, unity, and equality of Father and Son, puts these astonishing words on the lips of Jesus : " Therefore doth the Father love me : because I lay down my life, that I may take it again. No man taketh it away from me : but I lay it down of myself. And I have power to lay it down : and I have power to take it up again. This commandment have I received of my Father " (Jn 10, 17-18; see also 2, 19-22). And yet we have not said enough. Christ has such a sovereign hold on life and can resurrect Himself because *He Himself is the Resurrection and the Life* (11, 25). Therefore, He can perform the Father's will, raising the dead and giving eternal life to His faithful. " Now this is the will of the Father who sent me : that of all that he hath given me, I should lose nothing; but should raise it up again in the last day " (6, 39).

In this perspective the appearances of the Risen Christ are really *the beginning of the last day.* The last Resurrection is already here, but only in the presence of the One who resurrected Himself and will resurrect all men at the proper hour.

155

Firstfruits, Chief, Second Adam — these expressions refer to the same mystery. It is the beginning of the end in the person of Him who has already effected it in Himself and will effect it in all men. The new presence of the Risen Christ is really the anticipation of the last day, the concrete promise of the general resurrection, the source of all new life in the Holy Spirit. Christ's Resurrection is thus a *presence*, a *prophecy* and a *magnificent finale*. It situates all Christian time between Easter and the Parousia, between a past and a future which are unified in it. It inaugurates *the* mysterious dimension of Christian eschatology, in which the future is already present, and the end already achieved at the beginning. But to delineate the nature of this eschatology, we must retrace our steps and study the redemptive act which inaugurates this New Time.

7

Christ's Presence in Time

We must now synthesize the foregoing material in order to see Christ's relationship to time in its true perspective. Of course, even an inspired person could not grasp all the dimensions of this relationship. For this is the mystery of Christ the Savior Himself. St. Paul tells us that through the Holy Spirit Christians receive the power " to comprehend, with all the saints, what is the breadth, and length, and height, and depth " (Eph 3, 18). But he says this to express (in Stoic terminology) the cosmic role of Christ in all its transcendent depth and vastness; to emphasize that we can " know also the charity of Christ, " — the core of the mystery — " which surpasseth all knowledge " (3, 19). But even in this negative approach we can glimpse the panorama which God's message has laid out before us.

157

The Redemptive Act as the Mystery of Unity

Man's vocation is rooted in one fact — he *is loved by God*. His vocation, then, is *to love God*. Man's history begins in a state of innocence. God made man sinless, capable of being transformed by love. He wants men to be His friends, to be His own sons. The history of mankind is the story of man's response to God's love. But man, by definition, is the creature who can say no. His ability to say *no* makes his *yes* more valuable. Man can challenge everything : economic, social and political conditions, his place in the world, his life and the lives of others, even God and his own relationship with God.

Man makes these decisions of acceptance or rejection at the deepest point of his being, the *inviolable point* where he thinks and wills. There he can even challenge his vocation of loving God and say no. In the Bible, no matter what desire or good may be involved, *sin* is always *basically the rejection of* God, the attempt to treat Him as an equal, the refusal to say yes. Thus sin makes man guilty, condemned, miserable. It causes a deep-rooted privation in his soul, separating him from God, his fellow-men, and even himself. It is a refusal which surpasses time, because it profanes, alienates, and distorts the inviolable point of his being.

Furthermore, sin is *irreparable* as far as man is concerned. It is one of the characteristic marks of his existence. He can demolish but not rebuild; he can kill but not bring life back. The love which God has for man, the love to which He calls him, is a divine gift. It is the love which passes among the three divine Persons and is meant to pass between God and man through the communication of grace. When man rejects this love and refuses to love God, he shatters something which belongs only to God, a pure gift to which he has no claim. Spiritually he is dead, and a dead man cannot revive himself.

But *God wills to revive the dead man*, to restore his dried bones. The Redemption does precisely this. God unbelievably takes the initiative and grants another favor. He re-creates the being who has been de-created by sin. The Redemption is God's act of love which gives pardon, salvation, and life by enabling man to love Him once more. Man is *placed between God's gift and His pardon.* The whole Bible recounts the history of this love — the promise, the covenant, the repeated reconciliations of the indocile, faithless, ungrateful people through judgment and pardon. Salvation is possible for man only when he consents to be judged, recognizes himself as a sinner, and begs for pardon. God wills that man be brought back to life by a *conversion.* When *the inviolable point* of man has been reorientated, redemption is accomplished. It is always a difficult, painful process, because man must renounce his challenge, his refusal. He must renounce a part of his spiritual freedom. *In this sense,* he must renounce himself. Only through this death can he enter life, pardoned and transfigured, in the new joy of loving God. For all this God has willed that there be a Redeemer. He is to embody the whole process of redemption — revelation, judgment, pardon, conversion, and the redeeming fulfillment of the entire creation.

Jesus Christ, the Incarnate Son of God, who was crucified and rose from the dead, *is the Redemption.* There is a Redemption-time, because *a Redeemer is inserted in human time* and His action inaugurates this time. Sin represents man's terrible power to disorganize reality. So the Redemption is a mystery of reorganization and unification. Three aspects must be underlined.

First, the Redemption is *a mysterious concentration.* The strands of God's plan are woven tighter and converge toward Jesus Christ — mankind, the chosen people, the " remnant, " Christ. He is the central focal point of the human race He enters. From the beginning there is only one plan of salvation and it is fulfilled in Jesus Christ. There is only one Savior, Jesus Christ, the God-Man. He is the perfect model of the earlier mediators and the mysterious object in which Israel placed her hope. There is only one redemptive act, the oblation of Jesus Christ, it springs from the divinized point in His psyche where He contemplates His Father and offers

Himself to Him from the moment of the Incarnation to the Cross and the Resurrection. All humanity and time itself are subsumed in this act which re-creates them in the very person of their Creator. To say that Jesus Christ is the Redemption is *to assert that love is the whole meaning of the Redemption!* [1] The eternal *agape* is the source of the Redemption : " God so loved the world, as to give his only begotten Son : that whosoever believeth in him may not perish, but may have life everlasting " (Jn 3, 16). It accomplishes the Redemption : " Christ also hath loved us and hath delivered himself for us " (Eph 5, 2). It is also the end-point at which all men will be united in love, " as thou, Father, in me, and I in thee " (Jn 17, 21). The whole process is concentrated in Jesus because He is the visible manifestation of *the agape* (1 Jn 4, 10). In Him the Father ransoms sinful mankind and re-creates a humanity which loves Him. By " believing in this love, " man enters the salvation-world (1 Jn 4, 16). Opposed to sin and its destructive power stands the unique point, the heart of the Lamb " who taketh away the sin of the world " (Jn 1, 29). There the divine salvific power is concentrated for time and eternity.

The Redemption has a second mysterious aspect : *The Cross as the mystery of God in Christ.* St. Paul sums it up in this formula : " *God indeed was in Christ, reconciling the world to himself* " (2 Cor 5, 19). This reconciliation has a *fearsome aspect* — expiation. Christ enters a sinful world and gives testimony of His Father. He encounters those " Jews " who typify sinful mankind in John's eyes. Through them Jesus collides with the power of evil. Sin brings hatred, shame, blood-spilling and death into the world. When the " Prince of this world has his hour, " the Jews seize Christ, condemn and crucify Him. Jesus is subjected to the curse of sin and killed. But this reconciliation has *another aspect* also — victory. Christ's death is the seed of His Resurrection.

---

[1] We are not opposing love to justice. The *agape* takes sinful man seriously; thus it establishes justice and sees it accomplished.

Tomorrow, sprinkled with His own blood, He will enter the eternal sanctuary. The Passion is freely accepted and offered with a pure love which surpasses stoic resignation. It is the fulfillment of the Father's will. His hatred of sin does not equal His love for His Son. The Passion offers His Son to Him and thus destroys the reign of sin, death, and hell. Christ on the Cross " draws all men to Himself. " His humiliation is the means of His exaltation. The Cross is already the " obscure Parousia " of which St. Justin speaks. That is why St. John ends his account of the Passion with a solemn prediction of the imminent triumph. With the eye of faith and with repentant souls, men *shall look on Him whom they pierced* (Jn 19, 37).

God was in Christ reconciling the world to Himself. But *the Redemption is accomplished in the human consciousness of Jesus Christ.* Christ on the Cross is the Savior performing His sacrificial act. In this act God's love for men encounters men's love for God. *This encounter is the Redemption.* God loves us and gives Christ to us. Through Christ's oblation He envelops us in His pardoning and saving love. Christ as the Savior receives the fullness of divine *agape*, demonstrates it, and fulfills its purpose. With complete generosity He offers His body and soul, because " greater love than this no man hath, that a man lay down his life for his friends " (Jn 15, 13). But there is also the love of man for God. The " Son of Man " loves God. A man offers God a sacrifice of perfect love. This is the *satisfaction* rendered by Jesus Christ. He is the head of all humanity. All men are linked to Him by their true vocation and subsumed in His knowledge and love. [2]

---

[2] It is difficult to delineate *the exact form* of Christ's knowledge on the Cross. Even in His desolation He knows that He is *the* Prophet, the eternal High Priest, the Son of Man come down from heaven, the Lord of the kingdom, the well-beloved Son. To say that He has only a vague, general concept of mankind is to make Him *just another man* and to forget His true nature and the things which He bore in His consciousness. To say that He knows each man for whom He is dying in a distinct concept is probably attributing the impossible to Him and restricting His knowledge

Christ and mankind form one " mystical person. " In Christ, therefore, all men love God and their love atones for sin and glorifies them. This is what is meant by the merits of Jesus Christ. These *two movements* of reciprocal love *are parts of the same act,* the act in which Christ delivers Himself to the Father as an offering for us. The Redemption is the union of these two loves in the psyche of the crucified Christ. It brings about a definitive spiritual unity between God and men *within its efficacious principle.* Man *becomes capable of fulfilling his vocation* — to love God and men in Jesus Christ. God saves us by giving us His own Son, by making Him our head, and by loving us through Him who sacrifices Himself for us. *In* Christ we have Redemption (Col 1, 14). In Him God reconciles the world to Himself.

Sin separates man from his Source, his End, and his fraternal Communion. It turns man in upon himself, upon a desolate solitude, an interior wasteland. It drives him to indulge in vanity and external " amusement. " The Cross does the exact opposite. It *restores his interior life.* Now it is " dynamic and fecund. " [3] Man can contemplate, love, and offer himself without reserve. He has a sovereign interior life which is expressed in the mystery of expiation. It unites men with God through an act of love and sacrifice by which " man joins God in holy comradeship, " as St. Augustine said.

Finally, the Redemption has a note of *universality* in the *Resurrection.* The Father's response, the Resurrection, completes the divine plan of universal salvation. It represents divine judgment flooding the sinful world with the light of salvation or damnation (Jn 16, 8-11). It brings Christ back from death — I " was dead, and behold I am living for ever

to a *banal level.* We get a different perspective from the evangelists. The words in Luke, " You will be with Me in paradise "; in John, " Behold your son, behold your mother, " and, " It is consummated, " point toward a *simple, omnipotent* knowledge of His mission and its " content, " toward a knowledge by way of unity. Here more than anywhere else the theologian must remember *the various levels* of Christ's *psyche.*

[3] PIUS XII, *Christmas Message,* 1955.

162

and ever " (Ap 1, 18). It frees Christ from His " fleshly " link with the universe and immerses Him in divine glory, the source of transfigured mankind. It is the definitive exaltation of the Son (Rom 1, 4) which confers all His privileges on Him and makes Him the Head of the human race, its High-Priest, and its King. It makes Him that " *quickening spirit* " (1 Cor 15, 45), the source of eternal Redemption, of the new creation and of the " day of grace " for all men.

Christ is now " the Firstfruits " of a re-created world, the germinal cell of a redeemed universe. He is now the omnipotent intercessor, the sovereign eternal mediator, the man in whom " the power of an indissoluble life " (Heb 7, 16) is concentrated. Thus Christ *draws humanity in all its aspects to Himself*. His labors, His tears, and His death cover the physical aspects. His joy, His anguish, and His fearful distaste of death cover the psychic aspects. His contemplation, His free choice, and His love cover the spiritual aspects. Christ sank into the dark abyss of sin [4] and rose victorious. Now the hearts of men shrouded in darkness can rise to the light through the Risen Christ. When man is touched by Christ, everything *can be transfigured* (except sin) and will be *transfigured* some day.

Christ also *draws all men to Himself* in order to fashion His Body — the nucleus of the new world. He takes hold of interpersonal relationships in all their aspects in order to correct them, purify them, and transform them. We shall examine His activities as Mediator in the work of the Church. But we can see that it is always the divine *agape* which is at work in Christ, bringing about a transforming encounter between man and God, and between man and man.

Thus the Risen Christ *draws the entire universe* [5] *to Himself*. It is the body of His Body. He does not transform it intrinsically, but He does use it for His purposes. He organizes it gradually for His Kingdom. During the time in which

---

[4] See the fine text of the *Pseudo-Epiphanius* cited by URS VON BALTHASAR, *Dieu et l'Homme d'aujourd'hui* (Paris 1958), pp. 258-262.

[5] Cf. the remarkable article of S. LYONNET, " Rédemption de l'univers, " *LV*, 48, pp. 43-62.

His people are not yet resurrected, the universe is swept up in His wake and rushed headlong toward the marvelous transformation which will culminate in a new heaven and a new earth. St. Paul states that "in him dwelleth all the fullness of the Godhead corporeally" (Col 2, 9). According to some competent scholars, [6] the word "corporeally" contains the three aspects it has in Paul's epistles written in captivity. In other words, divinity resides in Christ's own glorified body, in His Mystical Body, the Church composed of redeemed mankind, and in the cosmic body, the re-created universe which awaits the final conquest of sin and the ultimate transformation. If we accept this interpretation, the full unifying effect of the agape is seen. Time itself is transformed into eternity because everything is perfected and made one.

The Eternal Present of the Risen Christ

Now we must try to understand the eternal present of the Risen Christ and His redemptive mediation. The glorious Christ seated at the Father's right hand is the source of the "saving grace" which envelops mankind at every "present moment." [7]

Christ's Eternal Act

The *eternalized point* in Christ has produced its full effect. Christ has become a "life-giving spirit." He is a glorified man submerged in the eternity of God, specifically, in the eternity of the Word. All His knowledge, all His love, and all His power combine to form one divine act. Now He is subject to only one measuring principle, the perfect unity of eternity. Christ's *ephapax* assumes its infinite meaning. It is no longer an event inserted into time and salvation-history.

---

[6] For example, P. BENOIT, "Corps, Tête et Plérôme," *RB* (1956) pp. 5 ff.

[7] This makes Christ a "secret source of existence" as Newman saw so well.

It is now an event which establishes this time and salvation-history.

The Epistle to the Hebrews delineates this point very clearly. Redemption was impossible during the Old Testament. It was a time of *repetition* (7, 23-26; 9, 25-26). The priests appeared and disappeared one after another. The sacrifices were offered daily as incessant pleas for salvation which had not yet been granted. By contrast, the New Testament is a time of *achievement* in which there is *no repetition*. Christ offers Himself only once (Heb 9, 25-27) to erase sin (9, 26-28). It is enough for always, because He offers Himself " in the spirit of eternity. " [8] And since He is perfect High Priest, His offering has infinite value. He is the priest who " continueth forever " (Heb 7, 24), and His sacrifice is unique, definitive, and eternal.

Since Christ's priesthood is eternal, it is *always at work*. Christ entered the eternal sanctuary once, by His own blood " having obtained eternal redemption " (Heb 9, 12). The permanent efficacy of His sacrifice stems from its infinite value. " He continueth forever " (7, 24) are words applied to the perdurance of God Himself. [9] He is " always living " to intercede for men (7, 25). He is a priest at work in an eternal present, *appearing now (for us) before God* (9, 24). This " now " contrasts with the endless repetition of the ancient liturgy and designates the eternal present of the day of grace, the permanence of His intercession until the day of His glorious Parousia (9, 28). While generations pass away, Christ the High Priest remains " yesterday, and today : and the same forever " (13, 8). As the eternal Mediator, Christ pervades human time, [10] " meriting grace and distributing it. " He sanctifies His people (13, 12), nourishing and feeding them (13, 20). This is His " glory for ever and ever " (13, 21). [11]

[8] On the meaning of this expression cf. C. SPICQ, *Ép. aux Hébreux*, II, pp. 258-259.

[9] Cf. the texts quoted by SPICQ, *op. cit.*, II, p. 197.

[10] *Ibid.*, p. 436.

[11] *Ibid.*, p. 422.

In Christ's Psyche

If we connect these themes to Paul's statements concerning Christ's role in creation, redemption, and the resurrection of the dead (Col 1, 15-20; 1 Cor 15, 20-24, 44-49), we discover the *all-pervading efficacy* of the Risen Christ's eternal present. In the divine plan, all creative and redemptive causality passes through the psyche of the God-Man, the unique focal point which transcends human time and relates it to salvation-time. In the developing universe God sustains the world, saves men, and forms the Mystical Body of His Son *through a human intellect and will*. The psyche of the Risen Christ is the efficacious source of human and cosmic redemption. But it is also a mysterious source situated *outside* the universe yet *at the heart* of the redeemed world. Everything takes place at the right hand of God, *at this infinitely simple point* where Christ stands and intercedes for us. All time is concentrated and rooted in this eternal instant, this *Nunc stans*. Christ's is the only human psyche which inaugurates and dominates the whole expanse of time.

Christ is the God-Man whose *human* mind and will *personally* concur with the simple infinite *divine* decree which measures cosmic and spiritual time. All creative and redemptive causality and divine omnipotence itself is gathered by Christ's psyche and " applied " to the entire universe. His " personal act of grace " inaugurates Redemption for every individual. [12] God's omnipotent power saves us through

---

[12] St. Thomas explains that through His human will Christ is both the " active and passive " instrument of Redemption (" sic instrumentum divinum, ut moveretur per propriam voluntatem, " 3ª, 18, 1, 2); that He acts thus through divine power (" actione Christi operantur in virtute divina, " 3ª, 48, 6, c, 1, 3); that this power (because of His conjoined divinity) becomes His own (" Christus operatus est nostram salutem, quasi ex propria virtute, " 3ª, 18, 1, 2); and that this theandric power touches us " not through His human *nature*, but *only through the action of the person* of Christ " (3ª, 8, 5, 1ᵐ. Cf. 2ᵐ and 8, 3, c).

Christ's *deliberate, free and sacred redemptive act.* Even though its effects are manifold, it is a perfectly simple act. In His psyche there is no past or future. *In it* everything *is* in the present — the world, mankind, Redemption and Glorification. For with Christ and in Christ, [13] the Father " hath raised us up together, and hath made us sit together in the heavenly places " (Eph 2, 6). The end of time, in which the Redemption will be fully completed, already exists in Jesus Christ who stands at the Father's right hand. Christ's Resurrection *signals* the *beginning* of this process and is a *pledge* of its development. And for us the resurrection of the Virgin Mary in turn is a sign and a pledge which depends on the Resurrection of Christ. It is true that *at least one human creature* is already resurrected and reigns in heaven with Christ. It is a bright promise for us. The miracle of her entrance into eternity corresponds to the wondrous favors granted her in time — her Immaculate Conception, her divine Maternity, her role as Mediatrix of grace. It shows us the infinite efficacy and complexity of Christ's eternal present.

Christ as the Universal Man

Because all creative and redemptive causality passes through Christ, He is, in the strict sense, the universal man. All mankind is summed up in Him. This theme has pervaded human thought from the distant past until now. Many have pointed out [14] that this eschatological hope dominated the thought of Marx. Man " makes himself " by challenging matter and by community of effort, briefly by " work. " The result is not achieved at once but only gradually. Human nature becomes more concrete through the struggles and contradictions of history. This self-creation is completed in the *revolutionary act of the communist man.* Only this act can

[13] " With " designates the temporal result of Christ's salvific act; " in " designates the eternal source and result of the temporal process.

[14] Most recently J. Y. CALVEZ, *La Pensée de Karl Marx* (Paris 1956), *passim* (see pp. 527-529, 538-553, 596-600).

fully realize the potentialities of the species. Man becomes a concrete individual and a universal figure. Specifically, it is the proletariat which realizes this hope. This despised class of hopeless men is the " embodiment of total misery. " [15] But it revolts and overcomes its misery by overcoming the bourgeoisie. In so doing it sees the meaning of its own action and *realizes the true nature of man.* It becomes the true mediator of salvation and reconciles man with nature and society. Its revolutionary activity is the means by which man realizes himself, because it gives meaning to everything and is not restricted to anything in particular. [16] The proletariat is, then, the center of history. Its revolutionary action is the moment of history which summarizes the historical dialectic. The proletariat is the consummation of the historical process and its ultimate meaning. Its particular individual act is coextensive with the historical process of becoming. The proletariat becomes the universal individual, the infinite finite being, the concrete universal.

We are not going to criticize the Marxist myth here. [17] But we can see that it etches a portrait — distorted by hatred — of Jesus Christ. *He is the real meaning of Marxist eschatology.* He is *the only universal man,* because He alone measures human existence and human history. He alone is really infinite. He is the man who *is* God, whose human psyche is part of the Son of God, " true God of true God, " eternal and infinite like His Father. This man is *the measurer of humanity* in its perfection, its happiness, and its plenitude. All the individuals who form mankind find their living " Idea, " their magnetic pole, and their personal center in this infinite-finite being, the God-Man.

Furthermore, the full plenitude of the divine *agape* resides in Christ. We cannot take in at a glance eternity and the

[15] CALVEZ, p. 596.

[16] " According to Marx, the working class has three marks which make it an exact replica of the Church : unity, universality, and a salvific mission in history. " G. FESSARD, *Études,* (Jan. 1960), p. 49.

[17] See the criticisms of P. CALVEZ, *op. cit.,* pp. 603 ff.

168

whole temporal process it unfolds. But we must say with St. Paul that the Father blesses us, chooses us, and predestines us in Jesus Christ from all eternity (Eph 1, 3-11; Rom 8, 28-30). In other words, the Father from all eternity sees in His Son the perfect image of Himself and the normative image of all mankind. He gazes on this image with love, and this is eternal life. In the heart of the divine *agape*, *this image* is *the real norm of all men*, of their worth and their development.

But the *agape* breaks through into time in the Incarnate Word. He is subjected to man's sinful condition and becomes a slave too. He accepts human suffering and experiences its tragic depths. He suffers, and is really dead until the " third day. " He measures the unbearable tension, the terrible gap between God and sinful man. *He measures it, not by overlooking it but by becoming a part of it and passing through it.* He does what only God can do, making " the impossible possible. " He passes through death and rises in glory. In the paschal mystery " the human condition is completely altered, " [18] because in one man's death and Resurrection, all mankind dies and rises. He has *enabled* mankind to span the abyss of sin and death and enter the Kingdom of eternal life.

Finally Christ is the man whose love *draws all men to Himself* until the end of time. Through the Church, He gathers all men into the unity of His Incarnate Person. He makes them willing and active members of His own Body. [19] He shares His own life with them " in a divine way. " This life itself is a divine one and it is shared " unto all the fulness of God " (Eph 3, 19). In other words, it is *the full realization of God in man and man in God*. During the passage of the centuries, He knits His own into a formidable structure. With love and hope they build His Body through labors, sufferings, and death. And finally they " meet into the unity of faith and of the knowledge of the Son of God, unto a perfect

[18] St. THOMAS, *De Veritate*, 29, 7, 10m.

[19] The " Body, " in Semitic literature and in St. Paul, practically designates the Incarnate Person.

169

man, unto the measure of the age of the fulness of Christ "
(Eph 4, 13). The only " finite-infinite, " the only " concrete
universal " is Christ the Person becoming Christ the universal
man. And only through an act of His human psyche — the
simple, unique, eternal redemptive act — does He save and
perfect those who accept His love by faith.

The Pre-Incarnation Period

We must now examine Christ's presence in time *from the
beginning of the human race* until His birth. The Bible does
not deal with this question directly. But it does provide
guide-posts which clarify the problem even without solving it.

The Eternal Plan in Time

God chose us *in Christ* before the foundation of the world. [20]
This was God's eternal plan for creation. In this " productive

---

[20] " In the New Testament, the word *katabole* along with *Kosmos* is
used as *chronological measure* before or after creation. " (C. Spicq, *Agape*,
III, p. 213, note 6.) Here we might do well to consider a fine text of Maxim
the Confessor. He explains that the union of divinity and humanity (without
any change in God) is " the blessed end of the world and recapitulates
all things in God. " Then he adds : " This is the mystery which envelops
the centuries and reveals the great decision of God who is infinite and exists
before time. The *Logos* of God becomes a messenger in becoming man;
He makes manifest the innermost depths of the Father's goodness; and
*He has revealed in Himself the purpose for which all created things were brought
into existence.* All creatures and all the ages were given a beginning and
an end in Christ, for Christ, or rather, for the mystery of Christ. For the
(hypostatic) union was conceived before time, before finiteness and infinity,
measure and immensity, limit and unlimitedness, creator and creation,
rest and motion. This union is effected in Christ at the end of time; it
accomplishes God's foreknowledge; thus finite things moving continually
toward themselves and others, find their stability in Him in whom they
are all judged worthy to subsist " (*Quaest. ad Thal.* 60, *PG* 90, 621 AC).
(Cf. 624 C : " *Christ is not fore-known as God but as man,* i.e., insofar as He
is made incarnate for men. Anything which exists eternally, exists outside
any cause or any reason. It cannot, therefore be fore-known... ")

thought, " this *scientia artifex*, the universe finds its transcendent cause. But it is a project which will start at some point in time and experience changing fortunes before it is finally finished. Humanity too is made up of individuals with free wills and control over their destiny. They too must attain self-fulfillment. The divine plan does not have a strangle-hold on man's development. On the contrary, it inaugurates and preserves the development of man.

From all eternity the Triune God wills to create, conserve and sanctify the world. The Father is the blessed source of the Son. He is perfectly and completely expressed in His Word; and *at the same time* we may say that He is " the Father of Our Lord Jesus Christ, " " who had brought many children into glory " (Heb 2, 10). The Son is the perfect image of the Father. At the same time He is also the One the Father wills to give to human beings, and the One who freely offers Himself as the Savior and the archetype of redeemed mankind. The Holy Spirit is the mutual love coursing between the Father and the Son. At the same time He is the One They will to communicate to us, the One who wills to give us the life of tender filial adoption. The Divine Persons *Themselves* are not affected by this salvific will. But Their will produces, *as Their created expression*, a spiritual creature totally dependent on Them, and fully capable of being united with Them. The creature produced by Their love is " enveloped " in the eternity of the divine *agape*.

The Eternal Plan in Christ

But the divine plan is actually realized in Christ. From all eternity the Word stands before His Father as the *Verbum Incarnandum* who must be made flesh, die, and rise again. From one viewpoint He is the Word, the perfect image of the Father. From another viewpoint He is the Word through which the Father wills to raise up and sustain creatures in His omnipotence, the type of man His Father wishes to make. Strictly speaking, Christ is the *goal* of the divine plan, the

171

heavenly man. [21]   And the earthly man, made in the image of God, is only a faint replica of Him (1 Cor 15, 45-47; Rom 5, 14).   Christ is the " second Adam, " the eschatological Adam (1 Cor 15, 47), the Adam " who was to come " (Rom 5, 14) to atone for the sin of the first Adam.   Christ is " the Son of Man " whom the Father contemplates in heaven from all eternity, and who will come down from heaven in order to ascend again.   After Christ foretells the Eucharist, He says to His disciples (Jn 6, 62-63) : " Does this scandalize you ?   If then you shall see the Son of man *ascend up where he was before* ? "   From all eternity He is the Divine Person in whom and through whom the divine plan is inaugurated, carried out, and brought to fulfillment.   There is no *Other* in heaven who will be made incarnate, die, and rise again. There is only *Christ Himself* who personally vivifies mankind, enkindles grace in it, and gives meaning and value to the precursors who announce His coming.

We recognize Him *as the source of mankind* and the focal point of successive human generations.   Adam is " a figure of him who was to come " (Rom 5, 14).   He has been made " to the image of God " (Gn 1, 27) and the perfect image of God is the heavenly man, [22] Christ (Col 1, 15).   Adam is also the anti-type of the second Adam, the one whose disobedience

[21] On this point see J. Bonsirven, *Théologie du Nouveau Testament* (Paris 1951), pp. 254-257; the careful study of O. Cullmann, *Christologie du Nouveau Testament* (Neuchâtel-Paris 1958), pp. 118-165.   Eng. trans. *Christology of the New Testament* (Philadelphia : Westminster, 1959).   And cf. H. de Lubac, commenting on Origen : " Christ was both God and man, preexistent and incarnate.   He gave Israel types and figures of Himself before His appearance in the flesh.   But it is only after His appearance that they themselves are able to have their full significance for us *de jure* and *de facto*.   And it is He alone who gives it to them. "   *Histoire et Esprit* (Paris 1950), p. 276.

[22] If the *morphe* of Phil 2, 6 corresponds to Gn 1, 26 (cf. O. Cullmann, *Christologie*, pp. 152-153) then *morphe* and *eikon* have practically the same meaning; and it is significant to see both words reappear in Rom 8, 29 : " whom he fore-knew, he also predestinated to be made conformable *(summorphous)* to the image *(eikonos)* of his Son. "

172

destroyed what the obedience of the second will magnificently restore. Christ is present in Adam in two ways. He is the perfect fulfillment of the first Adam and the redemption of the sinful Adam. [23] After Adam, Abel is also a figure of Christ the Mediator. [24] He is the first innocent victim whose blood is unjustly spilt, and this makes him a figure of Him who is to come. Our Lord Himself places Abel at the head of the list : " Behold I send to you prophets and wise men and scribes : and some of them you will put to death and crucify : and some you will scourge in your synagogues and persecute from city to city. That upon you may come all the just blood that hath been shed upon the earth, from the blood of Abel the just — " (Mt 23, 34-35). Obviously, in Christ's eyes, this series of sacrifices must be completed by His own " just blood. " The Epistle to the Hebrews takes up this theme and completes it. Abel is the just man who offers the better sacrifice and by faith he speaks to us today (11, 4). He foretells the perfect sacrifice of " Jesus the mediator of the new testament " and the " blood which speaketh better than that of Abel " (12, 24). In the liturgy this holy figure is placed before Abraham and Melchisedech in the Canon of the Mass. Christ is present in Abel as the sovereign Priest who recalls this mysterious figure and his " better " sacrifice, and makes his just blood the image of His own sacrifice. The *Verbum Incarnandum* begins the redemption of the Incarnate Word in Abel.

[23] Commenting on Ap 12 Père LYONNET writes : " Is not Christ the perfect image of God pre-figured by Adam, *to whom Satan refused homage* ? " (my emphasis) *D. SP.* XVIII-XIX, art. " Démon, " col. 15. Cf. the comment of P. EVDOKIMOV regarding Gregory Nazianzen's remark about " the suffering God " : " This is the expression of St. Gregory the theologian who contemplates the immolated Lamb before the Incarnation and insists on the Passion of a Being who cannot suffer by definition. " (*L'Orthodoxie*, Paris-Neuchâtel 1959, p. 221, note 66.)

[24] On this point see J. DANIÉLOU in *Holy Pagans of the Old Testament* (Baltimore : Helicon, 1957) pp. 29 ff. As we know, the story of Cain and Abel (Gn 4) has a theological purpose, and so it is made the conclusion of the drama in Eden.

There is no question of time involved in this presence of the *Verbum Incarnandum*. It is a sovereign eternal presence which determines the acts which will participate in it. It is the presence of the eternal plan enveloping the universe and unfolding in time. It is the presence of the eternal Person who is the mediator of creation, redemption, and the time which measures them. But if Christ is present at the very beginning, it is even more certain that He perdures during the course of human development, during the period of sadness, misery, blood-spilling and hope which follows original sin and the first promise. The vast expanse of human time [25] is no obstacle to Christian faith. Just as the *human spirit* discovers and measures this broad ocean of time, so through faith in the Word of God it can relate time to its source, its center, and its end, Jesus Christ. The human spirit is not in danger of being bewildered, though the imagination may be. All time is *embraced* by God in Christ, *orientated* by God toward Christ, and *uplifted* by God's grace in Christ. Cosmic time is salvation-time, and the *Verbum Incarnandum* can embrace it without being weakened or overwhelmed. For His power and His presence are divine.

The problem of time enters when the *Verbum Incarnandum* becomes the *Verbum Incarnatum*, and personally enters human time. At that moment His past and His future as a human being are concentrated in His present. The past becomes a preparation for Him and the future becomes His time of development. This is the radical novelty of the Incarnation. Christ *determines the past and the future*. He is the fulfillment of the past and the anticipation of the future. But Christ is also the Eternal One breaking through into time. Even in the novelty of this unique *ephapax*, there is *absolute continuity*

[25] Whatever it may be — 600,000 years for example. If scientists agree with the views of A. LEROY-GOURHAN (" L'Illusion technologique, " *La Technique et l'Homme*, Paris 1960) positing a " tool-making brain " and a " reflective brain " in man (only the latter being truly human), then there would be two incommensurable time-spans for mankind (see chap. 3) and the time-span of man *as an incarnate spiritual being* would be reduced.

174

between what precedes and what follows the Incarnation. The eternal divine plan is being realized in the mystery of Christ. When the *Verbum Incarnandum* becomes the Incarnate Word, eternity envelops time more tightly than ever in its unity.

And when Christ's human consciousness becomes aware of His own true nature, when He realizes that He is the Word, He becomes fully aware of *the mission* His Father has given Him. He realizes that He is the unique center of humanity — past, present, and future. We cannot insist too strongly on Christ's temporal relation to His own past and His own future. But this does not deny Christ's efficacious presence at the beginning of the human race. Cosmic time and history are rooted in the *Verbum Incarnandum. The first man* is a figure of Him who is to come. *The history of the Incarnation has already begun.* In the eyes of faith, " a thousand years are as one day, and one day is as a thousand years. " Even 600,000 years are as one day, a preparation for the day of the Incarnate Lord. The day of man's creation is established, measured, and redeemed by the day of the Son of Man.

The eye of faith does not telescope the vast expanse of human time. *It* simply *measures it by the Word of God* It measures human time just as it measures man, seeing in him a non-entity destined for sanctification. It knows that nothing can really prepare the coming of the Word Incarnate except God's wisdom and love. If paleontologists speak about 600,000 years of human history, the mind of faith knows that God Himself has regulated this period of preparation. The march of evolution toward man, man's call, his sin — all this is enveloped in God's omnipotent *agape*. Neither the Word of God nor faith tells us directly why the preparation is so lengthy. But it does reveal God's wisdom. *The human psyche* [26] *develops* gradually over these countless millennia. The wisdom of Egypt, Greece, India, and China is timeless and magnificent. God directs many aspects of human development toward the advent of His Son — civilization, moral

[26] Except the " brain. "

175

conscience, religious aspirations. And even during this development, man *experiences his profound misery*, the impossibility of self-realization, and the evil which stains and corrupts him, bringing sorrow and death. His mind is never " pure. " The various levels of his psyche (moral, religious, familial, tribal, national) do not develop integrally, not even in the chosen people. [27] Through this mixed process of growth and decay, *God forms His people.* They are more confused than the rest of humanity. They are called more explicitly, yet they sin more. Their assent and their dissent reach new heights. They are more unfaithful and yet they nurture great saints. They are a people in whom mankind is first fulfilled, and they produce Mary, the Mother of Jesus. Then the fullness of time comes and the God-Man takes up His dwelling among men.

Eschatological Time

At the present time eschatology is a widely used notion. But it is a vague notion, subject to many different interpretations. So we must carefully define the eschatological time inaugurated in Jesus Christ. [28] It seems that this time is to be defined *in terms of three facts* : the presence of the Risen Christ, His promised return, and the time of salvation between these two events. The first inaugurates salvation-time, the second completes it.

[27] On this slow process of development see R. MARITAIN, *Histoire d'Abraham* (Paris 1947) and A. GELIN, *Problèmes d'Ancien Testament* (Lyon 1952), pp. 71 ff. The former discusses the shift from a moral consciousness to a theological consciousness in Abraham.

[28] Eschatology refers to two distinct realities : (1) *the final event* — Christ's return and its implications (B. RIGAUX, *Les Épîtres aux Thessaloniciens*, Paris 1956, p. 195) : Eschatological hope envisions " a divine intervention which will radically alter man's state and his relations with God "; (2) *the relationship between the present and the final event* (rooted in the Risen Christ). We are concerned with the second point.

176

Its Structure

In the Christian faith, eschatological time is rooted completely in the presence of the Risen Christ. It is not rooted in a divine promise or a divine decision, but in *a Person who is present.* Christ is " seated at the Father's right hand, " not to await the end from afar, but to pour forth the Holy Spirit (Acts 2, 33), and thus fulfill His role of eternal mediator. " He is. . . always living to make intercession for us " (Heb 7, 25), in the full existence of an eternal instant. Now His sovereign " intercession " is not the tearful supplication of His " earthly days, " nor even a simple prayer. It is the presence of Christ the victim before God, now radiating the glory of the Son (Heb 9, 24, 26). It is *the royal manifestation of the Mediator's free will,* the very act of eternal mediation. [29]

Christ is enthroned as God's Son and is fully eternal. Now His sovereign presence before God can inaugurate and unfold salvation-time by an act which is itself eternal. He is really present to all human generations and can influence their critical moments. That is why His last words, according to St. Matthew, do not speak of His departure or return but of His *presence.* " Behold I am with you all days, [30] even to the consummation of the world " (28, 21). [31] St. John, typically, synthesizes and delves deeper. For him " all days " means *the one day* of mutual spiritual presence. Christ is in His own, and the disciples are with Him and the Father. " In that day you shall know that I am in my Father : and you in me, and I in you. " [32] This presence establishes the salvation-mystery, salvation-time, and the day of grace. Salvation is

[29] St. John gives us a hint of this will in 17, 24. On the nature of this intercession, one can see a collection of patristic texts and a commentary in P. DE LA TAILLE, *The Mystery of Faith* (London: Sheed, 1940), pp. 121 ff.

[30] An Aramaic expression meaning " always. "

[31] *Aiôn* simply means the continuation of the world from its creation to its end. (Cf. Mt 13, 39, 40, 41 and SASSE, *s.v. TWNT*, pp. 207 ff.). It could be translated " until the end of the world. "

[32] Jn 14, 20. Cf. P. MOLLAT, *BJ*, p. 159, notes *d* and *c*.

accomplished because "the streams of living water" flow from the pierced side of the Risen Christ, because the organism of salvation is instituted forever, and because the New Covenant between man and God has been sealed forever in the man Jesus Christ, the eternal mediator.

But this presence foretells another. The Lord has promised to return and *consummate* the work of salvation. Christ's presence in the Church is veiled and fragile as long as Christians walk through the trials and shadows of time, longing for invisible eternal things (2 Cor 4, 16-18). Hampered by their bodies, they "are absent from the Lord" (2 Cor 5, 6). Salvation is not achieved today, but tomorrow. Present realities are only a *beginning* and must be completed some day. Here below we experience only a part of the Redemption. The salvation won by the glorified Christ is tentative and uncertain. We do not yet conform totally to Christ. We must have faith before we can attain the full vision. We are wretched members of Christ's glorified Body, sinful members of the Church which is the Mystical Body of the perfect man. Church-time and cosmic time unfold within the unity of the new transformed world. And so, at the moment of Christ's Ascension the angels solemnly proclaim His return : " This Jesus who is taken up from you into heaven shall so come, as you have seen him going into heaven " (Acts 1, 11). [33] We do not intend to study the Parousia here. We only want to indicate that it involves the wondrous manifestation of the Son of Man coming in His Father's glory, the Resurrection of the dead (both the just and the unjust), the last judgment, and the birth of the " new earth " through Him who is " Alpha and Omega, the first and the last, the beginning and the end. " [34] This hidden and unknown turn means *the end of this world in its essential aspects*. For it fulfills the divine promise by

[33] BOISMARD'S translation, *Lumière et Vie*, XI *(Le Retour du Christ)*, p. 58.

[34] On these expressions cf. Mk 8, 28; Mt 16, 27; Lk 11, 31-32; Jn 5, 26-30; Mt 13, 36-43 and 25, 31 ff.; Ap 22, 13.

passing judgment. The terrible battle which took place in time is over. Christ's enemies are vanquished and He gives the Kingdom to His Father. Salvation-time is completed and cosmic time is ended. The transfigured world has appeared. This is the second pillar, the extreme limit of Christian eschatology. In the eye of Christ, the Resurrection and the Parousia are one. In terms of this world, they are two events which *open, close* and thus *measure* Christian time.

Between these two events, salvation-time is *definitively* established. All time is " intermediary, " so this characteristic cannot be the peculiar property of eschatological time. The latter is fully characterized by the real personal presence of the Risen Christ. This presence has *three aspects*. It is linked to Christ's passion and death : I am " alive, and was dead. And behold I am living for ever and ever " (Ap 1, 18). It is linked to the Parousia. And finally, it is linked to men journeying on earth. To them Christ communicates His risen life " all days " through the Spirit. This is the " veiled Parousia " which forms His body here below. [35] Eschatological time is *a series of relationships* (earthly and heavenly). It is Christocentric because it is necessarily connected to the Resurrection, the Parousia, and the eternal present of the Risen Christ. [36] It is orientated toward the Parousia and Paradise. And the source of this dynamic orientation is the Holy Spirit.

[35] On Jn 14, 18.20, cf. the note of P. MOLLAT, *BJ*, 159, *d* — " I will not leave you orphans : I will come to you — In that day you shall know that I am in my Father... " " ' Day ' can be a long period of time. Here it designates the entire period following Christ's Resurrection. "

[36] This is strikingly apparent in the *Appearances* of the Risen Lord. The disciples on the road to Emmaus converse about the Crucified One. They live in His hidden presence; and when they recognize Him, they yearn for His return. Mary Magdalen looks for the body of the Crucified; she recognizes the Living One by His call; but He sends her back to the other world — then to return — for full communion with Him. Peter (in Jn 21) is before " the Lord "; the latter reminds him of His Passion by His triple question and confirms him in his pastoral office, which will result in martyrdom; but regarding St. John, He reaffirms His coming as the mystery which governs history.

He is a guaranteed pledge of our future resurrection, and directs the world *from within* toward its glorious transfiguration. This dynamic orientation is the very essence of eschatological time. It measures the existential movement of mankind toward its end.

Its Function

Eschatological time has three main functions. First, it is an *efficacious means* of redemption for the individual, the Church, the human race, and the universe. It is not so by itself. But Christ makes it a condition for redemption. By means of time Christ calls men, pardons them, conforms them to Himself, and offers them to the Father. In time man must freely choose to accept faith and salvation, to be converted, and to renew his fidelity constantly. In time Christ the Lord *gradually realizes* the eternal plan of Redemption, and manifests the infinite richness of the divine *agape* and the fullness of grace which He possesses. The divine form of man is molded gradually each day until it conforms to Christ. Finally, eschatological time is *the sovereign measure* of man's *spiritual development.* It endures until this development is complete. It will end when salvation is accomplished, when *we have become what we shall be,* and we shall be like God, because we shall see Him as He is (1 Jn 3, 2).

We do not know when the end will be. Nor can we discover the various forms of this development. The " significant moments " are here and gone before we realize it. We are creatures marked for salvation. We participate in the measuring of spiritual development; but the measure itself, Christ the Redeemer, escapes our comprehension.

Its Mysteriousness

Eschatological time is especially mysterious. The Risen Christ is the center of time. He is *incarnate, yet transcendent.* Thus He dominates and regulates time. As the eternal Word He opens and closes cosmic time through His Father's activity. As the Incarnate Word He carries time in His human mind.

180

Adam becomes a figure of Him, and He makes human history the period between Adam and His own return. But we do not know *how* He does this. It is the very mystery of Redemption accomplished in the Risen Christ. We cannot discover the foundations of this mystery. The divine message shows us the preparations for Christ and the work He accomplished. But the last revelations of the Risen Christ to His disciples have not been given to us. We find traces of them in the first apostolic preaching. But these are seeds which are to grow in the Church during the salvation-period.

Furthermore, Christ told us that He would return, but He *refused to specify the day and the hour*. " It is not for you to know the times or moments, which the Father hath put in his own power " (Acts 1, 7). The end is hidden from us. [37] For man on earth, this is a part of the mystery shared in eternity by the Father and the Son. The Spirit is not meant to reveal it to us. The primitive Christians, flushed with the youthful impatience of love, were preoccupied with Christ's return. In the sacred repasts they shared with the invisible Risen Christ, they undoubtedly expected Him to return at any instant and consummate everything. St. Peter and St. Paul enlightened them somewhat on this point and St. John enlightened them even more. [38] Henceforth in the Eucharist they would proclaim the death of the Lord *until He comes*, *without knowing when* this would be. Their certainty and their uncertainty are part of the mystery of faith. They know His

---

[37] The events narrated in the eschatological discourse (Mt 24, 3 ff.) have no chronological order. They refer to a time of trial and tribulation which will last until the Last Judgment. As Père MOLLAT writes, the synoptic writers teach us two things about the Last Judgment : " it will be sudden and unexpected " (" Jugement, " *DBS*, cols. 1357-1358).

[38] " The author of the Apocalypse was enlightened by the Holy Spirit and by life in the Church. He understands better than the writers of the Old Testament that one must avoid confusing the destruction of Jerusalem with the end of the world. When Jesus informs him that His return is near, He is affirming a *truth of faith, not a date* " (my emphasis). A. FEUILLET " Le Chapitre X de l'Apocalypse, " *Sacra Pagina* (1959), II, p. 427.

return cannot be known. Christ *is* the source, the center, and the end of time. But the day of His return is *hidden* from us.

It is more important for us to know that He who measures the salvation-time is truly present to us and dwells in His own, in His Mystical Body. His presence makes our time eschatological. He who has come and is to come again, is present and dwells with us. His presence *establishes* eschatological time by opening it, sustaining it, and closing it. His presence gives it *its efficacious meaning* by making it an instrument of salvation. His presence *structures it* so that the past and future process of redemption takes root in a sinful world called to salvation. And so we come to the time of the Church.

III

The Church and Time

8

The Church on Earth

The Church's time is a spiritual time which derives from the glorified Christ and permeates His Mystical Body. It is *established from on high* by the Father's will, by Christ's human and divine wills, and by the Spirit They send to create Their Kingdom. But it is continued in the Church and in the consciousness of Christians.[1] It is *Christocentric*, sacred, salvific. It has its own meaning, its own rhythm, its own proper effect. It *envelops* cosmic time *and is enveloped* in turn by this time which is so different, so inimical, and yet so

---

[1] The Church certainly had a long pre-history. Cf. Y. CONGAR, " Ecclesia ab Abel, " *Festschrift für K. Adam* (1952), pp. 79-108; also the fine chapter (8) of H. DE LUBAC, *Catholicism* (New York : Sheed, 1958); J. DANIÉLOU, *Théologie du Judéo-Christianisme* (Paris 1958), chap. 10. Instead of tracing the Church from its earliest beginnings we focus on it when it is already fully constituted. We shall treat only a few essential points, and list only those references which are absolutely necessary.

185

compatible. In this chapter we can only outline the essential aspects of this complex time.

The Mission from Above

A. ESCHATOLOGICAL

The Church's time is eschatological in the sense we have already defined. Christ's presence and the eternal reality of the redemptive act inaugurate and regulate a time which begins with the Resurrection and will end with the Parousia. The dynamic relationship between these " events " determines the full meaning of the Church's time. And *the Holy Spirit is the vital force* behind it. He is the eschatological gift, who leaps into messianic time from the depths of eternity. He is the pledge and the first-fruits of the full Redemption and the Resurrection of the dead. From the beginning to the end He is the vital unifying force in the Church — *Spiritus qui unit Ecclesiam.* [2] In Him we find the force which unifies the time of the Church Militant. [3] The Church is necessarily involved in time, because she is nothing else but the *form* which the redemptive act assumes to reach men on earth and envelop them — that is, to save them. [4]

Blessed

The Church's eschatological time is a time of benediction. During it the Promise of old is fulfilled in the gift of the

[2] St. THOMAS, e.g. *ST*, III[a], 68, 9, 2[m].

[3] St. Irenaeus insisted on this point long ago. After emphasizing that the same God established both communities and both covenants (*Adv. Haer.* 4, 32, 2 and 33, 1. *PG* 7, 1071 ff.), he discusses the individual Christian : " The truly spiritual disciple receives the Spirit of God who has always been present to men in God's favors, predicting the future, recalling the past, and illuminating the present. Such a man is able to judge all things... " On God's unifying plan cf. H. DE LUBAC, *Histoire et Esprit*, pp. 404-405.

[4] On the secret, creative role of the Spirit in the Church, cf. NEWMAN.

Spirit. God promised Abraham that in him all the nations of the earth would be blessed (Gn 12, 3). This blessing refers first to the holy land which is only a figure of the Kingdom. But in the prophetic books it comes to be the promise of the messianic gift, the Spirit. It is finally fulfilled by Christ who " ascends " into heaven with a gesture of benediction clearly delineated by St. Luke : " and lifting up his hands, he blessed them. And it came to pass, whilst he blessed them, he departed from them and was carried up to heaven " (Lk 24, 50-51). Christ's blessing is the sign and the source of the promised Spirit, *in whom is joined both the promise and the blessing.* He is the promise and the living blessing. St. Peter explains that Christ, " having received of the Father the promise of the Holy Ghost, he hath poured forth this " (Acts 2, 33). Then, recalling the promise made to Abraham, he says : " To you first, God, raising up his Son, hath sent him to bless you : that every one may convert himself from his wickedness " (Acts 3, 26). [5] St. Paul takes up this theme forcefully in the Epistle to the Galatians. [6] " The scripture, foreseeing that God justifieth the Gentiles by faith, told unto Abraham before : ' In thee shall all nations be blessed. ' Therefore, they that are of faith shall be blessed with faithful Abraham " (Gal 3, 8-9). This blessing, the gift of the Spirit, comes to us through Christ. " Christ hath redeemed us from the curse of the law. . . That the blessing of Abraham might come on the Gentiles. . . that we may receive the promise of the Spirit by faith " (Gal 3, 13-14). The Spirit takes root in the depths of the human heart. Faith gives man a " new heart. " The Spirit's presence at the heart of the Church is a source of re-creation. The time of the mission is inaugurated for sinful man by the blessing promised to Abraham and conferred by Jesus Christ.

[5] On the texts from Acts, see the comments of J. DUPONT, *BJ*.

[6] On these texts, see the *Commentary* of LAGRANGE, pp. 65-67, 73-74; also BOISMARD, " La Foi selon saint Paul, " *LV*, 22, pp. 81-82.

B. COMMUNICATED FROM ABOVE

The Church's time by definition is the time of the mission. Its essential features are indicated in the closing words of St. Matthew's Gospel. [7] The Apostles have a mission which entails certain activities on their part. It is a mission sustained by the active presence of Christ Himself. " All power is given to me in heaven and in earth. Going therefore, teach ye all nations : baptizing them in the name of the Father and of the Son and of the Holy Ghost. Teaching them to observe all things whatsoever I have commanded you. And behold I am with you all days, even to the consummation of the world " (Mt 28, 18-20). [8] Even Christ's action in choosing the Twelve is eschatological, not only because of the mission entrusted to them (Mt 19, 28; Lk 22, 29-30), but also because of the number twelve itself. [9] During Christ's life on earth there were scarcely even three Hebrew tribes. Only at the end of time will the twelve tribes be gathered to form the eschatological number of the saved — 144,000 from each tribe. St. John gives us a more important formula : " Peace be to you. As the Father hath sent me, I also send you. When he had said this, he breathed on them; and he said to them : Receive ye the Holy Ghost " (Jn 20, 21-22). The text refers explicitly to the *second creation*, [10] which perfects the first. And it is accomplished by the Holy Spirit. The work of the Twelve will purify and renew God's people through the rites instituted by Christ. It is the dawn of creation once again.

---

[7] J. JEREMIAS (*Jésus et les Païens*, Neuchâtel-Paris, pp. 32-33) follows O. MICHEL and interprets the passage as one of royal enthronement. And SPICQ (commenting on Jn 13, 35) stresses that *mathetes* (disciple) is the loftiest title for a Christian because it indicates that he shares in the Master's way of life, cf. *Agape*, 3 (1959), pp. 175-176.

[8] The exegete JEREMIAS, seeing underlying Aramaisms in this text, translates it : " I am with you always until the end of the world. "

[9] Cf. J. JEREMIAS, *op. cit.*, pp. 16-17.

[10] Cf. J. SCHMITT, " Simples remarques sur le fragment Jn 10, 22-23, " *Mel. Andrieu* (= *RevSR*), 1956, pp. 415-423. He repeats D. MOLLAT, *BJ*.

The Divine Mediator

These are the words of Christ the Mediator, [11] the Head of His own Mystical Body and its members. Christ now lives in the bosom of His Father, in Eternity. From there He establishes and envelops the Church's time. *Between Him and the Church there is always a direct, vertical, transcendent relationship.* Christ forms His Mystical Body by this " personal act of grace " which calls and sanctifies its members and conforms them to Him. The Church's time is rooted entirely in the eternity of Christ and in the sovereign intercession of the eternal Priest.

Christ communicates His plenitude to His own in order to draw them to Himself (Jn 12, 31-33). But He does not descend into time again. Instead, the Church mounts toward eternity as it is *created in Christ* at every instant. We can still speak of Christ's time. But now it is the time of the Church and of Christians rooted in Christ's eternity, enveloped in it, and orientated toward it. It is the time inaugurated in Christ's consciousness and carried there forever.

Human Mediators

However, the Body of Christ is also formed by acts of human mediators. The Father wills them, the Son injects them into history and the Spirit actualizes them by His own power. These acts *prolong Christ's eternal mediation in history*. They are summed up in *three features* of the Church which Cardinal Newman clearly saw [12] — its hierarchical structure, its dogmatic corpus, and its sacramental system. Christ chooses men and gives them the power and the duty of continuing His mission " until the end of the world. " In exerting their authority, they are to be, like Him, servants of God and other men. Christ culminates a long prophetic tradition (Heb 1, 1) and reveals the divine plan. His human words express the plan

---

[11] " With these words Christ reveals Himself as the mediator between God and men " (St. Thomas, *in Jn.* 10, lect. 4, note 4).

[12] E.g. in *Apologia Pro Vita Sua*, Part IV.

of salvation, the divine message which is both a revelation and a command — " the power of God unto salvation to every one that believeth " (Rom 1, 16). Finally, Christ injects salvific actions into the world of human actions. They are joined to human objects and human words express their meaning. These Sacraments and the divine message are entrusted to those He has appointed as guardians. And they transmit them to others.

The Day of Grace

In the strictest sense of the word, man becomes a channel of Christ's grace. [13] *A truly human kind of time* is established. It is both social and personal in its organized unified levels. Its actions unfold in history to regulate and measure the life of redeemed man. But it remains *rooted in the Redeemer's eternal act.* It is the day of grace, in which time and eternity meet in a marvelous embrace. And it is ever present in the Church because of the eternal present of the Risen Christ. The Lord calls out unceasingly to human generations in the *today of salvation* — yesterday, now, and tomorrow (cf. Heb 3, 7-10; 4, 1-10).

It was in a present that God called the Israelites in the desert : " To-day if you shall hear his voice, harden not your hearts : as in the provocation " (Ps 94, 8-9). The day of grace is made present every day by God. He set another day after the provocation in the desert : " Again he limiteth a certain day, saying in David. . . 'To-day if you shall hear his voice' " (Heb 4, 7). And now in the Church it is a permament day of grace, rooted in the eternal priesthood of Christ. Christians must be faithful every day, " While it is said : ' To-day if you shall hear his voice. . . ' " (Heb 3, 15). The time of the Church, then, is *spiritual* yet *incarnate.* We cannot comprehend the divine elements which structure it, but we can comprehend its human ingredients. These ingredients remain essentially

---

[13] Cf. the fine article of Rousselot, " Intellectualisme, " *Dictionnaire Apologétique de la Foi Catholique,* cols. 1075-1076.

the same although they are expressed in different ways. They are the strange external trappings of the unique, eternal redemptive act.

C. THE MISSION AND THE CHURCH

At every instant the mission is willingly accepted and continued by the Church on a human level which Christ has carefully organized and arranged.

The Church's Mission

The *raison d'être* of the Church's *journey on earth* is the mission. The Church has been sent even as Christ was sent. " Missionary activity " is an essential part of the Church's make-up and development. In a sense, the mission envelops everything — the message, the sacraments, the hierarchy, the preaching of the Gospel. All these realities continue the mission of Christ. The mission is the vital force which hurtles the Church through space and time from Pentecost to the Parousia, and enables her to penetrate the hearts of men, purifying and saving the upright of heart. This vital force, activated and suffused by the Holy Spirit, *makes* the Church what she is meant to be. It too is eschatological. In fact it is nothing else but the will of Christ insofar as it is accepted and fulfilled by men. It is the continuation of Christ's mission [14] which establishes the Church of God, the Church of men.

Three Levels

The mission is not fulfilled through human thoughts and actions alone. It is also fulfilled through a triple hierarchy. The Father wills something and accomplishes it, first, through Christ. The God-Man performs His task so perfectly and so thoroughly that there is nothing more to add. Yet Christ

[14] The Church's mission must be linked closely to Christ's mission. This is the basic fact which determines the various meanings of the word " mission. " On this point see Msgr. JOURNET, *The Church of the Word Incarnate* (New York : Sheed, 1955), II.

in turn sends the twelve Apostles, not one person but a group headed by Peter. They are the witnesses chosen by the Father from all eternity. They lived in a " unique moment "; " all the time that the Lord Jesus came in and went out among us, beginning from the baptism of John, until the day wherein he was taken up from us " (Acts 1, 21-22). Christ is the unique and permanent Head of the Church and the Apostles are the foundation stones established by Him (Eph 2, 20). They are also *unique* because of this choice and their prolonged contact with Christ. They have received the fullness of the Holy Spirit, the power and the obligation of spreading the divine message and building the Church. They must *endure*, because their mission and their essential functions must last until the end of time. They choose *successors*, the bishops, who are consecrated to function as priests, teachers, and rulers. The episcopal body is, then, the apostolic body. [15]

Complex Duration

This new period is extremely complex because *it transcends time and yet is immersed in it*. The apostolic charge is transmitted in episcopal consecration. Through this action repeated through time and space, the unique priesthood is passed on and *the ordo episcoporum* is perpetuated. [16] The sacrament of Orders is *the sacrament* of *apostolic succession*, the sacrament *of the apostolic mission*. [17] This " repetition " in time is radically different from the ritual " repetition " of the Old Testament. The latter was a sign of expectation and impotence. The former is a sign of fulfillment and accomplishment in the midst of the last period of expectation.

This period is characterized by *its permanence in the Holy Spirit and in the hearts of men*. The mission is always the

[15] *Ibid.*, I, chap. 10.

[16] Cf. B. BOTTE, " L'Ordo episcoporum, " *Études sur le Sacrement de l'Ordre* (Paris 1958).

[17] Cf. the excellent article of L. M. DEWAILLY, " Mission de l'Église et Apostolicité, " *RSPT* (1948), pp. 3 ff.

same, because Christ is always its source and its final end. The same graces are continually given to men; the same powers establish mediative functions. It is all part of the New Creation brought about by the power of the Holy Spirit at Pentecost. But this continuity persists on the human side also. Men change but their relationship to the divine mission does not. The first unseen miracle performed by the Holy Spirit is to insure that both consecrators and consecrated [18] choose to be faithful to the actions of the Fathers, the Apostles, and Christ. *Through the Holy Spirit, the human will remains firm and steadfast,* and thus the visible succession becomes a means of indestructible permanence. [19] The Spirit was conferred through the permanent mediation of Christ. Thus, this secret Pentecost, endlessly repeated in the Church, is rooted in the presence of the Risen Christ and His eternal Redemptive Act. And yet, Christ's human will only chooses to accomplish the eternal will of the Father. And so we must hearken back to Tertullian's famous phrase : *ecclesiae ab apostolis, apostoli a Christo, Christus a Deo.* [20] The continuing succession derives its meaning and value from its source in eternity.

But the Church's mission does not stop here. Since the Church is missionary by the very nature of her functions, *the whole Church is affected.* The baptized and the confirmed are faithful to their consecration only insofar as their way of life gives testimony to the Church's mission. This is evident in the earliest times when the first converts are " sanctified " and receive the strength (Acts 2, 42-47; 4, 24-31) to persevere in the faith, in fraternal charity, and in the worship of God.

---

[18] For the problems posed by certain periods of Church history, see the apt reflections of Y. CONGAR, " Faits, problèmes et réflexions, " *La Maison-Dieu,* 14, pp. 107-128.

[19] On the " mystery " of the bishop's presence, NEWMAN wrote : " The presence of each bishop reminds us of the trials and struggles, the defeats and victories, the hopes and fears throughout the centuries. " At the same time, " it is the pledge of a daring combat today, of a bold profession of faith, and of a joyous martyrdom if it becomes necessary. "

[20] *De Praescriptione,* 21, 4; 37, 1.

Dispersed by persecution, they "went about preaching the word of God" (Acts 8, 4).

Time and the Mission

Time is, then, one of the basic dimensions of the mission for two reasons. First, Christ plants *a seed* on this earth and entrusts it to men. Thus, the Church is involved in a process of growth. The whole edifice must develop if it is to fulfill its mission and realize its "goal." Secondly, the Church is sent "to preach the Gospel *to every creature.*" She is involved in the history of the universe. She must branch out in space and meet every new generation. To fulfill her mission, the Church will need the whole span of time.

Historians date certain aspects of the Church's development. They mark the organization of the episcopacy and the claim of Roman primacy. They show how the churches developed in free communion, and how the rites developed in the various liturgies. They describe the unexpected problems and dangerous crises which necessitated deep thought and new definitions for the preservation and development of the original doctrine. *Christ establishes the Church and she gradually grows into an organized edifice.* Institution, manifestation, growth, organization [21] — these are the essential phases of the Church's development. Once the basic structure is realized, the Church continues to grow and adapt in order "to make disciples of all nations."

However, this mission-period involved in human time is rooted at every moment in the eternal redemptive act. The *divine agape* is the vital force which gives meaning and efficacy to its unforeseen, recurrent rhythms. Passing from the Father to the Son and then to the Holy Spirit (who has been given to us), it forms the Mystical Body and nurtures it among men until

[21] We do not refer to a structure which is permanently fixed. For it continues to grow and to adapt. J. GUITTON had devoted much thought to this problem from the philosophical viewpoint and shows a profound knowledge of the historical data. The result is his fine book, *Church and The Gospel* (Chicago : Regnery, 1961).

194

it reaches its full stature for all eternity. The missionperiod is the time when infinite Love is at work in the world to save it.

The Church and the World

The Church is associated with men and the universe. She is a wayfarer until the end of time. She bears all the marks of a continuing, difficult journey. She starts, stops, moves on. She retreats, advances, and impatiently holds her ground. There are periods of persecution and periods of blissful growth. By her very nature the Church is involved in human time. The eschatological character of the Church's time involves tensions and dangerous contradictions. There are both harmonious and discordant rhythms whose major components alone are visible to the eye of faith.

A. CHURCH – TIME AND COSMIC TIME

The meeting of these two kinds of time is mysterious but not contradictory in itself. *Fundamentally,* cosmic time is at the service of the Church. It will endure until the Church is fully perfected. Hence, the rhythms of cosmic time are utilized by the Church. The various phases of the Christ-mystery are associated with these rhythms although Christ remains the guiding norm of Church-time. The liturgy repeatedly unfolds the historical events of the unique redemptive mystery in a rhythmical way. It shows that *the Church dwells in cosmic time,* gives it real spiritual value, and unifies cosmic and Christian development by inserting cosmic realities into the Church.

This is the immense blessing which the Church confers on the world. Because Christ dwelt on earth for a very short period of time, the entire universe in all its vastness is saved from absurdity. And through the Church its temporal rhythms are transfigured and suffused with an eternal blessing. All this remains a mystery, because cosmic repetition is at the same time a continual *progression* in which the Church Militant is built. It is mysterious because the cosmos, though sanctified, can remain *indifferent* to the influence of Christ and the Church. In short, because here we *believe* what we do not see.

Furthermore, we do not know how long the Church will remain in cosmic time. The Church envelops cosmic time and marches toward a predicted but hidden climax. We do not know the day or the hour of this climax. Perhaps, if we believe St. Paul, it will be known only by those who are living when time passes into eternity " in the twinkling of an eye. " They will not experience death but they will experience all the shattering implications of death. In any case, there is no quarrel between cosmic time and Church-time. For cosmic time belongs completely to Christ, and Church-time has been established by Him through the powers conferred on Him at His Resurrection.

B. ENTANGLEMENTS OF HUMAN TIMES

The Church is made up of Christians who are also members of human societies. The time of a group is always a complex amalgam of many rhythms and many kinds of time. [22] Any human society is motivated by some spiritual principle which gives it meaning. This is the decisive factor in the encounter between the Church and men. We shall discuss only some of the forces involved, remembering that they combine to form a complex amalgam.

Two Specific Times

The problem involves two kinds of time. They are quite *distinct* because they measure *two radically different goals*. One is a natural goal of human life concerned with the advancement of culture and civilization. [23] Man is to build a human

---

[22] We refer to *cosmic* rhythms, *economic* rhythms, *social* rhythms, *political* rhythms, and *religious* rhythms.

[23] We use the word in the first meaning given by LALANDE (*Vocabulaire Philosophique*) : " A civilization is an integrated complex of social phenomena. It is composed of religious, moral, esthetic, and intellectual factors which can be passed from generation to generation " (5th ed., p. 138). It is interesting that the religious factor is put first. The German distinction between civilization and culture is not accepted by French scholars.

196

city in the midst of an ordered fraternal universe. The other goal is the divine plan working in time. Man is to build a mysterious city which will anticipate the heavenly city. In Christ, men are to commune with each other and with God, and they are to inaugurate eternal life here on earth by building the invisible heavenly Jerusalem. These two kinds of time are irreducible because they measure two different paths (one is realized on earth, the other is a passage from earth to heaven), and because they are intrinsically different owing to the differing nature of their objects.

However, these two kinds of time are *inextricably linked.* The goals which they measure are, according to the divine plan, ordered to one another. Civilization is to form men capable of receiving Christ's message. The superabundant gifts of the Church are to aid men in discovering their true dimensions as human beings. In the case of Christians, these two time-spans are lived by the same individuals, who are also members of the same human society. Non-Christians, too, live in both time-spans. They are not strangers to Christ who calls them from within, nor to the Church which is " sent " to effect their salvation.

Two Opposing Times

However, these two time-spans are also *enemies;* and so their intermingling is extremely dangerous. The Church is plunged into a world [24] which cannot help but be impure. This world fights the Church, because men are beleaguered by the power of sin even as the Church is suffused with the power of grace. Sinful man is a hidden fortress of " the Prince of this world, " which he will hold until the end of time; the Church is the fortress of redeemed men who are able to call upon the omnipotence of the divine Savior. Intrinsically,

[24] In the New Testament the *world* is an ambiguous term because it refers to : (1) mankind as it really is, tainted by sin and enveloped by Christ's grace; (2) the men who have rejected God and fight against Christ and the Church.

these two time-spans are not only irreducible but also contradictory. It is true that the time of sin is suffused with the
day of grace at every moment. But it is also true that Church-
time is daily attacked by sin in this " world " of " iniquity "
and evil forces. Throughout history the time of regeneration
mingles with the time of damnation. It is impossible to mark
them off clearly, because there are God's children in the world
and there are the devil's children in the Church. Even in the
heart of Christians pulse the two inimical rhythms. Now
the Church does not seem to be the leaven in the dough
but rather the growing wheat-stalk which the chaff tries to
choke.

These two time-spans are distinct, linked, and opposed,
first, insofar as they regulate the rhythms of *two sociological
groups*. The Church and the world encounter each other in
many different groups. That is why their encounter is so
violent and why the process of evangelization has a tragic
aspect. Every association of human beings has its own
complexity and involves at least three levels of action [25] — the
level of instinct or collective consciousness, the level of reason
or " society, " and the level of common ideals or " community. "
The tension among these three levels is a permanent one
because it is imbedded in the very structure of human
associations. It is difficult to maintain equilibrium, because
sin makes these forces potential enemies. The first two tend
to be at odds and can only be reconciled by the third.

In the " world " (mankind as distinct from the Church),
the heaviest weight is the basic impulses rooted in the soil,
the race, the flesh, and the blood. The strongest constraint
is exerted by the law, which is always in danger of imposing
a false and brutal justice. The ideal of civic peace and order
— the only ultimate — is upheld only by a feeble but
indestructible spark. All these forces, which are good in
themselves but vitiated by sin, cannot be integrated harmo-

[25] Cf. " Les composantes du groupe humain, " *Économie et Humanisme*
(May-June), 1955.

niously without the grace of Christ. That is why worldly time is discordant, chaotic, and painful.

In the Church, on the other hand, everything depends on heaven, because everything comes from the divine *agape* which gathers the children of God, purifies them, and saves them through Jesus Christ. But, everything must descend to the other levels, on a commonplane. The juridic and social order must be revivified so that it may be administered in love. The instincts and the collective consciousness must be tamed and integrated so that they do not disrupt society and the ideal of communion. [26] The tension always exists, equilibrium is always threatened, and there is always danger of a split into hostile factions. From the time of St. Paul until the present day there are countless examples. Christians in the Church are imperfect and so the Church Militant is imperfect. There are great sinners and scandal-givers. Even just Christians sin daily, and the saints are tortured by the thought that they are not perfectly innocent. Christians as a group fall into sin and often split into different sects. Indeed, wheat and chaff do grow up together. The Church and the world! Two inimical realities, two discordant time-spans which meet and intermingle. They fuse and separate to form a complex amalgam. We cannot simplify this complex but we can single out two of its enduring traits.

Reconciliation and Warfare

A. RECONCILIATION

The Church begins in a world already existing with its own structure, orientation, and rhythms — in short, with its own culture, however pitiable and undeveloped it may be. At the very beginning the Church comes face to face with three worlds

---

[26] This is one of the Church's most aggravating problems in certain countries, and it crops up repeatedly in many different places.

— the Jewish world, the Greco-Roman world, and the Oriental world. The situation becomes more complex as the Church expands and the world grows. And yet the Church has a mission. She must " make disciples " of these people and *Christianize* the world. She exists in a time of human and spiritual reconciliation. This period has different phases — after people are discovered, contact must be established. When the proper preparation has been made, the process of evangelization can begin. Then the people are sanctified and native churches can be established.

Slowness of Approach

It is a complex operation which is never repeated in exactly the same way in different places. It must be emphasized that there is *necessarily* a *slow* process of reconciliation before the process of evangelization. [27] When the Church approaches a non-Christian people, she must adapt to their way of life. Whether it is the tribes of the Amazon or the fast-growing cities of our own country, the Church must immerse herself in this unknown world and adapt to the people's viewpoint if she is to civilize and convert them. The job may be done quickly at times. The conversion of a chief may lead to the conversion of his people; armies may force the conversion of a nation by the sword; the white man may take control of the native population. But the essential task remains to be done because the souls of the people have not yet been converted. [28] This task, which is of prime importance for the future of a particular church, is usually long and difficult.

At times the Church encounters *a group which is so poor and backward* that the time for evangelization has not yet

---

[27] St. Thomas has an interesting comment on the gradual growth and application of human law : " it strives to lead men to virtue gradually, not all at once *(subito)* ; thus it does not immediately impose the standards of a virtuous man on a barbarous society, e.g., refraining from evil of all sorts " (*ST*, I^a II^{ae}, 96, 2, 2).

[28] This is true in certain areas which are nominally Catholic, e.g., Latin America. On the problems alluded to here, a series of excellent monographs can be found in *Parole et Mission.*

come. The Church must prepare the soil as the farmer does, rooting up stones and shrubbery, and watering it in order to plant the seed. This would certainly be true for the Indians of the Amazon, with whom the dialogue is practically impossible. " One could scarcely draw up a suitable presentation of the Gospel except possibly for the children of the little Indians who are born today. " [29] At times the situation is just the opposite. The Church encounters today whole groups of people whose outlook has been *completely revolutionized*. In dealing with men of the machine age, or Marxists whose spiritual outlook has become completely distorted, the Church may have to reform the spirit before she can begin to speak of Christ.

Sometimes the Church encounters a class of human beings whose way of life differs from that of others. In many places the working class today lives in a civilization which it is helping to build but which is not made for it. Sometimes the Church meets deeply rooted sociological situations, and she must prepare the process of Christianization by amazing steps. Thus the chiefs in black Africa who practice polygamy are drawn toward the Church by rites of formal engagement. [30] The Church may have to acclimate herself to difficult living conditions. Those missionaries who became nomads in order to convert the Mongols found the best way. Today, in the face of urban

[29] See CARVALHO and LÉPARGNEUR, " Ébranlement des cultures, " *Parole et Mission* (1960), p. 264. This statement would be too general if we did not add two restrictions. First, most so-called civilized people are dominated by " primitive " emotions and are no better than non-civilized people. Even practicing Christians — and saints too — are subject to the laws of the flesh. We are all brothers as far as our animal nature is concerned. But, on the other hand, we cannot underestimate the powers of God's grace. A new convert can suddenly extricate himself from those instincts which are most deeply rooted in his tribe. A newly converted Papuan chieftain was assassinated because he was a Christian, but he forbade his clan to take vengeance. Cf. A. DUPEYRAT, *Vingt et un ans chez les Papous* (Paris 1952), chap 24.

[30] On these pro-catechumens see *Parole et Mission*, 8, pp. 133-136; also pp. 106 ff. on those who are not yet ready to receive the sacraments.

201

migrations prompted by economic conditions, the Church may be overwhelmed with huge masses for which she cannot provide priests or proper facilities. Sometimes the Church encounters a religious group which considers itself superior. The Islamites preach the One God and are scandalized by the Christian doctrine of the Trinity. They regard political and military force as an act of divine homage and view charity as a sign of weakness. [31]

Previously, we said that there is no contradiction between cosmic time and Church-time. But the man of the machine age puts everything in doubt — cosmic time as well as sociological time. He affects cosmic time directly. [32] His way of living is transformed by three processes which we may call rationalization, collectivization, and acceleration. He refuses to be a prisoner of space and does not live by the rhythms of the cosmos. He upsets the usual routine of day and night. He works and takes his leisure at night. He attends the movies or dances until dawn. He shortens his work-week and fills his leisure time with activities which hinder his religious observance and detract from the meaning of Sunday. He throws the seasons into disorder. Winter finds him cavorting in the snow and summer finds him off on vacation. He pays no heed to the mysterious natural activities — planting the seed or reaping the harvest.

He lives more and more in group-activities. Social constraints dominate his outlook. Daily travel to and from work, weekend leisure, annual vacation, — everything is strictly organized. Organization controls the movements of men. Men crowd together in huge edifices, strangers to each other. The " human spawn " is massed together on a shrinking planet. Social or political activity would be impossible without mass demonstrations. Indeed, in totalitarian countries it takes

[31] Cf. J. JOMIER, " L'Emprise de l'Islam sur les âmes, " *Parole et Mission*, 9, pp. 230-243.

[32] Cf. P. A. BLOND, " L'homme d'aujourd'hui et le travail, " *La Maison-Dieu*, 65 (1961), pp. 6-11; L. CHEVALLIER, " Athéisme du monde technique, " *La technique et l'homme* (Paris 1960), pp. 136-143.

the form of collective liturgies. Solitude, silence, and individuality are on the verge of extinction. They are becoming
a luxury. The individual human being is becoming an ant
in this gigantic collectivity.

Finally, machines are accelerating the rhythm of life.
Man moves from place to place more quickly. Airplanes,
radio and television afford him more experiences in a few
hours than man could formerly get in days or even months.
He is being clocked more closely with each passing day. His
job has its infernal rhythm. The years become shorter and
close in on him. Economic projects spread out over five, ten,
or fifteen years.

There is more. He is continually hurrying to catch up.
Sensational discoveries and their revolutionary applications
worked out at a mad pitch have accelerated history so much
that man has no time to stop, reflect, and take stock.
He becomes a nomad in a sense that the pastoral clans and
tribal gypsies could never have imagined. Workers flood the
cities. The ranks of the poor swell and then migrate. There
is a huge turnover in the military and the ranks of the
public servants. Technicians shift periodically and rapidly to
distant places. " The settled world returns to a nomadic
existence. "

Challenge of the Approach

Thus the Church faces a world in which the traditional modes
of life and work are challenged. Each time she must prepare
a new manner of approach. She works in *a newly orientated
period of evangelization*. But all these new kinds of existence
have only one unifying principle — the Church must bring
Christ to the world. The project takes different forms because
human societies experience internal and external changes.
History has its periods of springtime (its " epochs " as Peguy
calls them), when mankind undergoes a wondrous growth.
The Church must anticipate them and guide their direction.
There are times when whole civilizations — which are mortal,

after all [33] — decline and disappear. Then the Church must disengage herself from the dying in order to save what is coming to birth. Remember what St. Augustine said about the fall of the Roman world. And, finally, there are "critical points" [34] in history when people united in a common civilization separate, establish their own culture, and live in their separate worlds. Then the Church must propound the doctrine of catholicity, so as not to appear as the inimical religion of a strange group.

The different modes of human existence threaten Church-time. If the Church fails to adapt, a new way of life may start without her and in opposition to her. The Church's *presence* in the world always involves the danger of *conflict* and *rupture*. We are well aware that political, cultural, and religious factors played a part in the "oriental schisms," [35] the Byzantine separation, [36] and the western schisms. But when the family has broken up, when the sheep are scattered, the process of reconciliation must begin again. The Church starts over, fully aware that she does not know when the reconciliation will take place. Yet she must prepare it over the centuries with persistent hope and fraternal love. Today we are almost certainly at one of these "critical points." The reconciliation of the separated brethren no longer seems impossible to men of good will.

B. WARFARE

The previous considerations prove that Church-time is not wholly a period of peaceful reconciliation. It is also a time of warfare. The Church must fight against sin, the devil,

[33] In spite of recent comments to the contrary. For "machines" do not constitute a civilization.

[34] On this point see the apt reflections of H. I. DALMAIS, "Le Temps et l'Église," *L'Église et les Églises* (Chevetogne 1956), II, pp. 84 ff.

[35] Cf. the important study of C. MOELLER, "Réflexions sur les schismes à l'époque des premiers conciles," *L'Église et les Églises*, I, pp. 241-260.

[36] Y. CONGAR has researched this very carefully, and gives a clear explanation of it in "Notes sur le 'Schisme oriental,'" *op. cit.*, I, pp. 1-95.

and the world which submits to these evils. The forces of sin and evil are also part of human projects. The great ancient civilizations were built at the cost of many human lives. The pyramids of Egypt and the temples of Central America bear eloquent testimony of this. Today, economic life is ruled by harsh figures and power corrupts the political arena. [37] Emotions enslave the masses. Greed rules the maladjusted human heart. Thus the Church must be cautious and she must fight. She, therefore, threatens the fragile equilibrium between men. The world knows this. It opposes the Church and begins to persecute her. The early Christians did not refuse to *serve* the emperor, but they refused to *adore* him. They compromised the most sacred aspect of the *Pax Romana*. There was only one thing to do. These " atheists " had to be suppressed. The world will be stained by sin until the last day and the Church will always be on the Cross : " They have persecuted me, they will also persecute you " (Jn 15, 20). We can see how far the modern totalitarian regimes have carried the process of suppression and destruction. And when they collapse, other beasts will take their place.

Christian Warfare

This warfare is even more tragic because the Church Militant is also infected with sin. Christians confront a tainted world with unpurified hearts. [38] The enemy is within as well as

[37] We do not wish to cause misunderstanding on this point. The State is an *essential part* of human society. It is the organ which promotes the common good. As such it is not a device of the devil, but something willed by God. However, it is more vulnerable to evil pressures and worldly perversions. It then becomes an instrument for evil. This is most apparent in St. John's Gospel, especially in the trial of Jesus. Pilate tries to do his duty at first and to save the innocent man. But he gives in to the fanatical pressure of the " Jews " (the " world "). He frees the guilty one and crucifies the innocent one. On the New Testament viewpoint see the remarkable article of H. SCHLIER, " L'État selon le Nouveau Testament, " *LV*, 49, pp. 99-122. Here we are referring to the State dominated by violence.

[38] These statements do not refer to *the essence* of the Church nor to her *esse* insofar as they are the immediate enduring result of Christ's redemptive

without. Christians are the first to tarnish the Church. When the " wise, " the " powerful, " and the " great " are Christians too, they attempt to use the Church instead of serving her. She becomes a means of dominating others. The common folk are content " to sin like everyone else. " Thus, the sinful world drags the Church along, woos it toward the standards of the group, and tends to form a closed Catholicism — a contradiction in terms. The world seeks to destroy the vitality and the liberty of the salvation-period. *Sociologically* speaking, the Church becomes " the churches. " This multiplicity involves historical and dogmatic differences which cause scandal and stain the cloak of Catholic unity. The dubious goals of the wordly city vitiate the Church's spiritual project. The story of Christ begins all over again. The rulers with their political ambitions and the masses with their worldly hopes try to use the Church for their own ends. The ecclesiastical structure sags, spiritual and temporal confusion develops, and sin becomes a part of Christian society.

The Church's Project of Salvation

The Church's mission, however, does not change. In the final reckoning, she must take hope in the Holy Spirit and transform human time into salvation-time. The actual encounter makes this a difficult task. The world is convinced

---

act. In this sense, as Msgr. JOURNET has pointed out, there is no sin in the Church. Our statements refer to what we may call the *existence* of the Church, i. e., *the way in which Christians receive the esse of the Church and realize her essence.* In this sense the Church, unfortunately, is tainted by sin. Y. CONGAR also distinguishes between the structure of the Church and her actual life in *Vraie et fausse réforme dans l'Église* (1950), chap. 1; also C. MOELLER, *L'Église et les Églises*, I, pp. 242 ff.; BRUNET, " Église, " *D. Sp.*, col. 401. We are reminded of St. Augustine's texts, e.g., *Retract.*, 1, 7, note 5. There he cites Eph 5, 25-27 and says : " However, as long as the Church remains on earth, she says ' forgive us our trespasses. ' She is not pure and spotless here below. But the gifts she has received here below lead her to heavenly glory and perfection. " St. Augustine also " explains " his *De Moribus Ecclesiae* and his *De Baptismo* (*ibid.*, II, 18). This is one of his frequent themes in *Enarrationes in Psalmos* (e.g. *in Psalm.* 99, 12-13).

that human beings change and make themselves better. The collective consciousness is obsessed with the " philosophy of history. " The conquest of matter achieved by technology dominates man's thinking. The emotions come to play a dominant role and are not regulated by spiritual ideals. The result is anguish, fear, sexual obsession, and psychic imbalance. Human existence becomes one of mass dependence. The technological societies become more alike and the undeveloped nations revolt against their poverty and misery. In short, it is obvious that a new world is arising before our eyes.

This new spirit is vitiated by certain terrible forces. Today, atheism is not only a way of thinking but *a way of living*. It is tied in with the new technological civilization and involves a complete reversal of values. It takes different forms — in Russia, America, and Scandinavia — and silently " takes possession " of large masses of humanity. Communism, too, represents a shrewd and formidable crusade of destruction. It brings a sudden end to centuries of cultural and technical backwardness. It aims to reform man by separating him from God, and to destroy the Catholic Church by persecution and subversion. We behold an unbelievable transformation, a deliberate attempt at anti-creation brought about by the suppression of Christian churches in many lands.

But the Church is not destroyed, because the Lord dwells in her and protects her always. She is involved in a period of struggle in which she must keep constant vigil and devote herself entirely to preaching for Christ. It is a period of judgment, because she must understand, evaluate and " prove all things : hold fast that which is good " (1 Thes 5, 21). She must give testimony now more than ever before, by revealing the Lord's countenance to men who are strangers to it. In purity, fidelity, and fraternal love, [39] she must preserve the pristine Christian values in the hearts of modern men. It is

[39] See the judicious comments on this point made by a specialist in Russian Communism, Madame PELTIER-ZAMOYSKA, in *Informations catholiques internationales* (March 1, 1960).

a time for "strength in faith," because the Church is persecuted and faith must be nurtured secretly in the hearts of men. She confesses her faith openly when she can, and in sorrow and hope she offers up the blood of her sons. At times she is forced to watch their souls depart from a shattered psyche. It is a period of silent suffocation, dislocation, and suppression. Where are the churches of St. Paul, St. Cyprian, and St. Augustine? Where are the churches of Scandinavia, China, and the Ukraine? Swept away years ago or centuries ago. But the Church is an immense Body, and a localized wound will never kill her. The face of the world changes continuously. The dying seed is the harbinger of a new harvest. In the sacrifice of suffering and love, in the silence of persecution and annihilation, the life-giving Word resounds in the hearts of men.

Christ's Time Prolonged

For Church-time is not the kind of time which we understand; it is the time of the eternal Christ. In the continuing struggle, the call to acceptance or rejection remains. No matter how it may *appear* on the surface, Church-time has only one source, one center, and one goal — Jesus Christ. Her essential mission is *to incorporate men into Christ*. Church-time, as the time of Christ, is a period dominated by God's unarmed sovereign omnipotence. This omnipotence is concentrated in Jesus Christ and is, therefore, present in the hearts of Christians. *The weakness of God is stronger than men!* (1 Cor 1, 25). But only by faith can we see the Spirit resurrecting the Church from the dark night of the tomb. Only by faith can we see this rejuvenating principle suffusing the Church " as a rich vein suffuses an ore-deposit. " [40] Through faith also are many aspects of this mysterious time-span revealed.

Christ's Passion is prolonged in this time-span until the end of the world. Churches are persecuted, Christians undergo sufferings, and unknown souls offer themselves as a redemptive

[40] St. IRENAEUS, *Adv. Haereses*, III, 27, 1 (*PG* 7, 966).

oblation. The intercession begun by Abraham and Moses and consummated by Christ — " Always living to make intercession for us " (Heb 7, 25) — is prolonged, through His eternal act, by the anointed ones and all the members of the Church Militant. Holiness works in secret as the vital force in the world. For it restores sinful mankind to equilibrium and roots up certain dangerous attachments. By prolonging Christ's oblation, it restores human solidarity and puts it at the service of grace. " Where sin abounded, grace did more abound " (Rom 5, 20). Who can say how much the spiritual rejuvenation of the world is abetted by such people as Theresa of the Child Jesus, Charles de Foucauld, Père Peyriguère, Abbé Tong, Père Tsang and the Chinese martyrs? What effect does a Père Lebbe have on China, an Abbé Monchanin on India, and a Père Candau on Japan? These few names are known to us. But the saints of the Catholic Church are as numerous as the stars. The Christian sees holiness in some and conjectures about a few others. But he knows that the universe is peopled by an invisible multitude of holy ones.

Strength in Weakness

All these facts are *summed up in the unifying presence* of Christ the Savior. His presence in the Eucharist proclaims the mystery of death and Resurrection until He comes again. This is the sacred focal point where everything acquires meaning, where the day of grace envelops the works of iniquity, where human solidarity is orientated toward God, and *where sinful cosmic time* seesaws in salvation-time. St. Paul has pointed out all the aspects of this warfare. He tells us that the most mysterious realities of creation — death and life, present and future — are sometimes bitter enemies and sometimes aids given by God Himself. [41] In other words, the world is *both at once*. The Church is always faced with these two aspects. Man is free to see either side, but the grace of Christ remains

[41] Enemies in Rom 8, 35-39; aids in 1 Cor 3, 22 ff. Cf. HUBY, *La Première Épître aux Corinthiens* (Paris 1946), pp. 116-117.

to give us victory over the world, or better yet, to put it at the service of salvation.

Church-time is shockingly weak. It has only " poor weapons " and the " armor of light. " But with *the force of the power of Christ* it silently suffuses sin-tainted time and envelops cosmic time. At the appointed moment, it inaugurates the personal salvation-time of each soul of good will. And, at long last, it elevates all cosmic activity and brings the universe to the consummation envisioned by St. Paul : *All are yours ; and you are Christ's ; and Christ is God's* (1 Cor 3, 22-23). The eye of faith believes all this but does not see it here below. Reconciliation and warfare, birth and death, contamination and purification, integration and rupture — these processes coexist while the Church lives in the world. They cannot be analyzed or fully integrated by a human mind. *Only the psyche of the Risen Christ can embrace this continuing activity. Only His eternity can subsume this time-span* and derive eternal fruit from it. Church-time is *immersed* in cosmic time. This is a permanent fact of the Christian drama. But, in the last analysis, cosmic time is made to be enveloped by Church-time. The latter endures while this world passes away.

The Journey to Eternity

The Church springs from the Risen Christ and returns to Him continuously. And the time-span which measures this journey returns to its source in eternity. In the process of expansion which we have analyzed to some extent, there is an *ascending* movement which is at the very heart of Church-time. This movement marks Church-time as *a journey to eternity* in three respects. [42]

In the first place, Church-time is a period of passing from unbelief to faith, and from sin to conversion. After acknowledging Christ, men are to enter the Kingdom through

[42] Later we shall expand on certain points which are only mentioned here.

210

repentance and Baptism. In short, Church-time is a period of passing *from death to eternal life*. It does not matter whether we are dealing with a baptized child, an adult convert, or a reformed Christian. Death and resurrection in Christ are a basic, permanent constituent of Church-time. In this sense, the Church is a body of people who are continually reborn, a consecrated group which journeys toward eternity every day.

Faith grows and continually deepens — *ex fide in fidem*. [43] Christians enter more and more deeply into the Kingdom and into eternity. The search for God and Christ, the quest after evangelical perfection, the discovery of the mysterious *agape* and its full dimensions — all these activities involve an infinite journey for Christians and for the Church. The process of search alternates continuously with the act of discovery. Each person follows his path and enters more fully into the mystery of Christ's death and Resurrection. The Church is forever propelled by a hidden, efficacious impulse toward an existence transformed by Jesus Christ.

Finally, at the " moment, " fixed by God, the time comes to enter eternity once and for all. For the individual Christian it is the hour when he *passes from this world to his Father*. Each day many experience this " final hour. " It is another permanent aspect of Church-time. In the person of the dying Christian, the Church passes from earth to heaven, from exile to her Father's house, from infancy to maturity, from imperfection to perfection. The pilgrims far from the Lord are reunited with their brothers for all time. They come at last to " the heavenly Jerusalem, and to the company of many thousands of angels, and to the church of the firstborn, " through the blood and glory of Jesus Christ (Heb 12, 22-23). But they enter eternity to plunge into the enduring source of the Church's life and to take part in the salvation of the Church Militant in a radically new way.

[43] Rom 1, 17. Cf. the commentary of LAGRANGE, *in h.l.*, p. 20; also of HUBY, pp. 68-69.

Thus, the journey to the Lord involves a *threefold* passage. Each member makes the unique passage into permanent union. Church-time, at its *deepest level,* provides *access to eternity.* The Church's perpetual beginning in time and eternity will be completed at the Parousia, the last epiphany and the last judgment, when all men will rise to life or to condemnation. All cosmic and spiritual growth in time leads to this moment.

The entire Mystical Body with its various members is involved in the process of birth, growth, and death. It experiences periods of advance and periods of set-back, periods of conversion from sin to grace and from grace to sin, periods of spiritual elevation and periods of decline. In short, it experiences conflicting movements which we cannot fully comprehend. But we know that these uncertainties are not like sea-waves which " begin over and over. " They ebb and flow over one another in the vast ocean of the Church which daily mounts closer to her glorious King, her Savior, and her eternal Spouse. Hence the Church is primarily an invisible reality — *the assembly of the saints in paradise.* As human generations succeed one another, the Church grows to maturity. The millions of faithful of one generation form one small part of the Body which is developing above. As Newman said, we are one reborn generation among fifty others. Today, " fifty times more saints have been signed with the seal of immortality. They must fight here below to obtain immortality above. " If one is willing to listen, he can hear *the angelic chant rising from the ship of salvation.* The Church, at every instant, is moving to the Father and to her dwelling in eternity.

It is a mysterious, sacred, silent time. The Kingdom sprouts like a plant in the night. The work of sowing and harvesting goes on and the Bread of Life nourishes men. The permanent *objective* is to bring men to salvation. The animating *force* is fraternal charity. The *efficacious means* is Christ's mediation through the power of the Holy Spirit. Only the psyche of the Risen Christ could establish and envelop this time-span in which is prepared the mysterious epiphany which will transform us for all eternity.

9

The Structure of Church-Time

We have just noted several characteristics of Church-time. But we are still left with the difficult task of analyzing *its structure.* [1] The Church is a living organism as her common titles indicate : Mystical Body of Christ, Spouse of Christ, Mother of the Faithful, Family of God. She is the most mysterious organism of all, existing in a time-span where the Lord's Incarnation is continued through the power of the Holy Spirit. The spiritual factors involved in this time-span are very complex. Only by *cutting* into this intricate complex can we hope to isolate its three essential components.

[1] We define a structure as a hierarchical complex ordered and unified in some specific way.

The Word of God

Words are a universe in themselves. They bridge the gap between persons. Since they imply a communication between at least two persons, they are signs of an idea to be communicated, outlines of an endless dialogue, and harbingers of a communion of life and thought. In short, they are one of the *mysteries of time*. But when they are part of the Word of God, they are a unique universe. We must now examine the role of this universe in the Church.

Word and Scripture

The Word of God has been *given to the Church*. It represents the dialogue between God and His people (through His inspired prophets) over a long period of time. *God, who at sundry times and in divers manners, spoke in times past to the fathers by the prophets, last of all, in these days has spoken to us by His Son* (Heb 1, 1-2). The final words of the divine message, revealing the deepest secrets and the most astonishing prophecies, are conveyed in the human speech of the Incarnate God. The Apostles listen and accept them. They ponder these words under the guidance of the Holy Spirit and then explain them in their preaching. These words pronounced in the fullness of time, are given a somewhat fixed form by being written down in what is to become the New Testament. When the last Apostle dies, the period of revelation is over. God has told men what they must know and do in order to be saved. For one or two generations the divine message was heard as "the living Word" glowing with vitality. Now it becomes the *Scripture* [2] and is fixed forever.

But the Scripture cannot be disassociated from the Church which proclaims it and explains its true meaning. Scripture and Tradition combine to form *one complex structure*. Many

---

[2] Cf. D. VAN DEN EYNDE, *Les normes de l'enseignement chrétien...* (1933), I, chap. 3 and II, chap. 1.

men spoke the Word of God and wrote it down. But it was God Himself who was speaking. He continues to speak and to beget sons through " the Gospel preserved in all its purity by the Church. " [3] We can see God's multi-faceted initiative and the historical development written between the lines of " Holy Scripture. " Every time we approach this work, it plunges us into the *unique moment* — which lasted for centuries — in which God gradually revealed Himself and inspired men to write His Word down; and it also takes us through this " moment " — already past — and plunges us into *the eternity* of Christ's revelatory and redemptive *act*. The eternal present of Christ establishes the past and the future of revelation.

Word and Faith

The time of the self-revealing Word has run its course. But this *does not mean that the time of a book has begun*. What has begun is the time of apostolic preaching in the Church. In other words, with the aid of the Holy Spirit, the apostolic body (the bishops united with Peter) preaches the words of Scripture with fidelity, authority, and effectiveness. The divine message is *written* down so that it may be *spoken* to the faithful — primarily at the Eucharistic banquet, but also at all the gatherings which are a preparation for it or a continuation of it.

---

[3] *Council of Trent, Sess.* IV, *init.* On this enormous problem we can only refer to some recent studies : C. MOELLER, " Tradition et Œcuménisme, " *Irenikon* (1962), pp. 337-370; C. BAUMGARTNER, " Tradition et Magistère, " *RSR* (1953), pp. 161-187; the articles of M. J. LE GUILLOU, P. DE VOOGHT, J. R. GEISELMANN on " Écriture et Tradition, " *Istina* (1958), pp. 161-214; H. DE LUBAC, " Le problème du développement du dogme, " *RSR* (1948), pp. 130-160; E. ORTIGUES, " Écriture et traditions apostoliques au concile de Trente, " *RSR* (1949), pp. 271 ff.; A. LÉONARD, " La foi, principe fondamental du développement du dogme, " *RSPT* (1957), pp. 276-286; J. H. WALGRAVE, *Newman the Theologian* (New York : Sheed, 1960); and the well-documented comments of Y. CONGAR, " Traditions apostoliques non écrites et suffisance de l'écriture, " *Istina*, 3 (1959), pp. 279-306; H. HOLSTEIN, " La Tradition d'après le Concile de Trente, " *RSR*, 3 (1959), pp. 367-390; P. VOOGHT, " Écriture et Tradition d'après des études catholiques récentes, " *Istina* (1958), pp. 173-196.

The Word of God proclaimed in the Church is " the power of God unto salvation to every one that believeth. " [4]

But the divine message is spoken to someone. And so it is also the time for the *hearing of the Word*. It is, in other words, the time for faith. The pastors of the flock had to " listen " to the Word for a long time before they transmitted it to others. They, too, have " received " and understood it in the same sense as the Church herself. They explain the message and their explanation is catholic insofar as it accords with the tradition of the Church. The baptized hear the message with the ears of faith (Gal 3, 2). They accept it in order to be converted, and meditate on it in order to conform themselves to Christ. They allow it to form them into the assembly of the faithful " begotten by God. " *This relationship between the divine Word and Faith*, between proclamation and acceptance, is one of the Church's component structures. It establishes one level of Church-time. The unique divine message must be multiplied insofar as it is preached to various Christian and non-Christian groups. The mission to preach to every creature involves countless repeated communications in time and space. But these communications are still part of the Church's mission and are rooted in Christ's act of revelation. He aids His Church (both pastors and flock) with His Spirit, and continues to reveal Himself in her through the unique eternal act which establishes and unifies the manifold expressions of the one catholic message till the end of time. [5]

The time for God's Word, then, is founded by this reciprocal relationship between an *ever-present, eternal reality* and *continuous repetitions in time*. We discover that duality is essential to the basic structure of the Church. She is the Body of Christ, one with Him; it is always God who speaks

[4] Rom 1, 16. The same theme is found in St. John, of course; cf. H. van den Bussche, *Le Discours après la Cène* (Paris 1959), pp. 106-107. Also the book written by an Eastern rite monk, *Jesus, A Dialogue with the Saviour* (New York : Desclée, 1963).

[5] Of course, the ramifications of this principle involve the infallibility of the Church, of the apostolic body, and of the Roman Pontiff.

216

through her — *tanquam Deo exhortante per nos* (2 Cor 5, 20.) She is the Spouse of Christ, necessarily distinct from Him. She preaches through her leaders, listens through her faithful, and lives the Word of God through the lives of both her leaders and her faithful. This Word is both a written and a spoken one. *Scripture and Tradition* are *two inseparable functions ;* first, because each implies the other : Scripture originates in the apostolic tradition, and the Church's tradition has the role of preaching and explaining Scripture; [6] secondly, because they are simultaneously lived by the Church : she believes the Word, prays it, celebrates it, and testifies to it, always preserving the meaning which the Fathers attached to it; thirdly, because both are subject to the eternal subsistent Word [7] who is revealed through them by the Holy Spirit in order that His Body may be wholly united and completely faithful.

Word and the Church's Psyche

Finally, the Word of God is carried in the psyche of the Church. The words of St. Luke regarding the Virgin Mary, a type of the Church, are particularly apropos. She " kept all these words, pondering them in her heart " (Lk 2, 19). It is extremely difficult to define the exact nature of this psyche, and yet it is necessary to introduce it at this point. [8]   Let us

[6] The first is " constitutive " *(traditio constitutiva)*, the second continues and explicates *(traditio continuativa, explicativa).*   Cf. C. BAUMGARTNER *op. cit.*, p. 165, note 11 and pp. 169 ff.; H. CROUZEL, " Origène devant l'incarnation et devant l'histoire, " *BLE*, 4 (1960), pp. 84 ff.

[7] This is one of the major differences between Christianity and Islamism. The latter is a religion based on a book. Cf. Y. MOUBARAC, " La naissance de l'Islam, " *LV*, 25 (1956), p. 9 : " In the eyes of his followers, the founder of Islamism does not have the same personal importance as Jesus has for Christians. Conversely, the Koran is much more important to them than the Gospels are to Christians or the Bible to the Israelites. "

[8] The word flows spontaneously from the pens of the theologians. Cf. H. DE LUBAC, *op. cit.*, p. 134 (citing Bainvel, de Grandmaison, Pinard, Lebreton, Gardeil); C. BAUMGARTNER, *op. cit.*, pp. 173-174.   The *letter of the Dutch Bishops* on the Council (Christmas, 1960) declares that the Council seeks " to maintain contact with the *growing consciousness of the universal Church* " (cited in *Études*, April 1961, p. 105).

217

say that it is *the Holy Spirit insofar as He is immediately communicated*, universally, to the Body as a whole, and individually to each member, through the hierarchy, the Word, and the Sacraments. This psyche is the fruit of an efficacious relationship with the Spirit. Hence it is *by no means a metaphor*, but rather a profound reality. It exists only in the act by which the Holy Spirit communicates His theandric being to the Church. Its clarity, its unity, and its universality are absolutely unique. Hence this psyche is *supra-personal* and *supra-social*. It is not enlightening like an intellectual perception, but brightly illuminating like the indefinable feeling of a sovereign presence and communion, the presence of the Trinity revealed in Jesus Christ. [9] Its invisible unifying principle is the Holy Spirit. Through Him Christ's *ego* is revealed forming His own body. Its visible unifying principle is the universal (catholic) unity of the Mystical Body itself as expressed by the apostolic hierarchy and summed up in its living center, the sovereign Pontiff. The Church's psyche exists only in *this* indestructible *union and distinction* between the Spirit and His Spouse, the Head and His members, the blessed Trinity and the creation which participates in it, i.e., the Church of Christ.

Thus, *Scripture is cradled in the psyche of the whole Church* which sustains and protects it, and is protected by it in turn. The Church listens to it, ponders it, and draws nourishment from it. Thanks to the Spirit, the Church comprehends the mystery of Scripture, animates and vivifies it with the impulses of her own heart, and then preaches it to the world. The apostolic hierarchy alone interprets Scripture authoritatively. But these interpretations *become part of the Church's life*. Each day they are taken up by the magisterium and lived by the Christian people. Scripture and Tradition are complementary and inseparable. Together they make the unique Word of God a living reality. If Scripture structures the

---

[9] We have attempted to explain under what conditions this is possible and orthodox in our book: *The Christian Experience* (New York : Sheed, 1954).

Church, it is because the Church sustains it, guards it, and communicates it as the priceless pearl and the sacred deposit.

Hence the infallible interventions of the magisterium are an extreme example of the relationship between Scripture and Tradition. They are exceptional occurrences which rarely define the dogmatic meaning of a scriptural text. They represent the special, solemn moments in which — under the veil of faith — the presence of the Spirit is made manifest, and eternity is made present in time. For most of the time, the Church lives the divine Word with the aid of the Spirit. She draws nourishment from this daily bread in the security of a universal faith — *securus judicat orbis terrarum.*

Memory

It now becomes apparent that the aid of the Holy Spirit establishes memory and prophecy in the Church. To speak of a spiritual psyche is to speak of a memory. Once again we are *not dealing with a metaphor* but *with a mystery.* The memory of the Church is the Holy Spirit and her own organic structures — the immutable Scripture, the episcopal hierarchy which interprets it and preaches it, and the faithful who listen to it. The faithful live the message of Scripture, and by the reactions of their common psyche — *sensus communis fidelium* — they preserve and support it. Often they pave the way for an official interpretation. [10] When a new problem arises or a new appeal is sounded, when a doctrine begins to blossom and spread gradually, when a great crisis befalls the Church (sometimes affecting her for centuries), the Church stops to reflect on Scripture and to recall the past with the aid of the Holy Spirit. [11]

The Church recalls the past through the primitive confessions of faith, the traditional liturgies, and the truths so dearly

[10] Cf. C. BAUMGARTNER, *op. cit.*, pp. 174-175, 184-185.

[11] Apropos of this recollection (Jn 14, 25-31) which is an interior understanding of revelation, H. VAN DEN BUSSCHE writes : " This understanding is not restricted to the first witnesses of the faith nor to the hierarchy. It is granted to every one of the faithful until the end of time. " *(Le Discours d'adieu de Jésus)* (Paris 1959), pp. 94-95.

aquired and formulated in the councils. She remembers the lengthy struggles, the blood of martyrs, and the unbroken chain of great witnesses. When she ponders the Word — the *unum Verbum perfectum* — she returns to the fountainhead. [12] She fords the current and sees the living waters become a mighty stream. She forms a *judgment in the day of grace*, in the light of the Holy Spirit. In this act of recollection, the past returns. The Church establishes contact not only with her own beginnings in time, her birth and development, but also with her eternal source, the Holy Spirit communicated by Christ yesterday, today, and tomorrow. In her memory, where " faith is activated by love, " truth grows and blossoms like a plant in the sunlight. *It changes so that it may remain the same,* [13] because it is unique. It is the mystery of God communicated in Jesus Christ. This mystery was *fully revealed* in the first days of the Church. But it will *never be fully expressed in formulas*, because the Church as a whole could not possibly comprehend it all before the end of time. Only the psyche of the Risen Christ can comprehend it fully. Insofar as the Church has not yet reunited with His psyche in the Beatific Vision, insofar as she has not yet become " the perfect man, " she is still seeking, discovering and clarifying aspects of this truth. And unfortunately, she is also allowing certain aspects to be buried in the darkness of obscurity. The Spirit must help the Church to discover and ponder these aspects once again, to grow along with the body of Christian dogma. [14] The remarkable thing is that in questioning Scripture and Tradition, the Church is questioning *its immutable faith*, the faith which remains the same yesterday, today,

[12] The image is nicely developed in NEWMAN, *On the Development of Christian Doctrine.*

[13] *Ibid.*

[14] Apropos of Scripture, which is not the mystery but the word through which it is revealed, Newman wrote : " After all our efforts, at the end of our life and even on the last day of the Church, (Scripture) will still be virgin territory full of hills and valleys, forests and streams, hiding wondrous treasures all around us. " *Ibid.*

and tomorrow, thanks to the Holy Spirit. When two different Popes decided to define the Immaculate Conception and the Assumption, they not only examined Scripture and Tradition, but also questioned the bishops about the *living* faith of their *present-day* churches.

Prophecy

Every psyche is open to the future. The Word of God is also prophetic. In the Church there remains the Spirit of the prophets, which is nothing else but the Spirit of Christ. [15] But here again we find a strange situation. The Church *does not know the secrets of the future.* They have not been revealed to her and they are not a part of her spiritual resources (cf. Acts 1, 6-8). Though a corner of the veil may be raised slightly, the rest remains in doubt. It is not so much intended " to inform " us as to make us live the evangelical attitude par excellence : " Watch ye therefore, because you know not the day nor the hour " (Mt 25, 13). Not only the end of history, but also her own historical development in all its aspects — empirical, human, spiritual and salvific — is hidden from the Church. And yet the Church *knows the mystery of the future,* the silent, invisible, mysterious, but permanent and fruitful return of Christ the Savior. She knows what is involved in waiting and preparing for His return — trials, temptations, and persecutions. The Kingdom will progress and experience setbacks. Individual churches will appear and disappear, and pass through periods of greatness and decline. All these fortunes must be accepted with faith and hope, with patience and fortitude, with joy and sorrow. " You became followers of us and of the Lord : receiving the word in much tribulation, with joy of the Holy Ghost " (1 Thes 1, 6). This is the permanent " pattern " (*ib.* 7).

Thus the Word of God is prophetic because it *reveals the meaning of everything to come, even though the actual events*

[15] We exclude the *charisms* of prophecy *in the strict sense,* although they have a definite role to play in the history of the Church. It is very difficult to mark them out.

are unknown. The veil of faith is not lifted here below. That is why the Church and the saints are cautious about revelations, visions, and predictions of the future. [16] But at the same time the Church is certain that the future, no matter what form it may take, is in the hands of the Lord; that she is indefectible and indestructible amid changing human events because she represents Christ's presence among men; that the all-powerful Word, ever the same and yet ever new, will be preached until the end of time. In short, she knows that the redemptive word of Christ will always be a part of cosmic time, not only as its explanation but also as its guiding principle, linking it to its source and its final end. His redemptive work gives cosmic time a transcendent value which respects the multiplying of its positive rhythmns and unifies them in their movement toward one end. But time is needed for all this!

These Words which come from God to men must remain *humbly subject to the Spirit.* When they take the form of a dogmatic definition, as in the nineteenth and twentieth centuries, we know that they are the Word of God. But their full significance will be revealed only when they have long exerted a reforming influence on the hearts of Christians and the Church of tomorrow. When we are dealing with human words which try to express the truths of Christianity, to develop them and integrate them into human thought, *time* must be *taken into consideration.* When they are formulated too quickly without the proper maturation and correlations, or when they are left in an undeveloped form, in short, when they are too modernistic or too archaic, [17] they become errors or heresies.

---

[16] Cf. the classic and picturesque examples of A. POULAIN, *Des Graces d'Oraison.* Chaps. 20, 21.

[17] Cf. H. WALGRAVE, *op. cit.,* on Newman and the heretic, p. 199, and the references in footnote 49. Regarding the monophysites' refusal to accept dogmatic formulas, and their opposition to the formulas of Scripture and St. Cyril, cf. J. DANIÉLOU, " Bulletin d'Hist. des origines chrétiennes, " *RSR* (1955), pp. 594 ff.; also C. MOELLER, in *L'Église et les Églises,* pp. 242 ff.

The true Christian knows that the past and the future belong to God. " He can look ahead to the extent that he looks back. " In the present day of grace, he calmly *prepares the work of the next five centuries.* [18]

Silence

The Christian also speaks without words. In some cases this *silent testimony* is the most potent. For the Word of God is a divine act — *dicere Dei est facere.* [19] The man who accepts it, must live it and manifest it. Only then will the spoken word have full meaning. When the surroundings are inimical to the spoken word, when the priests and the faithful, the archbishop or the cardinal, are reduced to silent imprisonment, the Word still rings out through their sufferings and their fierce loyalty. This is the attitude of Jesus Himself — *Cœpit facere et docere* (cf. Acts 10, 37-39). And His attitude is our guide. There are silent churches and silent missions. The spoken word is weak, infrequent, and secret. But the person of the Word is more vividly present under the veil of humiliation and crucifixion — *Jesus autem tacebat.* The Word of God indicates His presence. When the members of Christ are undergoing their passion, His redemptive presence is expressed in the dark night of their silence, their sorrow, and their indefatigable hope.

The time of the Word is a time of life, death, and resurrection. The words pronounced by the Church in time assume different forms in time and space. But even in time they sustain time and do not pass away with it. " Heaven and earth shall pass away : but my word shall not pass away " (Mk 13, 31). These words are the humble yet omnipotent temporal expression of the eternal Word, the Son " upholding all things by the word of his power " (Heb 1, 3).

[18] NEWMAN, *op. cit.*, pp. 81-82.

[19] St. THOMAS, *in* 2 Cor, I, lect. 2, note 1 : " Dicere Dei est facere : dixit et facta sunt (Ps 32, 9). Unde benedicere Dei est bonum facere et bonum infundere. "

The Sacraments

This component of Christian time fulfills the promises involved in the time of the Word. The sacraments are *completely intrinsic* to a sacred universe. Through faith they accomplish the word. However, they also involve a human action on the material universe, which is not implied by the word. Thus sacramental time involves *a relationship between man and the world* in which there is an extraordinary transformation. The sacraments involve a material and spiritual encounter with Christ, an encounter which is the " sacrament " of an encounter with God.

At the heart of every sacrament, *the redemptive act is present* and " applied " to all human generations and to each human being throughout time.

Divine Sacramental Act

The sacramental act is, first of all, completely divine. Its efficacious source is the unique, eternal, redemptive act which is made present through it. Its concrete symbolism [20] derives from a *deliberate intention of Jesus Christ*. This intention is expressed through the sacramental rite, even though the Church may determine the exact words and actions to be used. Its proper effect is to communicate some specific aspect of the mystery of Christ to human beings, and thus to make them adopted sons of the Father conformed to Christ. There is a direct connection between Christ's " intention " and the effect of grace, between the eternal plan and the temporal action. The sacraments are truly " free acts " of the Lord enveloped in the unique redemptive will, which is perfectly free and eternal and transcends its results in time. The sacramental world is a world of free actions expressing the unique act of redemptive liberty.

[20] We do not say : *the material elements* (things, actions, words) of this symbolism, because they have evolved in the course of time.

On the other hand, the sacramental act is completely human. Its symbolism pierces to the depths of the soul and the universe. And since creation is the first stage of salvation, this symbolism is not alien to the real movement of man toward God. Every religion has its own symbolism, but this symbolism is based on a foundation common to all men. In every case *man's relationship with the world is involved.* [21] Christ makes use of an already existing symbolism (baptism, anointing, banquet). He makes use of a world in which man has already introduced the sacred element. And so He links man with cosmic time by inserting the latter into salvation-time.

The sacraments also require a " minister, " a consecrated man who performs the sacramental action. A necessary prerequisite is that he have *the intention of doing what Christ wills.* Only then is Christ's redemptive will fulfilled and His redemptive act rendered present. All this implies a need for faith and love to give the sacred act its full meaning and clearest expression. And finally it presupposes a sacred respect for the act which the redemptive power utilizes as a means. Through this sacred " act, " man and the entire universe become a means of salvation. However, the only valid minister of a sacrament is the man chosen by God, consecrated by the Church, and marked with the priestly character. [22] This character represents the permanent hold of the eternal High Priest on those He has chosen to continue His work and to render Him present among men. Time and eternity embrace once again.

[21] Cf. M. ÉLIADE, *Patterns in Comparative Religion* (New York : Sheed, 1958). On Baptism see (e.g.) L. BEIRNAERT, " Symbolisme mythique de l'eau dans le Baptême, " *La Maison-Dieu*, Nr. 22 (1950). For a provocative philosophical discussion, see P. RICOEUR, *Finitude et culpabilité* (Paris 1960), I, pp. 11-25 and 153-162.

[22] We must take due account of other cases. When a baptized person performs the rite of baptism, he does so by virtue of the baptismal character which gives him a share in the priesthood of Christ. In emergencies an unbeliever may do so through his connection with the Church by virtue of man's supernatural vocation in Christ.

The subject, too, must do his part. *A sacrament cannot be received in a state of absolute passivity.* [23] The subject must respond. He must know, accept, and will what is done. He must believe and love the Lord who calls him. Only then does the sacrament exist for him and realize in him its mystery of grace. Only then does the believer personally encounter the Risen Lord, enter into communion with the Trinity, and give glory to God.

Temporal Mystery

The sacraments, therefore, are a complex temporal mystery for two reasons. First, there is a *twofold relationship* implied in the very essence of the sacraments, a relationship between two men and a relationship between both men and their Savior. Two men are united by a specific religious intention, one as the minister of the sacrament, the other as the subject. The consecrated minister renders Christ present so that He may dwell in the subject and actualize His redemptive act in both. The free exercise of the sacramental rite involves certain responsibilities which mark the sacrament as *a focal point* of horizontal and vertical *relationships between time and eternity*.

Furthermore, the sacraments are entrusted to the Church, not to men. Through the hierarchy, she is charged with the task of guarding the sacraments and preserving the ideas which Christ intended to express through them. That explains why the externals of the sacraments have often changed in different, changing, cultural environments. External change has not threatened their authenticity, because the Church sees to it that they express the idea willed by Christ faithfully and ever more precisely. [24] But this is only the first step.

[23] Not even by new-born infants. They are baptized in the faith of the Church working through the priest, the god-parents and the parents. As we know, many pastoral problems ensue.

[24] This " precision " does *not* take place *in the order of reason* but *in the order of tradition and religious faith*. As we know, the ceremonies of Orders developed, and theologians disagreed on their essence and on the positions of the ecclesiastical magisterium (Council of Florence). When Pius XII (*Sacramentum ordinis*, 1947) for pastoral reasons officially determined the

The Whole Mystery of Christ

The sacraments involve the whole mystery of Christ. Thus they bring about the full measure of salvation in all its dimensions. For the community and the individual they always represent important *kairoi*. Each time the sacramental act is performed, the Lord lays a sovereign hand on the Church and a spiritual event of salvation-history is visibly realized.

The sacraments always involve the word of God because they are realized by it. Although they are completely subject to the Lord, they are divine actions performed with unique freedom and efficaciousness. In them Christ acts through His Church. Thus they actualize the day of grace and the *full mystery of Christ's temporal existence* — the past (His death and Resurrection), the present (the Risen Christ), and the future (the Christ to come). All this is possible because at the heart of the sacramental mystery lies the redemptive act. This act, which formerly produced effects in time from without, is now eternalized in Christ who stands at the Father's right hand. It draws to itself and to eternity all the men it touches in time and space, because the power of God has sustained and supported it ever since it was inserted into time. One eternal act, one divine power, one source of salvation, one Mystical Body — sacramental activity is immersed in this oneness. The many sacramental actions stem from this oneness, their source and their final end. [25] Human time is perpetually

matter and form of the sacrament on its three levels, he settled on the practice of apostolic times : the imposition of hands and the prayer to the Holy Spirit.

[25] Fr. SCHILLEBEECKX has explained this very clearly : " The whole redemptive mystery of Christ insofar as it is a divine action (not in its historical content) is rendered present in the sacraments. In them we are touched by the salvific power of the Incarnation. Obviously, then, the efficacious core of the sacraments is the eternal redemptive act of the Son of God. And this act is identical with the mystery-content *(Mysteriengehalt)* of Christ's salvific sacrifice on the Cross, with the mystery-content of the glorified Lord's salvific activity in heaven, and with the mysterious salvific *virtus* of the Sacraments. " The text is cited by P. GEFFRÉ, *RSPT*, 1959, p. 391. (We hope to see Schillebeeckx's book translated very soon.)

suffused with these acts which alter it radically and transform it invisibly. In them Church-time discovers one of its essential rhythms. In them it also discovers *its unique center, the Eucharist.*

Faith sees the Eucharist as the most obvious link between time and eternity. The Eucharist is a memorial, because it reproduces Christ's action during the Last Supper and presents the mystery of the crucified Christ (as does the Last Supper itself). It is an anticipation, because it gives us the Risen Christ and promises His glorious return. It is both a memorial and an anticipation, because it is the real presence of Christ, the King of Kings and Lord of Lords, who died, rose again, and is now seated at the Father's right hand. In short, it is both, because it is the presence of the act which redeemed us then, redeems us now, and will glorify us in the future. In the Eucharist, the eternal redemptive act establishes and directs salvation-time by a unique presence which is the focal point of everything else. The Eucharist inserts a divine force of life, love, and unity into the Church, the human race, and the universe itself. It is both a magnetic center of transfiguration and a final divinizing end. It takes place in the heart of the Christian assembly and continually renews their efforts of charity, prayer, and " communion. " Thus it makes the assembly a Christ-like community whose life and charity must enkindle and nourish the perpetual redemptive mission. [26] It makes Christian liberty an effective force in history. It makes cosmic time an integral part of salvation-time once again, and prepares the day and the hour when both will merge into the time-span of the New Heaven and the New Earth.

Thus the Eucharist is temporal because of its complex human aspects. It is the act of *this* human priest over *this* bread and *this* wine in *this* gathering of Christians; and the act of Consecration is temporal because of the words and actions

[26] If there were enough space we should have to indicate how each Mass is connected in time with the Old Testament (the liturgy of the message and the promise) and the New Testament (the liturgy of fulfillment involving a further promise).

which effect it. [27] However, through the Consecration Christ is made present, and His presence is neither spatial nor temporal. It is a " mysterious " presence, because of the relation of the consecrated species to the Body, Blood, and very Person of Jesus Christ. Through the Eucharistic sign Christ is present, because the sign itself represents an *efficacious link* with Christ as He is in eternity. Through the Eucharistic Consecration and Communion the Church and Christians are taken into Christ and become real members of His Body. In short, they draw near to the unity of eternity. In this typically human temporal activity, the Church becomes a contemporary of her Lord, because she is elevated to partake in His oblation, His love, and His life. The Church's temporal existence becomes here *a true process of eternalization,* [28] because Christ assumes it into His eternal present and so it returns to its source through the sacramental acts in time.

Liturgical Time

All this requires a slow and continuous education of the Christian people. They must be summoned by the divine message and united in fraternal love. In short, the Eucharist presupposes a specific time — liturgical time. [29] It is celebrated

---

[27] These too are subject to the laws of time; the words cannot be pronounced at a different time if the sacrament is to be valid.

[28] The liturgical texts indicate this at every turn. In the Leonine Sacramentary (*Sacrament. Veronense,* Mohlberg ed., 1956) : temporal aid is given in view of eternal joy (p. 12, Nr. 87); the Church gives time to receive eternity (12, 91); the sacrament sustains humanity and restores eternity (115, 912); Christians, driven from paradise, find access to eternal life once again (25, 194); they seek " *to experience eternal realities* through this temporal celebration " (26, 108)... And the marvelous text of Christmas-time develops the theme of the mutual exchange between God and man, demanding " *not only that our frailty assumed by the Word be worthy of perpetual honor,* but *also that its participation in eternity may make us eternal* " (161, 1260).

[29] On this point see the careful reflections of H. I. DALMAIS, *Initiation à la liturgie* (Paris 1958), pp. 85 ff. Eng. trans. *Introduction to the Liturgy* (Baltimore: Helicon, 1961). Also *Maison-Dieu,* Nr. 65 (1961).

in the heart of the liturgy where human time becomes the time of God's mystery.

The Church *shapes* the liturgy and liturgical time to express and communicate the mystery of Christ in accordance with God's dignity and man's nature. The liturgy is steeped in faith, and only by repentance, love, and adoration can man prepare himself for this mysterious encounter with the Lord. The Church centers the liturgy on the Eucharist, where the Lord is sacramentally present to form His purified sanctified Body. All liturgical celebrations and the entire Divine Office center on the Eucharist, and the people of God gather around it.

It is the Church which *develops and " fills "* liturgical time. She makes it a unique time-structuring edifice. By faith, the liturgy becomes a wondrous vital relationship with the full mystery of Christ, with His sorrowful fraternal past on earth and His judgment and resurrection in the future — through His eternal mediation in the present. But faith has *free rein* in coming to appreciate this relationship and its own place in this mystery. Thus liturgical time is complex insofar as faith may concentrate on this or that aspect of the Christian mystery. The structure remains the same but its contents are varied. And these varied contents can affect *the quality* of the structure and *the temporalization* of the Christian consciousness. At Christmas, for example, the Church's psyche views Christ as the little child who appeared once on earth. Of course, her worship is directed to Christ Himself living in His eternal present after rising from the dead; she views this first Epiphany as an announcement and a preparation for the final one. But she focuses on the permanent, universal, normative value of this first manifestation, and the liturgy underlines the birth of the Church to life in Christ throughout time, thanks to the all powerful Mediator.

Other aspects are more complex. Advent, for example, implies a coming already fulfilled at Bethlehem, a coming tomorrow at the Parousia, and a coming today in the salvation offered by the Church. The three advents are integrally linked in the time which they combine to structure. Other

230

periods underline the transcendence of this mystery-time. Pentecost implies the eternal presence of Christ " ascended " to the right hand of the Father from which He sends the Spirit; the first manifestation of the Holy Spirit on the day of Pentecost; and the permanent creative communication of the Spirit to His Body by the Lord of glory. This varied time forms a perpetual cycle of feasts which encircles the cultural and cosmic cycle and adopts its rhythms to order it to its own ends. It is immersed in its motion to give it new meaning. From within and without it makes the time of men the time of Christ the Savior.

Of course, *human time* marks the liturgy. The liturgy has evolved through the centuries. It varies from East to West and is changing before our eyes. Temporal change affects the very heart of the liturgy, i.e., the sacraments themselves. They develop and change in order to express more clearly the " idea " of the sacramental mystery. Once upon a time Baptism was conferred with a triple affirmation of faith in the Trinity joined to a triple immersion. Today it is conferred with a single formula and a single ablution. The rites of Confirmation have changed, and they are different in the West and the East. The rites of Ordination have developed considerably and we are only deciphering their history now. They are filled with symbolic words and actions in a time which looks for clear signs of the powers conferred. Pope Pius XII " determined " that only the primitive apostolic rite — the imposition of hands and the invocation of the Spirit — was necessary for the validity of the Ordination.

Yet with all these developments through history, the liturgy and its cycle of feasts has *one unvarying absolute :* the personal presence of the glorified Christ realized in the sacramental act, especially in the Eucharist. Every Eucharistic celebration renders present the sacrifice of the New Covenant which is eternal and indestructible because it is tied to the unity of the God-Man. Each Mass celebrates Christ's death and Resurrection. Each Sunday re-presents Easter in a rhythm which sustains, governs, and measures all other rhythms. Every

231

liturgical act until the end of time is united in some extra-ordinary way with the sacramental act in which the priest, the victim, and the sacrifice are always one and the same eternal mystery. And through its repetition in time, this mystery establishes the acts which participate in it and measures the steady growth of Christ's Body. If there is *an expanding universe*, this is it. Each sacramental act, linked with those which preceded it, is an expansion of the unique act which establishes them all and makes them bearers of eternal life, until the Body is fully developed and all God's children, scattered in space and time, are " gathered into one. "

Human Activity

Christ brings men into His Body and makes them sons of God in order to give divine increase to their being and their activity. Thus there is in the Church a time for human decisions centered in Jesus Christ, who creates and measures Church-time. This time of human decisions is always mysterious and unpredictable. Within the world of the divine word and the liturgy it establishes certain *kairoi*, essential moments of growth. Through man's free will, it accomplishes the eternal design which always coexists with these significant acts. This time has *two poles*. It is rooted in an *organic community* in which pastors and flock form one body. Thus the activity of the Spirit directly affects each individual member, [30] and at the same time the entire community of pastors and flock, so that the apostolic mission may be fulfilled.

The Apostolic Body

The first pole is composed of the decisions of the hierarchy, reached by careful deliberation or by divine inspiration. The

[30] Cf. PIUS XII, *The Mystical Body of Christ* (New York : America Press, 1955), pp. 29 and 38.

hierarchy has received the charge of ruling God's Church with love (Acts 20, 28). When their decisions are universal they inaugurate a new *kairos;* when their decisions are particular they continue or clarify an existing *kairos.* They plunge the Church's activity into man's activities in time in order to correct and Christianize them. They seek to resolve the Church's inner crises or her conflicts with the non-Christian world. They form one of the most obvious and most specific temporal aspects of the Catholic Church, because they are inextricably linked to a point in history and to the assistance of the Spirit. [31]

For example, the first important official stand was certainly taken at the " Council of Jerusalem, " [32] which represented something significant for the apostolic Church. This council freed pagans from the obligation of becoming Jews before becoming Christians. It marks the first official break with Judaism which was meant to preserve the true Christian message. It is followed by a whole series of local and ecumenical councils which show the influence of contemporary historical problems. For example, the great councils of the fourth and fifth centuries are summoned by the emperor who governs them and sometimes presides. Usually the oriental bishops alone are present. The Pope approves the convocation (more or less) and is present only through his delegates (perhaps just priests). Usually he does not confirm them explicitly. Such a system is inconceivable today, but even there *the essentials are already present.* The assembled bishops realize that they represent the universal Church. They are united with the legates of the Roman Pontiff who insure the unity of East and West. They realize that they represent the apostolic tradition and the unanimous faith of the Church. The " seed " is there, and the Church will become more aware

---

[31] With all the restrictions which must be added regarding the absolute, prudential and " biological " assistance of the Church. The terms come from Msgr. JOURNET, *op. cit.,* I, pp. 397 ff.

[32] Acts, 15, and the notes of J. DUPONT, *BJ*, pp. 133-141.

of it as it grows in her midst. Not all the councils are ecumenical in the same way.[33] They do not all have the same authority. The Council of Nicea enjoys a certain primacy. The first four councils " are sacred like the four Gospels, " but the fifth (553) is sacred " only insofar as it confirms and explicitates the first four. " At Ephesus no *de fide* definition was formulated; and St. Leo did not want any formulated at Chalcedon. In short, the notion of ecumenicity is probably " analogical. "

But at each of the great councils involving much work, much activity, and some tragedy at times, one thing ends and something else begins. Certain errors are rejected, certain truths are made precise, and ecclesiastical life is given a new boost. The process is irreversible and never completed. Many questions have been " decided " once and for all — Christ's divinity (Nicea), the hypostatic union (Chalcedon), the primacy of God's grace (Orange), justification and human liberty (Trent), the Pope's infallibility (Vatican I). But the Church continues to develop, the march of human ideas goes on, and the truths of Christianity blossom. New problems arise from older ones : the human psyche of Christ; the precise point of divergence between Catholics and Protestants on man's role in the work of salvation; the link which establishes the episcopal body between Western and Eastern Christians; the question of Mary's mediation, which is still not completely developed [34] even though Pius IX defined the Immaculate Conception and Pius XII defined the Assumption. Every

---

[33] Cf. C. MOELLER " Les schismes à l'époque des premiers conciles, " *L'Église et les Églises*, (Chevetogne 1954), pp. 252-253. The quotes are his. See an excellent survey in *Le Concile et les Conciles* (Chevetogne, Paris 1950). For the councils of the fourth and fifth centuries, cf. the study of P. CAMELOT, *ibid.*, pp. 45-74.

[34] Several weeks before his death, Pius XII said that the doctrines of " Mary, Mediatrix " of all grace and " Mary Co-redemptrix " were " not fully clear and certain. " This accounts for his reserve during his pontificate. (Cf. P. LEIBER in *Documentation catholique*, 1959, p. 165.)

definition is both an end and a beginning, an autumn and a springtime. [35]

The Inspired Ones

In addition to these decisions from the top, there is *initiative from the ranks below*. " Manifestations of the Spirit and of Power " in Christians chosen by God have always occurred in the Church, because Christ's Body is essentially " pneumatic. " The inspiration of the Spirit uplifting the humble little ones is a second unforeseen but permanent resource in the evangelical treasury of Church-time. When Christ feels it is necessary, the Spirit takes possession of a humble pure heart. He makes it glow with fire and bubble with living water and thrill to an unknown melody. It gradually grows to arouse the Church and move the hierarchy; and then, one day, a new *kairos* has begun. The sacred assembly of the martyrs; the flowering of monasticism in Egypt, Syria and the West; the earth-shaking divine tenderness embodied in the *Poverello ;* the consuming zeal of St. Dominic, whose tenderness, tears, and forceful truths saved the Church from the Cathari; the flowering of mystics in Flanders and the Rhineland; the epic of St. Teresa of Avila, St. Ignatius, St. Francis Xavier, and the missionaries up to our own day; Charles de Foucauld burying himself in the desert, and the harvest of his countless sons and daughters — the list could go on endlessly. Each of these inaugurated *a spiritual springtime*, a rediscovery of the Lord, a new quality in Church-time, a new " moment " in the Church's unique " Moment, " an unknown flowering season of Christ's richness. It is only after these unexpected revivals

[35] The ordinary magisterium of the Pope is being exercised more and more in the great encyclicals. Leo XIII treated the connections between the temporal order and the spiritual order. Pius X reacted against modernism. Benedict XV discussed the Missions, and Pius XI condemned modern totalitarian movements. Pius XII made even greater use of them. He wrote vigorously and frequently, treating the structure and life of the Church, and the crucial problems harassing the minds of men today.

have given a new impulse to Christian life that we can evaluate their full significance. But the same mystery is always involved. The flowering of sanctity is always a passage to the Lord, the insertion of time into eternity, and the anticipation of the new heaven and the new earth.

The Christian People

Between these two extremes, we must emphasize the role of the Christian people as such. One mistake would be to forget their presence at the great decisions of the councils. The hierarchy scrutinizes the living faith of the people and often refers to it explicitly. Each bishop represents a specific segment of the Christian people. He assumes their cares and weighs their decisions, considering their appeals, their misery, their anxiety, and their love. And thus he influences the outlook of the hierarchy. The bishops know that they are responsible to their flocks for their teachings, their planning, and their reforms, and that they must integrate these things into the life of their people. Where there is a bishop, there the Church is also; and the very essence of divine authority is *service to all*. The infallibility of conciliar decisions implies a slow temporal development [36] of the whole body, which existed before the council itself and was seeking answers to some questions. And these decisions play such an important role because they represent the insertion of eternal life into human time and Christian time, through the assistance of the Holy Spirit.

The daily life of the Church too involves the initiative of countless individuals (which we shall study later) and the wondrous growth of various apostolic activities. Man's liberty unites with the power of the Spirit to stage a new advance for the Kingdom of God. The start of the Y.C.W. and the development of Catholic Action; the rise of missionary

---

[36] Sometimes, unfortunately, it pre-supposes a state of corruption which forces the hierarchy to intervene.

groups and the secular institutes which organize them in different ways for greater solidity and effectiveness; the resourcefulness of the older religious orders; the increase of priestly societies linked to parishes or to militant groups; the biblical and liturgical revival — we can see so many examples of this aspect of Church life animated by the gifts of the Spirit and flooding the desert with living waters.

One Time-Period

But these three components form only *one unique temporal process.* They operate independently, and yet they are inextricably linked by faith to form the complex of Church-time. The divine Word leads to the Sacraments, the intrinsic " form, " and initiates apostolic activities. The sacraments presuppose that the Word has been accepted by faith, and enable us to live as Christians and to immerse ourselves in the efficacious action of Christ. The decisions of the hierarchy are meant to reflect faithfully the Word of God, the norms of Tradition, and the faith of the Christian people. They preserve and clarify the meaning and the use of the sacraments; they insure the correctness of evangelical expedients, mystical inspirations, and missionary activities. The great saints provide striking examples. The poor man of Assisi was completely obedient to the Pope and the bishops; even as he was rekindling the fervor of the Church, he manifested an unbelievably holy respect for the Word of God, the Eucharist, and even the most ignoble priests. [37] And he demanded the same attitude of his followers. In short, these three components unite to *form one complex time-period :* the time when Christ's Mystical Body is suffused with the Spirit, when the Church is journeying toward the Parousia, and when the eternal *agape* is being lived in the Body by the Spirit and the Spouse to bring all men and the world itself into the fullness of Christ.

[37] See the writings of the Saint, e.g., P. BAYART, *Saint François vous écrit* (Paris 1935), pp. 89-90, 139-140.

The Christian Universe

Let us repeat once more that time finds its source and its explanation in the eternal act of Christ. Time is neither cyclic nor linear. Nor is it a combination of both. Time, *at every instant*, is *established in men's psyches by an eternal Psyche*, by Him who is *the heart of the world and the Psyche of psyches* (Lequier). and since this redemptive act is present first and foremost in the Eucharist, we may have something else to learn from it.

The Eucharistic act is repeated countless times each day in accordance with Christ's own command. At first glance Christianity appears to be a religion of repetition. In fact, it is no such thing. *The universe of the myths is the universe of repetition*. The universe as it appeared to primitive peoples inspired the creation of myths. [38] Their intelligence was *in a darkened state*, as Maritain said, [39] immersed in a world of symbols from which it had not yet freed itself. They had not yet reached the point of real reflection. That is why they usually expressed their ideas in myths. These myths embody *man's existence in relation to the universe*. The great myths always have two elements — man and the sacred — because they express man's relationship to sacred realities.

Now repetition is one of the essential elements of this mythical universe. Creation is conceived as a drama : the victory of the gods over the " primeval " forces of confusion and terror. In short, creation transforms *chaos into cosmos*. But although these forces have been overcome, they have not been destroyed. Fragments of the primeval chaos remain

---

[38] Analyzed by M. ÉLIADE. Cf. *Patterns in Comparative Religion* (New York : Sheed and Ward, 1958) and *The Myth of the Eternal Return* (New York : Pantheon, 1954). Contemporary thought is re-evaluating the myth. We accept the phenomenological analysis of Éliade as such. But see the notes which follow.

[39] In *Quatre essais sur l'esprit dans sa condition charnelle* (Paris 1939), chap. 2 : " Signe et Symbole. " We must add the refreshing thoughts of P. RICOEUR, in *Finitude et Culpabilité* (Paris 1960), especially II, 153 ff.

to threaten the new order. The victory is never decisive, and so it must be defended repeatedly as long as men and the world endure. That is why *the act of creation is repeated* endlessly in the various mythical rites — " orgies, " feasts, sacrifices, and liturgies.

These cults periodically re-create the earth, which otherwise would return to chaos. The primitive man joins his god and ensures divine victory. In his " fear of history, " he sees time as an all-consuming force of destruction and tries to abolish it. He is transported back to the dawn of time, to the sacred instant on this side of time — *in illo tempore* [40] — which gave birth to the world. He celebrates his rites *in illo tempore* to re-present the power of that moment once again and to re-create the world out of chaos. The liturgical rite of repetition, then, has *direct cosmological* import. It creates the cosmos once again, regenerates it, and saves it from falling into chaos. It is, therefore, *anti-historical*. It casts time aside as a destroyer so that it may unite with the moment of the world's beginning and establish it anew. And it knows full well that this process will wear down and will have to be regenerated once again. Repetition, then, abolishes time to join the primitive " Great Time " and to regenerate a time which is always provisional, devoid of meaning, and slipping into nothingness. [41]

The Christian universe is quite *the opposite*. As Éliade has noted, *the biblical doctrine of creation* marks the first contrast. And it is even more significant that traces of a mythical universe remain here and there. [42] However these traces are only the images used as evidence. Even if one admits continuity on the plane of imagination, *the meaning*

[40] The expression is Éliade's — *passim*.

[41] Cf. ÉLIADE, *The Myth of the Eternal Return* (New York : Pantheon, 1954) p. 155.

[42] See the ideas and references of E. JACOB, *Théol. de l'A. T.*, pp. 110-121; also T. MAERTENS, *Les sept jours* (Bruges 1951), pp. 14-25; also the important article " Mythe, " *DBS*. There one will find a history of the confusing notions about the myth by J. HENNINGER, a proper view of the Old Testament by H. CAZELLES and of the New Testament by R. MARLÉ.

has been radically altered. [43]   In the Bible God creates by His Word and His Spirit.   His creation appears as He wills it to appear.   And He entrusts it to man only so that man by his free will may inscribe the history of his salvation on it. Even when mankind is so tainted by sin that God chooses to destroy it, He saves " a remnant, " and establishes creation itself as the framework and the eternal pledge of His Covenant with men.   Such an action *cannot be repeated*.   It would be absurd even to imagine such a thing.   Instead man *celebrates* the wonder and the richness of this action.   Because the world has been created by an omnipotent merciful God, every kind of mythical cosmogony is excluded.

Futhermore, the cosmos is made to permit and to symbolize God's Covenant with men, the salvation of a sinful race. Here is *the second contrast* with the universe of myths — *Christ*. As we have seen, He represents a fulfillment and a breakthrough.   He performs the perfect sacrifice which saves mankind; and His act, by definition, is unique.   Christ saves us once for always.   Here again, repetition is absolutely excluded.   No one can repeat the act of the God-Man.   To attempt it would be the worst blasphemy.   Christianity is *the religion of the Ephapax*, not the religion of repetition.

Now it is apparent that the Christian universe is *devoid* of any mythical cosmogony or salvation-history.   Thus it *is* truly a universe in time, a human race in history — a world growing and rising toward God.   If it has repetitious aspects, these repetitions do not attempt to repeat or renew the basic acts of creation and Redemption.   They are performed in a creation which has already been sovereignly completed, [44] and they can only actualize an eternal Redemption which was fully accomplished at the Resurrection of Christ.   The Eucharist is a perfect example.   It is repeated countless times every day. But it does not repeat the act of sacrifice.   Rather, it is

[43] In a similar view cf. P. Ricoeur, *op. cit.*, II, 191-192.

[44] But a creation entrusted to man to " perfect " it.   We have explained this above.

240

immersed in the salvific reality of this act. *It repeats this act symbolically*, through the signs chosen by Christ. It renders present the eternal act of mediation, through the sacrificed Body and the spilt Blood. This act is always a presence, a remembrance, and an anticipation. And so *it continues to immerse the Church in its unique inexhaustible Source*, the sacrifice of Jesus Christ in history and beyond history. The Eucharist, therefore, is a sacramental sacrifice. It is the efficacious sign, visible and repeated, of the unique sovereign Sacrifice.

The sacrifice is repeated *in the sacramental order*. In other words, "the sacrament of the sacrifice" is repeated. Each eucharistic celebration in time implies the presence of eternity and its effective life-giving unity. The Eucharist is the sacramental repetition of a mystery which is not repeated. It is performed repeatedly because man is *in via* and must commune daily with his Savior. This present act of repetition always evokes the past, and at solemn high Masses the deacon chants : *in illo tempore*. These words do not have mythical significance. Rather, they recall the *historical* life of Jesus of Nazareth, the normative type for all who live in the inspiration of faith. This return to the past is a return to Jesus Christ, the life-giving principle who stands at His Father's hand offering His eternal sacrifice for the salvation of His flock. The liturgy, for example, is truly a time when sacred acts are repeated and regulate the existential course of the Church. But this time has reality and complexity only insofar as it is rooted in eternity and suffused by it.

10

The Christian and Time

The time of each Christian is a spiritually incarnate time. It is lived in the grace of Christ, in the power of the Spirit, and in the communion of the Church. Thus it is profoundly a Church-time. It is rooted in the Word of God, nourished by the sacraments, and unfolded in a *kairos* opened by the Spirit at the heart of the Church's historical activity. But it is also a unique time, the time of a *vocation* lived in faith, of a call initiated always by God, but one to which man must freely respond. Thus the time of each Christian has several traits which are peculiar to the life of an individual. We shall indicate them now.

243

Predestination

This is the most serious problem of all. Is man's destiny a *fixed race*? Has God already chosen our destiny or *are we free to choose* for or against God? Does each human psyche inaugurate a meaningful time? Are we really " our own progenitors " by our free decisions in time? Does the dogma of predestination cast the shadow of doubt over everything? Let us try, at least, to associate this awesome problem with the mystery of time.

The Meaning of Christian Predestination

First of all, Christian predestination is not predestination as envisioned by the Greeks, for example, in the tragedies of Aeschylus. [1] The terrible events which take place here on earth — and which have real causes — are pre-determined in heaven; men are the prey of the avenging demon, " puppets in the hands of the gods, " victims of an inexorable fate. When a man is very great and when he *knows how*, he can struggle, and this is inspiring. But he fights against an invincible destiny. It is Christ who will have to deliver man from the *Heimarmene* — the terrible fatalism written into the course of the universe.

But Christian predestination is not that envisioned by the Israelites either. [2] In their view God has foreseen and determined everything. He has set times and hours by His immutable decrees. He has a book in which the history of the world has been written in advance. But such a view threatens to destroy human liberty — a thing so dear to the

---

[1] Cf. A. J. FESTUGIÈRE, *L'Enfant d'Agrigente*, pp. 14 ff.

[2] Cf. J. BONSIRVEN, *Le Judaïsme palestinien*, I, pp. 188-190. On the biblical view, see VAN IMSCHOOT, *Théologie...*, I, pp. 108-110; on Qumran, F. NOTSCHER, " Schicksalsglaube in Qumràn und Umwelt, " *Bib. Zeitschrift*, 2 (1959), and 1 (1960).

Pharisees — and leads to an extreme reaction [3] whereby " God's sovereignty is sacrificed for the sake of man's dignity. " [4]

Christian predestination differs radically from these two conceptions. This is apparent when it is integrated in the framework of God's salvific action. The Bible strongly emphasizes three major points. First, God's activity in the work of salvation has *absolute primacy and complete sovereignty*. It is God who calls and sanctifies, who stoops to convert the sinner and transform his heart, who repeatedly begins over after the sinner has fallen again. In short, it is God who initiates, sustains, and completes the process of salvation. St. John was only recapitulating the biblical teaching when he said : " In this is charity : not as though we had loved God, but because he hath first loved us, and sent his Son to be a propitiation for our sins. " [5] But this call *implies* and *awakes* in man the wondrous possibility of *free* response. Man can really say yes or no. God's countless appeals through His envoys, through Christ, and through His Church, His unseen appeal directly to men's hearts, all would be meaningless if man did not have this indestructible power. God calls, but does not force us. That is why the Church's interpretation of Scripture has always opposed any form of spiritual predestination and determinism. [6]

The Christian doctrine of predestination and reprobation results from these two premises. But one more fact must

[3] Either the decrees are able to be modified by prayer, or predestination depends on a pre-vision of one's merits; or else everything is determined except the use which man will make of his free will. J. BONSIRVEN, *op. cit.*, I, p. 190.

[4] J. BONSIRVEN, *op. cit.*, I, p. 191. There is also an Islamic view of predestination which we shall not examine here. In it there is no attempt to reconcile man's responsibility and God's absolute decree. Cf. L. GARDET, *Connaître l'Islam* (Paris 1958), pp. 25-26.

[5] 1 Jn 4, 10. The world of the *agape* is God Himself, and man shares in it only insofar as God permits him.

[6] These two points are, perhaps, the only dogmatic data underlying the well-known controversy on sufficient and efficacious grace. See A. MICHEL, " Grâce Suffisante, " *DTC.*

245

be emphasized. First there was the *election* of Israel, then the *election* of Christians. However, we must not interpret this word as our contemporaries usually do. Today, *choosing* a means or an end implies *excluding* other means or other ends. Choosing and rejecting are inextricably linked in our act of choice. But, in the Bible, election is not *the converse* of rejection. Israel becomes the " chosen people " by a wondrous act of God's love which establishes the Covenant. But she is chosen as the first-born who must convey God's name to others. The Jews, to be sure, often shut themselves up in this privilege and took terrible pride in it. But that does not alter the significance of the divine gesture. Israel's election involved a *mission* to serve God by serving all mankind. Insofar as they failed to do this, they compromised their election. Their special privileges involved an awesome responsibility. [7] And the prophets had to remind the people continually that both privileges and duties were involved, and that Israel would not go unpunished for blaspheming God's name among the nations. St. Paul takes up this theme in the well-known chapters of the Epistle to the Romans (9-11). [8] Israel is the chosen people and remains so in spite of her infidelity; even her infidelity is ordered to the salvation of the pagan nations. In the matter of salvation, God calls all men, Jew and Greek (10, 10-13). *He has enveloped all men in unbelief that he may have mercy on all* (11, 30-32). Instead of affirming an election which involves exclusion, Paul affirms the *inclusion* of all true sons of Abraham in the unique election of Jesus Christ.

[7] Cf. H. H. ROWLEY, *RHPR* (1950), pp. 327-328 : " Election is neither a merited reward nor a grace to be simply enjoyed. It is given in view of a mission. " Cf. *RB* (1951), pp. 147-148. Election involves service to God and men.

[8] For the present state of the question see S. LYONNET, *Quaestiones in Epist. ad Romanos*, II (Rome 1956). These chapters refer primarily to the nation as such, not to individuals. Even where individuals are discussed, their own eternal destiny is not considered, but rather their role in salvation-time and salvation-history.

Now predestination is centered in the heart of the revelation-mystery. It is *Christocentric and Trinitarian.* [9] It was never presented as an act of the One God, but as a decision of God in three Persons regarding man's eternal salvation in time. It is the decision of the Father " before the foundation of the world "; it is situated in Jesus Christ, the mediator of creation and redemption, in whom all men are called to salvation, and in whose image predestination is realized; it is accomplished by the gift of the Holy Spirit, who enables us to pass from earth to God. Thus it involves the divine relations of the Trinity, the exchange of life and love which is the Trinity. It is the act of a sovereignly gratuitous, generous, merciful love.

But predestination is also *ecclesial.* Paul never refers to it in purely individual terms. He always refers to the body of Christians, those whom the Father has called in Christ and who have responded, [10] those who form the Church, the Body of Christ : " Those " whom the Father has known in advance and predested (Rom 8, 29); " We " whom He has chosen in Christ before the foundation of the world and predestined to be adopted sons through Christ (Eph 1, 5)· Jesus Himself says : " Come, ye blessed of my Father, " for whom the Kingdom has been prepared before the foundation of the world (Mt 25, 34). This election is personal, because it is addressed to an *individual incorporated into the community of grace ;* [11] and the Church is predestined — as Israel was " chosen " — in view of the mission which is her intrinsic

[9] Cf. St. Paul's two principal texts : Rom 8, 28-34 and Eph 1, 3-14; also the text of Mt 25, 31-46. On St. John and predestination, see the excellent remarks of MOLLAT in " La Conversion, " *LV*, 47, pp. 95 ff.

[10] In the language of Paul, they are the *chosen.* The term refers to entrance into the Church, not into eternity. Cf. LAGRANGE, HUBY, LYONNET, etc.

[11] St. Paul takes up the language of the prophets (Gal 1, 15) and calls himself the *klêtos apostolos* (Rom 1, 1). Cf. O. CULLMANN, *Christ and Time* (Philadelphia : Westminster, 1958) p. 220. — But he is referring to his vocation to the apostolic mission.

purpose : to bring men to salvation in Jesus Christ. It is nothing but the divine *agape*, this eternal love, shared by the Trinity and extended to sinful mankind which has been redeemed by Jesus Christ. We cannot dissociate predestination, the plan of the eternal *agape*, and salvation-history. This is not an inescapable choice, an iron law or a fatalism. We are not confronted by a unique God whose transcendence terrifies wretched human beings; we are confronted by infinite Love, springing from the Father, finding expression in His Incarnate Son, and enveloping us through the Spirit, so that we may commune with the Trinity.

Eternal Predestination and Time

Hence predestination too is an eternal act. It is not in time but is, rather, *completely immanent in God*. To be sure, Scripture and the Church present it in formulas involving time. God fore-knows and pre-destines; He chooses and blesses before the creation of the world; the spotless Lamb is marked before the foundation of the world and revealed at the end of time (1 Pt 1, 20; cf. 2 Tm 1, 9-10); and Paul enthusiastically lists the series of divine acts leading to salvation : God fore-knows, pre-destines, calls, justifies, and glorifies (Rom 8, 28-30). But Paul does not situate himself in God's eternity and behold divine acts succeeding one another. He takes as his vantage point the Christian life as it is now, specifically, experience in the Spirit as it is described in chapter 8 of Romans. From there he ascends toward the invisible, mysterious, and indivisible source of our salvation. The expressions he uses are part of his Jewish heritage, and images which are necessary if our weak mind is to convey the meaning of this mystery. But he has no intention of speculating on the nature of eternity, nor of introducing a process of succession in God. [12] It is for

[12] " When St. Paul counts five divine decisions, he does not mean to connote successive acts in God; he speaks as a man, expressing in human fashion the unique eternal divine act. " J. BONSIRVEN, *Théologie du Nouveau Testament* (Paris 1951), p. 271.

248

the Church's theology to present this point clearly, insofar as it can.

Now we know that God is simple and eternal; that His acts do not succeed one another; that there is in Him no *ordo volitionum* because He is infinitely perfect, [13] and in one simple act He sees, decides, and performs; that He is not in time and therefore He cannot fore-see nor pre-destine, but merely see and accomplish; that predestination for Him is an act of thinking and willing totally enveloped in His own mystery; that only *the result* of this act is *in time,* [14] *forming, by its links with time,* an *ordo volitorum :* vocation, justification, glorification.

Predestination and Vocation

The *first temporal effect* of predestination is the vocation of the human being to faith and justice. It cannot be emphasized too much that St. Paul always sees predestination in this light. Predestination emerges in time as a call to liberty. It is an appeal repeated through time as long as a man lives, enveloped in the day of graces. Predestination *does not suppress* human liberty; it *establishes* [15] it. Without the act of personal liberty there is no true response to God, no possibility of justification, no Christian salvation. Predestination is a strictly eternal act, but *it implies the insight and welcome of human response.* [16]

---

[13] St. Thomas, *ST*, I[a], 19, 5 and 6.

[14] For St. Thomas (I[a], 23, 2, c and i), the act of predestination is eternal and so immanent in God that in itself it does not touch human beings : *non ponit aliquid in praedestinato.* It is the *exsecutio praedestinationis* which touches the subject first of all through *vocatio*, as St. Thomas explicitly indicates (*ibid.*, 2, c).

[15] Cf. H. Bouillard, *Karl Barth*, II, 162-163.

[16] See J. Maritain, *Existence and the Existent*, chap. 4 (New York : Doubleday, 1957). His views have recently been challenged by Nicolas (*Rev. Thom.*, 1960, pp. 199 ff.) who espoused a particular Thomistic position. We do not intend to join this controversy among theologians. We feel, however, that one must espouse such a position as that of Maritain, if one wishes to avoid the dreaded specter of antecedent reprobation. The *terminology* used is relatively secondary.

249

We know that God wills the salvation of all men, and that Christ died to ransom all men; that the last Judgment will assemble all nations (Mt 25, 32) before the Son of Man, [17] and that He will judge all men because they have met Him in their unfortunate brothers; that God so loved the world as to give His Son (Jn 3, 16), and that the blood of the Lamb suffices for " the whole world " (1 Jn 2, 2). But this universal salvific will is accomplished only *by man's free response*. Man must follow the grace working in him (Rom 2, 14-16). He must accept the love of truth (2 Thes 2, 10). In short, he must believe so as not to perish (Jn 3, 16). This is the tragic grandeur of human liberty.

From his Baptism to his death the Christian lives *in a time of judgment*, [18] of justification or condemnation as the case may be. He is judged every day on the basis of his fundamental choice; he will be judged definitively at his last hour, and this judgment will be his foretaste of the last general judgment. [19] If he says yes and perseveres in this choice, it is only by God's help. For it is God who calls, justifies, and saves us at the final moment. If he says no and persists in his refusal, he does so in spite of God's love, God's call, and the blood of His Son. Thus we notice a *radical anomaly*. God calls us to salvation but not to condemnation. He wills to save but never to lose. *God blesses but He does not curse.* Christ's words at the last judgment will be : " Come, ye blessed of My Father, receive the Kingdom prepared for you (by the Father) before the foundation of the world "; then " Depart from Me, ye cursed (but not by the Father) into eternal fire prepared for the devil and his angels " (for the first sinners, not for you). The first cause of good is God; the first cause of evil is man. The Church has always rejected " with horror "

[17] See J. Jeremias, *Jésus et les Païens;* also, T. Preiss, " Le Mystère du Fils de l'Homme, " *Dieu Vivant*, 8, pp. 17 ff.

[18] See the important article of Mollat, " Jugement dans le N. T., " *DBS*, pp. 1346-1394.

[19] See the passage of Thibaut cited by Huby, *La première Épître aux Corinthiens*, p. 174, n. 2.

— *cum omni detestatione* — the blasphemous [20] tenets of predestination-theologies. Her position is well stated in the Council of Kiersy : " If men are saved, it is the gift of Him who saves them; if others perish, it is because they have merited it. " [21] In other words, if men are saved, *Ipse prior ;* if men are lost, *homo prior.* But why does God permit some to be damned? We cannot give a direct answer to this question. We know that in God mercy is first and justice is second, the latter being enveloped by mercy. How are they connected in the case of damnation? We do not know. All we know is that we *cannot positively integrate* the two sides of the revealed mystery. We can only accept them and faithfully continue to adore and to petition the crucified Christ. Finally, man must remember that he is only " dust and ashes " in God's sight and has no right to ask such a question. " *Man, who art thou that repliest against God?* " (Rom 9, 20). The pieces do not fit together on the conceptual level; reason cannot provide an answer. Only profound adoration and courageous trust will suffice. In God's eyes there is predestination and there are predestined souls. But we do not have the light, the vision, nor the words to comprehend such a mystery.

We know that God truly wills the salvation of all men; that the grace of Christ touches and sovereignly envelops all men (Rom 5, 20-21); that the time of each man and of all human history until the Parousia is a time of penance, pardon, and salvation; that final impenitence is the punishment for many previous sins and for the obstinate rejection of God's last call. [22] Human time, then, is the time of existence " in them that are saved " or " in them that perish "

---

[20] Council of Orange, final declaration, *DB*, 200.

[21] Kiersy-sur-Oise (853), *DB*, 318.

[22] See the astonishing text of St. Thomas (*I Sent.*, d. 40, a. 4) which closes : " It is evident *(patet!)* that the first cause of the failure (of grace) is man alone; there is no such failure on God's part once we realize this. " Cf. Msgr. JOURNET, *Entretiens sur la Grâce* (Paris 1959), pp. 49-50, 67 : " If someone is not numbered among the predestined, it is because of a refusal for which he alone is responsible. "

(2 Cor 2, 15) as the result of a fundamental choice. Man is really " put in the hands of his own decisions " and capable of rejecting God. This is the dark side of a bright and glorious mystery — the mystery of man's collaboration with God. *The now of grace* is *the present of liberty*. God wants to save *men with free wills*. And so He demands that we work out our salvation : " Labour. . . that. . . you may make sure your calling and election. For doing these things, you shall not sin " (2 Pt 1, 10). When a man enters eternity, he does so with the fruits of his free will which was tainted by sin, redeemed, and saved. We can believe the words of St. Augustine to his flock : " Chosen or condemned, which do you want to be ? *Now it is up to you. . .* Make your choice while you have time. " [23]

Conversion

Human existence, therefore, is a time of conversion, which puts the very meaning of time at stake. Conversion introduces a new measure into spiritual existence and is realized on ascending levels. But from beginning to end it is basically *a participation in Christ's death and resurrection*. Dying in order to be reborn in Christ — this is the definition of conversion.

A. A REVOLUTION

This *metanoia* which opens the Gospel revolutionizes our existence. It is a passage *from unbelief to faith*, from death to life. Usually it is the result of a long process silently directed by the sovereign Lord. He knocks at the door of the sinful heart, touches it, and illuminates it. He calls upon it to counteract its base inclinations and gives it the desire to alter its life and reunite with the Lord. Faith, love, and

---

[23] Cited by PORTALIÉ, " Augustin, " *DTC*, col. 2401 (= *Enarratio in Psalm.* 36, 1; *PL*, 36, 356). Also cf. J. GUITTON commenting on St. Augustine in *Le Temps et l'Éternité...*, pp. 337 ff.

repentance grow together until the decisive hour when man must make his ultimate choice, say yes or no, and submit to God's pardon or condemnation.

Obviously this is a *temporal process* which can move more or less intermittently. It centers *on Christ,* for there is no conversion if our gaze is not focused on Him who has been pierced (Jn 20, 27-29) and who has risen to summon all men to His glory. Man enters the mystery of the Savior's past — He loved me and delivered Himself up for me; of His present — He calls me to pardon and to newness of life; and of His future — He wishes me to share His purity, His love, and His joy. Faith is, then, the gateway to the Savior's mystery in time and eternity. But it is also *a new perspective of oneself.* Our past life appears in its true light as a blot, an absurdity, an offense against God which crucified our Lord. Our future life appears as a wondrous hope practically within our grasp. Faith calls out to us : the Kingdom is at hand! it is for you! it needs you!

Here is the decisive point. Man must take the necessary step. He must dedicate his liberty. He must lose himself in order to save himself. He must submerge himself in Christ in order to die and rise. If a man says yes, he gathers up his sinful past and leaves it in the hands of Christ. He is welcomed by the Lord, revivified, and opened to eternal life in Jesus Christ. In this light Scheler's [24] fine analysis of repentance takes on amazing dimensions. For man lays hold of his past to change its meaning and to be reborn in the future only by consenting to God's personal call and by immersing himself in the ever-present mystery of Christ. Christ envelops him in His Cross, Resurrection, and Parousia, and draws him towards His eternity.

In that instant, *the meaning of time is changed.* Man is no longer bound by his past but freed by a transforming future.

---

[24] See chapter 3. This would be the place to contrast the Christian concept of conversion and that of Kant. The latter is a rational conversion which makes us members of an intelligible order. Cf. J. HAVET, *Kant et le Problème du Temps,* pp. 198-207.

His existence in time attains a new level, because grace elevates him to the risen life of Jesus Christ. There is *a new relationship between time and eternity.* Eternity previously had established an existence in which man was immersed in sin and separated from eternity. Now it inaugurates an existence in which man is incorporated into Christ and shares the eternal life of God. His *temporal existence,* too, is *radically changed* because its basic rhythm, its free development, and its true finality are literally transformed.

Now the complete conversion to the Christian faith takes place *through Baptism.* There, sinful man, linked to the first Adam, is buried with Christ and rises to a new life in Christ who is seated at the Father's right hand. There he becomes a new creature in a new creation devoted completely to the service of Christ and the service of God. [25] The changes of which we were speaking are effected *in a sacramental act,* through which man is inserted into the Body of Christ and becomes a son of God. In this act man shares in the *historical and transcendent* dimensions of the mystery of Christ. He lives in the present of the Risen Christ, he is immersed in the past of the paschal mystery, and he strives toward eschatological completion when his personal sanctity will be perfected in a perfectly holy Church, and when his body will rise in the risen Body of Christ. Thus man inherits the promise of his long past and his future in a presence which is rooted in an eternal act by his own free will.

The situation is similar in the case of the conversion of the Christian in the state of sin. The change is less radical, depending on his perseverance in faith and in hope. But it is still a complete change, because man passes *from spiritual death to spiritual life.* Conversion remains a revolutionary process by which the past is renewed in a transforming future. The sinner returns to the Lord and again enters the love of the Savior. He loses his self-centeredness and focuses on God

[25] On this point, see the study of MOLLAT, " Symboles baptismaux chez saint Paul, " *LV*, 26 (1956), pp. 61 ff.

in Jesus Christ. Conversion is man's entrance into the mystery of Christ's death and Resurrection, because it is God in Jesus Christ who enables him to repent, to reunite with Him, to surrender himself and plunge anew into eternal life.

In both cases we must underline *the level-gap* involved in the sudden passage from sin to grace. There is an ontological and temporal discontinuity between the former state and the latter one. In the supernatural order, the sinner left to his own resources will remain a sinner; only God's infinite power and tenderness can rescue him from his sinful state, draw him out of himself and regenerate him in Christ. It is the Father's eternal unchanging love which justifies the soul by transforming it within and enabling it to heed its call. [26] Now this internal principle of life is *a " temporal effect " of eternal love*, and we call it grace. This result of God's activity is a radically new entity; it does not stem from anything in man's sinful state; it is not brought about in the time-period when man is in sin; it comes from on high to inaugurate a new type of temporal existence, because it gives human time a new participation in eternity. [27] It is an instantaneous revolution, a radically new beginning, a rebirth, an entrance into the now of grace. Eternity lays a sovereign hold on time in a most formidable way. It gives us a new perspective on sin. We see it as a time when a life " filled " with eternal love disintegrates into an empty and broken life leading to dissipation and death; when the time of conversion becomes a time of judgment and condemnation.

B. FIDELITY THROUGH TIME'S DURATION

Because conversion marks a new beginning in time, it demands our fidelity in time. And in trying to preserve our fidelity we encounter three obstacles.

---

[26] On all this see St. THOMAS, *ST*, Iª-IIªe, 113, 2, 7 and 8; IIIª, 3, 1ᵐ.

[27] St. THOMAS, Iª, IIªe, 113, 7, 5ᵐ. Cf. the additions of GUERARD DES LAURIERS, *Dimensions de la foi* (Paris 1952), I, pp. 177 ff. and II, pp. 76-77.

First of all, we encounter *crises in the wear and tear of time.* Time wears on, or rather man is worn out during the course of time. A prolonged effort takes its toll on the body and on the spirit. Our powers of concentration and our ability to make decisions and carry them out become mere habits; the unending cycle of beginning anew begets hardening, boredom, and disgust. Then, too, *crises* appear. They may be physiological : puberty, menopause, old age, sickness; sociological : exams, choice of a profession, retirement, unemployment; interpersonal : introductions, marriage, bereavement, abandonment. Such crises threaten man's tenuous equilibrium, alter his sense of values, and force him to begin a new kind of temporal existence if he is to avoid collapse. Grace does not save us from these aspects of human existence, it helps us to integrate them into our life of faith. When a soul manages to preserve its resiliency and vitality in this difficult journey, it is, as it were, a miracle of God.

Sin too menaces the Christian who is still not completely converted to the Gospel. The grace of Baptism takes away all our sins, but the forces of greed still burn in our soul. Our risen life is only a beginning; we must serve God and continue to reject sin; we must strive after holiness and preserve our faith : " So *do you* also *reckon,* that you are dead to sin, but alive unto God, in Christ Jesus our Lord. Let not sin therefore reign in your mortal body " (Rom 6, 11-12). This text exemplifies how advice and command are interwoven in the Christian life; how *the new existence* of the baptized *inaugurates a new way of living* filled with obligations; *how the psyche must do its work* in the life of a true Christian; how the Risen Christ demands mortification from us. As long as we are pilgrims far from the Lord, we have only the *deposit* or *pledge* of the Spirit with which we must fight and grow : " Now we have received a share in the Holy Spirit that He may perfect us and prepare us for incorruptibility by enabling us to touch and possess God. " [28] We are only *the saved*

---

[28] St. IRENAEUS, *Adv. Haereses,* V, 8 (*PG,* 7, 1141-1142).

in hope, and by definition we are subject to the wiles and temptations of the devil. Temptation always involves more than ourselves and other men. It also involves the one who prowls about seeking his prey, who revels in our secret complicity; who uses the sins of one person to bring about the downfall of others. And we must be on guard against his traps and his blandishments until the very end.

Finally, the Christian must know, as his Lord does, *the spiritual trials*, " the pangs of rebirth " intended to conform him to his elder Brother. St. Paul developed the theology of these " messianic sufferings, " because he himself experienced all but one of them. The trials involved in conversion, in life within the Church, in Christian marriage; the temptations, setbacks, and persecutions of apostolic life; — all are part of Christian life here below. They are countless and difficult; they are threats to our faith and means of developing it; they are forces which enable the Church to deepen her life and her communion with Christ; they are part of the unique Redemption unfolding in time and calling men to God's consolation; they are a mysterious introduction to the joy of the Holy Spirit and the secret germ of eternal life. [29]

All this indicates the " dramatic " quality of our fidelity in time. [30] It is not merely a time of death and resurrection with Christ. It is a time which is never secure. Our fidelity is constantly threatened and sometimes breaks down. It is always rooted in the invisible Christ and demands that the Christian humbly and bravely work every day [31] in a time which will be fulfilled outside time only through the Spirit. The " faithful servant " must watch, for the enemy is always

[29] There are innumerable texts. E.g. : 1 Thes 1, 6; 3, 3; Rom 5, 3 ff.; 1 Cor 7, 28; 2 Cor *(thlipseis)* 1, 4-8; 2, 4 ff.; 4, 17 ff.; 6, 4 ff.; 7, 12-13; Phil 1, 17; 4, 14; Col 1, 23-25.

[30] On this theme in the Bible, see J. DUPLACY, " Fidélité, " *Catholicisme*, IV, cols. 1269-1275.

[31] Cf. the " terrible daily effort " referred to by Pius XI (at the beatification of brother Benilde); text in *Trouble et Lumière (Études Carmélitaines)* (Paris 1949), p. 180.

at the gates of his heart; he must pray, for only the Lord can keep him from " entering into temptation "; he must begin again every day, for each day has its own task, its own difficulty, and its own grace; he must stand firm in the face of storms and harrassments; repentant and hopeful, he must walk, *and advance*, in truth, [32] in love, and in holy fear. In other words, he must go forward and continue (in Christ) the journey through existence.

Thus man enters a time-for-patience (*hypomone*). Patience is the stabilizing force which enables us to persevere in our fidelity because it stems from Christ's fidelity and God's fidelity. This " patience " is always realized in the Holy Spirit in two different ways. First, through *the sacraments of fidelity*. Penance restores the Christian life. After the rupture effected by sin, Penance gives us a new present in Jesus Christ and links it with our holy past which had been interrupted but not destroyed. It is one of the miracles of Christian existence on earth. Then the Eucharist goes farther still. It establishes a new link with Baptism (which it perfects sacramentally) and purifies the faithful soul of its daily sins. The Holy Spirit continues this process by His secret activity. His inspirations " correct " and illumine the soul. If the soul is docile, the Spirit continues to give deeper unity to its earthly existence. Under His guidance liberty, which is " the proper use of free will, " becomes *the proper use of time*. Each soul must arrange its own spiritual itinerary; its fidelity consists of successive conversions which strike deeper and deeper; and these conversions mark the imprint of the Holy Spirit on its progress and immerse it ever more vitally into the life of the Church which they serve to enrich.

But this liberty is always fragile and threatened. The man who is trying to convert himself lives in holy fear as well as in joyous hope. " In the cool night he keeps watch, humming the praises of grace in order to resist the advance of sleep. " [33]

[32] Cf. J. DUPONT, *Essai sur la Christologie de saint Jean* (Bruges-Paris 1951), pp. 71-77.

[33] FABER, *Le Progrès de l'âme*, p. 365.

Every time he receives Holy Communion he says : " Lord Jesus Christ, never permit me to be separated from You. " For *man can remain faithful only because God is faithful.* He never presumes that he will remain faithful tomorrow. Fidelity is inscribed on God's heart alone, not on ours. In a strict sense, tomorrow belongs only to God, not to man. Man must prepare for it, but he has no right to demand it, to treat it as his, to expect it as a master (Lk 16, 21), or to glory in it apart from God. And since *only God can dispose of tomorrow,* man must trust in his heavenly Father who watches and guards him lovingly : " Be not therefore solicitous for tomorrow; for the morrow will be solicitous for itself. " [34]

Growth in the Holy Spirit

Conversion is an enduring dimension of Christian life. But it is not a straight-line process; it is, rather, an ascent toward Christ, an unlimited forward movement. It is not an indefinite punctualism but a vital process of development like that of a child. It develops into the " perfect man " who has attained his full physical and spiritual stature. The Christian, according to his vocation and the " measure " of his gifts, must write the history of his personal encounter with God in Christ. He must conform himself to Christ and fashion a tender heart open to the Holy Spirit " who has been given to him. " From Baptism itself Christian growth involves *work* and *docility*, activity and inspiration. And Christ, the Master of time and of life, gives man the time he needs to realize his vocation.

[34] Mt 6, 34 (cf. Jn 4, 13-17). Prv 27, 1 says : " Boast not for tomorrow, for thou knowest not what the day to come may bring forth. " Commenting on this text, Rabbi JOSEPH said : " ...You do not know what tomorrow will bring. Perhaps tomorrow you will exist no more, and yet you are worried about a world which will no longer exist as far as you are concerned. " *(Strack-Bill.* I, *in loc.).*

Growth in Time

This period of growth is a grace given to us by God. From birth to death it is *sovereignly measured out* by God's will, God's power, and God's love. And this starting point, this call which confers on every man his own *kairos*, finds its origin in Christ. That is why there are always " young saints " and " old saints " [35] in the Church. The former are perfect at twenty-five, the latter at eighty. But they did not make the choice. It is the Lord who chose them and they responded wondrously. The root-principle of this personal growth is the same in any case. It is " faith working through love, " a stable, permanent principle of deiform life, rooted in the center of the sanctified soul, developing and revealing the transforming presence of the Spirit in our activity. God *dwells* in man, man *dwells* in God, and from this communion (which St. John expresses in terms of eternity) springs the power of eternal life. The structure of Christian time is always the same : it is *the fusion of a choice in eternity* with *a response in time*.

Christian time involves temporal growth to such an extent that it is *linked to the bio-psychological development of man*. A spirit does not age, but an incarnate spirit does insofar as it is joined to a body. Youth, maturity, and old age leave their mark on the human being because of the animated body which puts it in contact with the world, and because of the responsibilities it must accept, carry out, and then pass on to others. And this process of development exerts a direct and profound influence on the exercise of faith by the intellect, the will, and the emotions. Spiritual training must take this *process* into account and it must describe the kind of faith proper to each stage of life. [36]

[35] The apt expression of DE GRANDMAISON. Towards the end of his life, Newman admired the " old saints " more and more.

[36] Interesting speculations are made by A. BRIEN in various writings, e.g. " Education et developpement de la foi suivant les âges de la vie, " *Cahiers du Clergé rural* (Dec. 1951, Jan. 1962). Also in the small book of LIÉGÉ, *Adultes dans le Christ* (Paris, 1959).

And so we encounter a problem. If man grows, ages, and dies, then his spiritual life must also grow. (Old people show a remarkable " wisdom. ") The Christian must advance " from faith unto faith " (Rom 1, 17), " from glory to glory " (2 Cor 3, 18), from childhood to manhood, from imperfection to perfection (1 Cor 13, 10-12), from corporeal diversity to " a consummation in unity " (see Jn 17, 23). Growth is a rule of Christian life and it affects not only individuals but the Church herself. She is not restricted within certain limits, because she has an infinite vision : to conform herself to Christ (Phil 3, 10-11), and to be perfect as her heavenly Father (Mt 5, 48). She envisions the conversion of every human faculty — " spirit, and soul, and body. " [37] She strives to illumine all man's aims with the light of God and to imbue all vital forces with His purity. She suffers setbacks and then moves forward, because earthly life is the growth period of God's children.

Spiritual Stages

When the Christian is faithful to the Spirit, he is purified and molded by the Lord until his death. And the traditional divisions of the spiritual life [38] are very sound in this regard. There are *beginners* of many different sorts who must develop the seed of a spiritual life in spite of sin, routine, and inexperience with the things of God. Then there are *advanced* souls who are already somewhat purified before God. They have resolved to renounce themselves and follow the Lord; and they have begun to develop a real interior life. And finally, there are *perfect* souls (in comparison with the other two groups). They are still wayfaring soldiers who fall into sin now and then. But they are truly docile to the Holy Spirit, devoted to God and to others, and striving for heroic sanctity.

[37] 1 Thes 5, 23. On the meaning of the expression see the treatment of B. RIGAUX, *in h.l.*, pp. 596-600.

[38] Cf. J. DE GUIBERT, *Theologia spiritualis* (Rome 1946), pp. 279-317.

These stages are quite diversified in time, and yet well integrated. For they bring about our growth in love which enables us to penetrate deeper into the grace of Baptism, to die to sin and live for God. And the result is that the " perfect " desire only one thing : to die and to be with Christ, or else to remain in the flesh (Phil 1, 21-26) *if God wills it ;* but at all events to be " found in him. . . That I may know him and the power of his resurrection and the fellowship of his sufferings : being made conformable to his death, if by any means I may attain to the resurrection which is from the dead, " to the transformation of " the body of our lowness " into " the body of his glory " (Phil 3, 9-11. 21). Such a vision has only one motivating force : the desire for eternity, the desire to be with Christ, through death. But it remains submissive to God's will and takes place in a time-period which opens out on the Cross and the Resurrection. It is completely suffused by this passionate movement toward an invisible goal, and totally consecrated to the service of others " for your furtherance and joy of faith " (Phil 1, 25).

On an even deeper level St. John recapitulates all this in the simple unity whereby *Christ dwells in man and man dwells in Christ :* " abide in me, and I in you " (Jn 15, 4). You abide in Me through faith and love, as in the One who upholds you eternally in His knowledge and His love and now gives you eternal life. I shall abide in you, the ones I sanctify and unite in love, so that you may be witnesses and that the world may believe in the Son who has been sent by the Father. By abiding in God, observing the commandments, and testifying to the Son and the Father, the Kingdom of God's children solidifies and grows into the perfect unity of the Trinity. Paradoxically, this *indwelling* (which is a characteristic of *eternity*) *involves* a process of *becoming*, and *eternal* life involves a period of *time* in which our resemblance to God develops and our sanctified life becomes more manifest. But eventually we reach perfection in the eternal vision of the Trinity. And so, " every one that hath this hope in him, sanctifieth himself, as he also is holy " (1 Jn 3, 3).

Activity in the World

Necessity of Presence

However, the Christian cannot grow unless he is actively present in the world. On the one hand, he is swept up in the Church's mission to save men, and he must take part in this mission if he is to be a real Christian. On the other hand, he is suffused with the theological virtues which drive him to share what he has received, and he must do this if he is to remain " faithful. " But he is also involved in the structures and the rhythms of the temporal world. His thinking and his activity as a Christian, like that of all men, is conditioned by " his bodily presence in the world, his physiological makeup and his cultural environment. " [39] His life as a Christian involves social relationships. His life in the world means contact with others. And so he necessarily lives a temporal existence segmented into various levels without any clear limits. Finally, the Christian finds Christ in the world too, and this also affects his outlook. The Lord identified Himself with the poor, the lowly, and the wretched. To serve them is to serve Christ Himself, and the Christian is judged daily on the love he shows for his brothers. Thus, the time of men has become *a time of Christ*. " It is marked by the secret presence of Him who is Lord of time and eternity. " [40]

Interior Life and Testimony

The Christian lives in the world in a unique way. His presence is rooted in Jesus Christ, the heart of the world. From this source it develops *in two* seemingly different *directions*. But they are really connected, because they both find their source in charity.

First, the Christian develops his *interior life*, chiefly by prayer. The Christian is really present in the world when

[39] A. Dondeyne, cited above (chap. 3), II, 465.

[40] T. Preiss, " Le Mystère du Fils de l'Homme, " *Dieu Vivant*, 8, p. 35. It is a remarkable article.

he recollects himself and " raises " his mind in search of God. But he can do this only if he takes part in the prayer of Christ and the Church. Even when he is not aware of it, he is borne up and sustained by this prayer, because it is the vital principle of his search for communion. On the one hand, it is a prayer of adoration, praise, and thanksgiving. The Christian plunges to the heart of his human vocation and reaches the sacred point where he is in communion with all men. There in Christ he can only " pray together with all the saints " for all mankind. It is also a prayer of petition and supplication on behalf of himself and all men treading the dangerous road to salvation or damnation. But it is still enveloped in the eternal intercession of the great High Priest. This prayer finds its real fulfillment in the communal celebration of the Eucharist. The assembled Christians offer praise and petitions in the unique sacrifice. They are nourished with the unique life-giving Bread which renews and deepens the unity of Christ's Body and the unity of its universal prayer. The world is enveloped in prayer and reorientated toward God.

Our interior life, therefore, immerses us in the One who calls all men to salvation and the fullness of life. [41] Christian prayer is a " vertical " ascent which reaffirms the relationship between time and eternity. This contact is the foundation-stone of Christian activity in the world. Without it all is lost, with it everything is possible. That is why those who are really most active in the world are hidden and secluded. The cloistered contemplatives devote all their attention to the One God who holds the hearts of men in His hands. Through their sacrificial intercession He reaches some particular soul, some particular group, or the threatened multitude.

[41] Prayer reaches the Eternal, overcoming time and enveloping the past and future. *Libera nos, Domine, ab omnibus malis praeteritis, praesentibus et futuris.* But private prayer is always limited, for three reasons : (1) it is completely subject to God's will; (2) it is never *the* universal prayer (only Christ has this privilege); (3) it is always conditioned by the purity and sincerity of the person's love. However, the saints show us how much of eternity can be imbued into the prayer of a member of Christ.

But why is Christian prayer also *a temporal activity*? Because it activates both the soul and the body. It must be "practiced." It must be nourished by reflection, expressed in words, and perfected by practice. To be sure, the Spirit still guides the journey. But He usually makes use of human resources. The Lord Himself taught us a prayer with human words. We learn prayer as we learn all great things; now and then the greatest contemplatives can only stammer with the simplest words. Our prayer does not penetrate into eternity suddenly and directly. It is too important and too profound to be learned so easily. Our prayer is woven from the fabric of our life and our interpersonal relationships. It involves the difficult task of uplifting our whole life, of starting again each day until our days are complete — Give us *this day* our *daily* bread.

Secondly, the activity of the Christian must be *a visible testimony*. His faith, his purity, his fidelity, and his justice must manifest his mysterious interior life. He must strive to understand others, to serve them, or simply to live peacefully with them. With purity and generosity he must take part in temporal activities. And it is always fraternal charity, the gift of God, which gives meaning to his actions, directs him, and enables him to judge rightly, to fight valiantly, and at times to die heroically. It is a time of difficulties and conflicts which is measured by the mission ("faith working through love") and which in turn reveals the joy and resiliency of Christian liberty.

Temporal Tension

The most amazing aspect of this activity is its *contradictory* character. It is bi-polar and is marked by a tension which St. Paul described so well.

First, *here time shrinks* before our eyes, "like a veil which is drawn back."[42] Marriage, sorrow, joy, earthly goods and

---

[42] E. B. ALLO, commenting on our text, 1 Cor 7, 29-31 (*Première Épître aux Corinthiens*, pp. 180-181). It seems difficult to exclude the history of individuals from this *kairos* as HUBY and PRAT try to do. Cf. PRAT, *Première Épître aux Corinthiens*, pp. 174-175, notes.

their use — all are part of a world whose " figure passes away. " By faith the Christian adheres to realities which do not pass away. The Spirit dwells in him as the hidden seed of eternal things. The gravest sin for him would be to cling to transitory things as if they were eternal; to use the instant as if it could satiate his desires; to act as if cosmic time were not the battleground of an eternal vocation. The Christian cannot be just an earthly man; while he is *on this earth, he must prepare the New Earth.* This involves a radical detachment, which is *not an evasion.* His real family, his true home, are above; but their earthly counterparts are very dear to him because they foreshadow eternal *realities.*

Thus the Christian *values* time very highly. His eternal destiny is worked out in time, and his free choices in time determine his entry into the Kingdom and the rate of his development as a human being. St. Paul also underlined this aspect in two texts (Eph 5, 15-16; Col 4, 4-5). The Christian must " make good use of the present time " (Osty) and " utilize fully " the *kairos* granted " for his own sanctification and the conversion of his neighbor. "[43] He is immersed " in an evil world " prone to violent passions, drunkenness, and debauchery. If he is to act as a Christian in the midst of human time, he must pray; he must keep his heart and his judgment intact; he must dwell in the light of " wisdom "; he must testify to the Spirit's presence in him by his chastity, his sobriety, his fraternal love, and his joy; he must act as one of the saved and " spend and be spent " for the work of the Kingdom (2 Cor 12, 15), helping to convert " them that perish " and to strengthen " them that are saved " (2 Cor 2, 15). Thus he gives deep meaning to his short stay on earth and stores up the fruits of eternal glory.

The " Now " of the Christian

The " now " of every Christian is marked by this tension between two realities. To say that time is eschatological is to

[43] Cf. J. HUBY (quoting F. BÜCHSEL, *TWNT*), *Les Épîtres de la captivité*, p. 222 (cf. p. 101, note 1).

take note of these two poles. *Real presence* (activity) *in the world* involves *contact with eternity*. But we must take note of another, deeper tension and connect it to this one. We must note the tension between the flesh and the spirit which marks the time of conversion. This is the *dramatic* element in the present of each Christian. It is never a purely Christocentric present. The Christian lives in a body, and his bodily life envelops his spiritual life. His life in Christ develops in the rhythm of time, because it is linked to a body and to the world.

The Christian never becomes completely spiritual. His body remains carnal and perishable. His soul is still " carnal " because of its attachment to the body and its desires, and because it is not fully impregnated with the Spirit. Some of the old man, some of the sinful tendencies still remain. The old desires can surge up once again and the Christian can fall back into a sinful life.

Every time the Christian commits a mortal sin, his former sinful present returns. His direct contact with the glorious Christ is broken, and the other two relationships crumble. [44] He begins a new present unconnected with the former one. His temporal existence descends to a lower level, fatally disconnected from the higher one on which he had been living. He has realized a possibility which is always present in our earthly existence. In this sinful present he chooses to reject Christ and anticipates his final damnation. He enters a state of spiritual death. It is a time of refusal, isolation, and destruction leading to eternal death.

This terrible possibility of separation, destruction, and condemnation is open to the redeemed Christian. It lies " submerged in the world " or lurks on the " horizon of his existence. " During the course of time it gives rise to dangerous allurements and wayward tendencies, to " temptations. " Another leader, another band of would-be companions, another kind of temporal existence lurks nearby and

---

[44] As long as one does not lose his faith, a real relationship remains. We are not concerned with this problem here.

threatens the present life of the Christian. They remind us of the possibility of revolt and continually attack us, insidiously or openly. They *disturb the rhythm* of our life and we find ourselves threatened by the allure of the old time of sin. The two conflicting rhythms are part of Christian existence and cast their shadow on the present of each Christian. [45] The time of sin is not the foundation-stone of Christian time because the latter is the deepest level of our temporal existence. The time of sin is an atmosphere of sinful forces pressuring our spiritual life and tempting our treacherous bodily powers to revolt. The present life of each Christian is an amalgam of relationships with Christ; but it is suffused by disruptive forces which seek to restore the time of sin.

All this indicates that the life of the Christian is menaced daily and must be saved from the morass of sin by Christ's power. It too must be redeemed from sin daily, because sin constantly tries to overcome our free will, the point at which we adhere to Christ. Our spiritual present is *a time for hope* not only because it looks toward its fulfillment in eternity, but also because it must be rescued daily from the menace of death. It is a time of thanksgiving, because we " are " saved; a time of supplication, because we are saved " only in hope "; a time of combat, because we are successful only if we " hold " firmly against the attacks of sin.

It is a present in which we adhere to Christ by remembering the Passion in which we share, and by awaiting His anticipated return. Faith works through love to build up the spiritual time of each Christian. And finally, it is a *salvation-present* " enveloped " in the eternal present of Christ the Savior.

Mystery of Christian Time

We must remember that *time remains mysterious for the Christian*, because he approaches the world and Christian time *through faith*, which opens salvation-time for him in the midst

---

[45] Cf. the remarks of G. STAEHLIN on this present which is a *continuing now* and a *now already past*, in *TWNT*, IV, 1107 ff.

of cosmic time. What Christ *sees*, the Christian *believes* on
His word. Revelation has told him that Christ inaugurates
salvation-time and that men must enter, live and die in this
time by faith, if they are to be saved. But the full dimensions
of this time, its individual and social aspects, its inner nature,
and its essential " moments " — all remain hidden in the
Father's eternal plan, in Christ's redemptive psyche, and in the
eternal life mysteriously communicated to the Church for the
sake of men. The Body of Christ develops during the
salvation-period, [46] and the Christian collaborates in this
development. But the source, the center, and the end of
this temporal development remains hidden from him. It is
not for him to know " the times and the moments which the
Father has set by His own power, " nor the " measures "
(of grace, of sin, and of holiness) which structure the salvation-
period. [47]

Thus the Christian lives in a salvation-period which he
cannot comprehend but in which he must believe. Hence his
psyche is *the battleground of an inevitable tension.* By his
activities as a member of the human race he lives in cosmic-
time. By faith he lives in the Church's salvation-time. Insofar
as his *psyche is in the world,* salvation-time seems to be inserted
in cosmic time; insofar as his *psyche sees God* by faith, cosmic
time seems to be enveloped in salvation-time.

Although faith gives unity to his life, the Christian cannot
synthesize cosmic time and salvation-time, just as the Church
cannot synthesize world history and salvation-history. The
rupture caused by sin and death remains. Mankind and the
world are not yet totally transformed; the " old world " of sin
within man and outside him is still a real menace. And thus
the two time-spans remain distinct. The Christian does not see
their ultimate unity; he sees them as being partly *complementary,*
partly *inimical,* and partly *unconnected.* Faith affirms their
unity, but the Christian can only hope to see it on the last day.

[46] Cf. BENOIT, " Corps, Tête et Plérôme, " *RB*, 42 (1956).
[47] BENOIT, *op. cit.*, p. 42, note 2.

However, a true synthesis of these time-periods can *be approached* here below more and more each day. At the spiritual center of his being, the Christian lives in Christ. Through his faith and his love he lives outside time and draws near to eternal life. He shares in the power from on high which unifies these two time-spans in the psyche of the Risen Christ. The more he lives in Christ, the better he can *transform* cosmic time into salvation-time. As he unites more closely with Christ, he links cosmic time more closely to salvation-time. *Insofar as he becomes eternal, he makes cosmic time an instrument of eternity.* Thus Christianity recognizes two extremes. The unrepentant sinner lives in one kind of time. He has rejected Christ. Torn loose from his connection with eternity, he lives a meaningless existence. But the saint lives in another kind of time. He is united with eternity and can integrate chaotic human time into " the knowledge and wisdom of God. " He seeks God above all else, and so he finds God in everything. *The course of the entire created world becomes ever more closely linked with the course of salvation-time.* In the end " everything becomes a grace. " The saint sees cosmic time as already transformed into salvation-time because his existence has been transformed in Jesus Christ. " I live, now not I : but Christ liveth in me " (Gal 2, 20). And *Christ inaugurates* salvation-time within me.

II

The Mystic and Time

The mystics arouse both passionate admiration and systematic disparagement. They are reproached for being unfaithful to the Bible and lacking in brotherly love. They seem to be completely wrapped up in their own experiences and to dwell outside time and history. [1] These criticisms are not really

---

[1] See the remarks of A. LÉONARD in his fine study " Recherches Phénoménologiques autour de l'Expérience mystique, " *SVS* (Nov. 15, 1952), pp. 435-436, 447-451; also A. NEHER, *L'Essence du Prophétisme* (Paris 1955). Neher clearly sees that the experiences of Christian mystics " are experiences of a real time " (p. 80), but he centers them around ecstasy. He states that the mystic, unlike the biblical prophet, ascends to God " by utilizing the means of discovering Him " (p. 98); the biblical Word is not to be equated with magic (!) nor with mystic experience (involving silence); prophetic time excludes mystic time (pp. 52-54, 261 ff.), for the former involves love *with* God while the latter involves love *in* God. However, in reading his pages on knowledge and love as found in prophetic experience, the Catholic theologian sees a direct anticipation of Christian mysticism. In his *Théologie de l'Ancien Testament*, E. JACOB writes : " God

well founded. For the mystics bring us to the mysterious heart of Christianity. The Father loves men, the Son redeems them, and the Holy Spirit transforms them, making them one with Christ and God. The mystic is the living *exemplar of this oneness* which is the mysterious fruit of Redemption.

Thus the relation of the mystic to time is a crucial and enlightening problem. Christian mysticism is a world in itself. It has different levels and different kinds of members in it. There are mystics of contemplation, mystics of action, and mystics of suffering. Each of the great mystics follows his own path, the path to which God calls him and which he must follow. We shall take as our example St. John of the Cross, a Doctor of the Church and one of the contemplative mystics. [2] Though it may be a difficult task, [3] we shall try to discern the essential characteristics of time as it was lived and expressed by him.

loves His people so as to accomplish His goal with them, the establishment of His kingdom in the world. This *eschatological orientation* preserved God's love in a mystical form because mysticism suppresses time while O. T. love involves a slow but sure education of God's people " (p. 89). O. CULLMANN thinks that mysticism involves " participation in an extra-temporal myth " not " in a past historical event " (*Christ et le Temps*, p. 157).

[2] I do not use the word " speculative. " In dealing with the great mystics such divisions as *speculative* mysticism and *psychological* mysticism seem to be quite inaccurate. Some mystics may tend to be more speculative, and others may be more psychological. But the true mystic is beyond such categories as " speculative " (even a Ruysbroeck) and " psychological " (even a Teresa of Avila).

[3] I leave aside the problems of textual criticism and take the texts as we have them. For the English translation cf. E. ALLISON PEERS, *The Complete Works of Saint John of the Cross* (London 1934-1935) 3 vols., cited by Book (or strophe) and chapter. *MC — Ascent of Mt. Carmel; LF — The Living Flame; DN — The Dark Night; SC — Spiritual Canticle.* For another bibliography cf. the thesis of H. SANSON, *L'Esprit humain selon saint Jean de la Croix* (Paris 1953), pp. 347-360. These pages were already drafted when the intensive study of G. MOREL appeared, *Le Sens de l'Existence selon saint Jean de la Croix* (Paris 1960), 3 vols. I should like to have benefited from them. At any rate, my aim here is different.

Mysticism and Eschatology

Mysticism and eschatology are fully "reconciled" in the New Testament. [4] The Lord has come and gone, but He will return. And Christians await His return, the time when the Kingdom will be fully revealed and all men will be judged. They already possess the deposit of the promise, the Holy Spirit and His gifts. The Christian who remains faithful enters more and more into the richness of Christ, and God Himself dwells in him. [5] This is precisely what happens to St. John of the Cross.

A. ESCHATOLOGICAL TIME

The marvelous experiences which he describes take place in eschatological time in the highest degree. The first Christians awaited the hour of Christ's return, to be taken away with Him and to see God face to face. The Beatific Vision is the direct goal of John's desires, his prayers, and his ascent. As he travels farther, he comes into closer communion with God and the Lord, and his desire for the Vision becomes more

[4] See J. Huby, *Mystiques paulinienne et johannique* (Paris 1946); D. Mollat, "Jugement," *DBS*, cols. 1374 ff. and 1392; A. Léonard, *op. cit.*, pp. 462 ff.; F. M. Braun, "Morale et Mystique à l'école de saint Jean," *Morale chrétienne et requêtes contemporaines* (Paris 1954).

[5] The opposition of "Christians" to mysticism is grounded in a doctrinal supposition. They imagine that the New Testament embodies only a "functional theology" regarding God and Christ, and that we have only a "functional" (not a real ontological) participation in the divine realities of the Kingdom. Such a view is open to serious question. Cf. L. Malevez (*op. cit.*, chap. 5) : " The Christian mystic seeks to become a true Christian fully united to God. A functional theology maintains that the mystic's desire for God does not conform to the Bible. But such a theology is really in danger of betraying the true spirit of the Bible " (pp. 284-285).

all-consuming. [6] Single-mindedness is a basic trait of St. John. This young Carmelite wished to become a Carthusian in order to serve God more perfectly. St. Teresa tried to hold him in her reformed order. He had only one reply : " Yes, but do not delay too long. " [7] This impatient love suffuses the life and work of St. John. He is not a lost man nor an idler. He is *a man with a goal*, a transfigured man living for the fullness of eternal life (*SC* XI, 2 ff.). He knows that he will obtain it only after death. As he goes on, becoming more submissive to God's will, he enkindles an ever stronger desire to die in order to be with God (*LF*, I, 6). " To be dissolved and to be with Christ " (Phil 1, 23), — that is his all consuming desire, the spark he tries to give to others. Here we see the *Marân atha* of the primitive Christian, lived with a purity and an intensity that is truly extraordinary.

John's itinerary is incomprehensible unless we connect it to his transcendent goal. Only this explains the urgency of his call to souls and the stages he describes in his exposé. This is the heart of the Christian mystery. Christian eschatology certainly has a social aspect. The people of God are to be saved and the royal Kingdom must be established. But the very fact that this kingdom is inhabited by persons indicates that eschatology also has a personal, individual aspect. [8] Everything on earth is ordered toward the salvation of individual persons who are immortal and capable of rising again. St. John of the Cross is understandable in this perspective. He offers us a view of the personal Parousia

[6] St. John expresses himself in terms of the Beatific Vision, because this is a biblical approach (cf. 1 Cor 13, 12; and 1 Jn 3, 2); also because Benedict XII defined it dogmatically in a famous constitution (1336, *DTC*, " Benoît XII " by X. M. LE BACHELET, pp. 658 ff.; cf. H. DE LUBAC, *Catholicism* (New York : Sheed, 1958), pp. 100 ff. Also the summary of H. RONDET, *Les Dogmes changent-ils?* (Paris 1960), pp. 25-35; finally, because it has become a common expression of Catholic theology.

[7] BRUNO DE JÉSUS-MARIE, *St. John of the Cross* (New York : Sheed, 1957). Also H. CHANDEBOIS, *Portrait de saint Jean de la Croix*, p. 35.

[8] Cf. the recent study of J. GALOT, " Eschatologie, " *Dict. Spir.*, XXVIII-XXIX, cols. 1019-1059.

which prefigures the final one. For St. John, Old and New Testament *eschatology directs the paths of the mystic* and pervades the time of his journey. From the time God begins to speak to His chosen soul, He has only one purpose : " All the gifts, both large and small, which God confers on the soul, are intended to elevate it to eternal life " (*SC*, III, 3). The course and the time of mystic experience are *rooted* in *eternity*.

B. DIVINE UNION

Mystic time is eschatological for still another reason. In the spiritual present the mystic anticipates and eventually effects *the closest approximation to the Beatific Vision which is possible here on earth*. From the very start of the Ascent, St. John expresses this in simple words — " divine union " (*Title*), " the highest state of perfection which we call the soul's union with God " (*Argument*), " perfect union with God through love " (*Prologue*). These words have profound meaning. When we read St. John we are amazed to find the themes of the Canticle and the Living Flame already mentioned in the Ascent. There we find a definition of transforming union (*SC*, II, 5) : " God communicates (to the soul) His supernatural existence so that it itself appears to be God, possessing what He does. When God distributes such a supernatural favor, the soul and God are so closely united that it and the things of God are one. The soul is transformed by this participation. It seems to be God rather than a soul and, indeed, it is *God by participation.* " [9]

This is the ultimate goal here below. After the dark night and the bewildering betrothal, the soul experiences the perfect peace of spiritual marriage. The soul has been stripped and refined, then renewed and transfigured in preparation for this immediate but imperfect union with God. Spiritual marriage is not the ultimate goal. It only prefigures the goal by way of anticipation. It is the *closest possible* union *here below*, as the Canticle repeats continuously. The soul is immersed

[9] Cf. *SC*, 28.

275

" in glory and love. "   Every time the Holy Spirit singes it
with the flames of divine love, " it seems that the soul is about
to enter eternal life " (*LF*, I), but it does not.   Although the
soul begs God to tear away the veil, the hour has not yet come.
The veil is very thick and interwoven with resistant fibers.
The mystic is still attached to other creatures and to his own
natural tendencies.   He is still a being of this world and of
time, composed of body and soul.   He cannot see God face
to face.   The soul longs for death and the sight of God.
" It dies of not dying " *(poem V)*.

The progress of the soul of the mystic is *measured*
intrinsically by this movement toward the Beatific Vision.
It is *the sole goal* of mystic consciousness.   The Christian is
orientated toward his final end by the anticipatory possession
of future realities and God Himself, through the Holy Spirit.
The life of the mystic is dominated more and more by the
Holy Spirit.   It is transformed gradually by God and the
mystic grows more aware of this transformation (in God and
by God).   Mysticism does not contradict eschatology.   In fact,
here below it is *the only perfect example* of a soul which has
been revived in Jesus Christ and has " become God by
participation. "   The revived soul becomes more divinized and
strives earnestly to detach itself from this life of misery and
enigma in order to attain the Beatific Vision.   Here there are
no *images* of the Parousia.   Images were a Jewish literary
device.   St. Paul gradually gave up this device, and St. John
uses them only in the Apocalypse.   In St. John's other writings,
only the *essential* message is presented : " When he shall appear
we shall be like to him : because we shall see him as he is "
(1 Jn 3, 2).   This is the meaning and the orientation of the
mysticism of St. John of the Cross, the eschatological time
which is presupposed in his writings.

C. FAITH

The only " proportionate " means of effecting this divine union
is faith, living faith rooted in hope and charity.   St. John

of the Cross associated each of the three theological virtues with a particular power of the soul and described in unforgettable fashion the purification of hope and charity. But at the same time he emphasized the *essential unity* of the divine act which communicates them and the *unique impulse* which drives the soul toward the Beatific Vision. That is why he speaks quite naturally of " the light of faith " which " *gives us hope* of eternal life " (*MC*, III, 27), and of " faith through which we love God without *possessing* Him " (*SC*, Prol.). He reiterates the rich biblical vocabulary. For him, faith envelops our spiritual life on earth.

Virtue of the Pilgrimage

Faith by definition is the virtue proper to beings journeying through time. In relation to the eternal day, it is the night through which we journey to God. Commenting on the mysterious knowledge conveyed by the passing days and nights (Ps 18, 3), St. John writes : " Day is God in His full beatitude. He is the Day which conveys to angels and to human souls (days also) His divine Word, His Son, that they may know Him and take their delight in Him. And *night is the faith of the Church Militant* which gives knowledge to the Church and to individual souls. It is night because it does not yet enjoy the transparent wisdom of the Beatific Vision " (*MC*, II, 13). Considering *the radical gap* between God and us, it is a dramatic communication : " God is on high and speaks from eternity; we are blind inhabitants of earth who understand only the ways of the flesh and time. " [10] Thus faith is the virtue proper to a wayfarer because it is basically an impulse in time toward eternity. The soul " walks by faith " as St. John loves to say. Faith is the measure and the time proper to the whole ascent to God.

---

[10] *MC*, II, 20. The text is directly concerned with personal revelations and the problems involved in their interpretation. However, it describes a more universal condition.

Only Proportionate Means

However, faith has this role for only one paradoxical reason; because it is *a communication of eternity which transfigures time*. It is the only proportionate means of union (*MC*, II, 9 and *passim*), because it secretly contains the reality which will be unveiled on the last day. St. John compares it to the earthen pots in which Gideon's troops hid their lights. At the end of life, faith will " break open " and reveal " the shining glory of divinity which it contained " (*MC*, II, 9; see also *SC*, XI, XII). The heavy cloud of obscurity is an essential part of faith. It makes use of fragmentary knowledge and images which give us, even as the memory and the will, a foretaste and a partial possession of created and divine realities. Yet this knowledge is to some extent an imperfect knowledge of God. Faith already possesses eternal life. It is *the* temporal virtue because it must detach, " disentangle " the soul from the cloud of obscurity, mold and purify it so that it may acquire a true knowledge of God. It calls us to strip ourselves of our present knowledge in order to acquire perfect knowledge. When our soul is transparent it will be illuminated.

" Obscure " Knowledge

This purification of our mind, our senses, and all the apparent supports of faith on earth is not an *intellectual* process. It can only be accomplished by love " because love of God makes us strip ourselves of all that is not compatible with God " (*MC*, II, 5). This purification of the soul must be complete. Day after day it must rise above worldly conversation and individual realities. Since faith is *a medium* for God, *who has no medium*, [11] it implies a complete negation of every " visible " object. It is a " negation " [12] intended to bring about

[11] *MC*, II, 4. This fine text should be read in its entirety.

[12] Compare this with the comments of St. BRETON on being and transcendence viewed phenomenologically : " Élan implies the negation of every object, transcendence over any categorization insofar as an object can be imagined or represented by a concept. " *Approches phénoménologiques de l'Idée d'Etre* (Lyon 1959), p. 112.

union with the Infinite who is both object and subject — God, the transcendent One in Three. St. John describes this slow journey in great detail. It is an extraordinary adventure in time and eternity, in which man abnegates all knowing, sensing, and feeling (*MC*, III, 2). The beginner and the initiated both experience the dark night of the senses and the dark night of the spirit. It is a journey from light to darkness, from particular objects to the universal, from the known to the unknown. It is, as the soul discovers, a journey from complex things to the simple being, from the many to the one, from appearances to the essential. In short, our interior self is conformed to God. The result is what St. John calls an obscure knowledge of God. The soul fixes its loving gaze on God as on a friend (*SC*, XII) and it waits for the inexpressible union between " two transparent spirits, " [13] the pure divine essence and itself. " [14]

This knowledge is really faith viewed with its light and dark patches (*MC*, II, 15). It is *obscure*, because clear perception gives way to a transcendent presence through love. It is *simple*, because the soul gradually ceases to perform

[13] Just as St. John does not advocate the destruction of the soul's powers and appetites, so he does not suggest that all conversation and all conceptualization be suppressed. The union of soul and body makes this impossible, just as it prevents the mystic from attaining direct vision. In fact the mystic must develop his interior life so deeply that he transcends these powers, discovers their true value, and finally (in spiritual marriage) re-discovers them above in the light of eternity. Recently this point was underlined once again by G. MOREL, *La Structure du Symbole chez saint Jean de la Croix* (Recherches et Débats, 29, *Le Symbole*, p. 76).

[14] St. John excludes the Beatific Vision as such from mystic experience. He views the substance of the bared soul (1) as purified and (2) as open to the transforming power of the divine substance. We are still waiting for the historians to show us the influence of " northern mysticism " on St. John's thought. He does not express himself with the refined precision of Ruysbroeck (cf. the profound study of Paul HENRY, " La Mystique trinitaire du Bx. Ruusbroec, " *RSR* (1951-1952), pp. 335-368; (1953), pp. 51-75). This is certainly not an indication that John's work is inferior. It merely shows that the two writers had different experiences, different environments, and different viewpoints.

individual acts and " devotes itself to one all-consuming act " of a higher order (*MC*, II, 12). It is *pure*, because fleshly habits and activities, as well as knowledge through faith, disappear as the soul and its powers are entirely transformed. St. John standing on Mount Carmel perceives the full eschatological significance of this journey. If the soul could shed the veils which surround it " and stand with the naked purity of a simple spirit, it would be transformed into the pure wisdom of the Son of God " (*MC*, II, 15). In the meantime, the *temporal process* involves definite stages in time. The journey leads to a more thorough purification and to a darker night. The blind soul plunges on, knowing nothing, feeling nothing, possessing nothing. It is " lost " (*DN*, II, 16). And yet its security, its progress, and its very salvation depend upon all this. For " God takes you by the hand and leads you like a blind man through places you would never have discovered and could never have crossed " *(ibid.)*. There is a *complete gap* between the hidden substance and the visible surface, between the terrible experience and the blessed reality. Faith gradually revolutionizes our temporal existence which will completely disappear on the last day. [15]

Faith, Hope, Charity

Faith is, then, *the source* of hope and charity. The three virtues form *one reality*. Hope and charity perfect faith, but *faith conditions them in this life*. Here we must hope without possessing, and love without seeing. Hope and charity are also involved in the process of purification. Thus St. John writes some astonishing chapters on the purification of the memory. The mystic must detach his memory from every sensible object in order to be united to God alone through faith and hope (*MC*, II, 3-5; 12). So, too, the will is purified when God " restrains all the sense-appetites and renders them

[15] From a different viewpoint we may say that at this point faith and theology *pass judgment* on tangible experience. They use the absence of tangible experience as the criterion of certitude and security and they show negation to be a dialectic necessity in the search for truth.

incapable of tasting earthly or heavenly things " (*DN*, II, 11). Thus all the powers of the soul are brought into wondrous harmony and imbued with a single-minded love. The soul " really " fulfills the great commandment *(ibid.)*.

D. GOD'S ROLE

It is essential to understand that *from beginning to end God dominates this process.* St. John's explanation of God's role is most significant. Mysticism is not an undertaking initiated by man. It is *God* who calls the mystic to eternity (*SC*, 24; *LF*, III, 2-3). There is a passivity surrounding the intense spiritual activity of the mystic, his efforts and his lofty act of consent. God alone determines the starting point and the goal of the mystic's experience. He alone arranges its stages, decides the severity of its trials, and determines the degree of transfiguration. For St. John, mystic time is *absolutely unique*, even in the framework of Christian life. There are two reasons for this.

First, *God does not usually interfere with the time-process.* When He chooses to unite the two extremes of grandeur and lowliness (Rom 13, 1; Wis 13, 1), He " does it in a smooth orderly way " (*MC*, II, 17). He forms, purifies, and elevates by degrees. " He *perfects man in a human way*, proceeding from the external to the internal " *(ibid.)*. This principle dominates the writings of St. John of the Cross even as it dominated his experiences. We find the same principle guiding the various aspects of salvation-history — the preparation for Christ in the Old Testament (*MC*, II, 22); the need for Christ the God-Man and for His Church *(ibid.)* ; the governing of men according to Christ's image and human reason *(ibid.)* ; the passage from infancy to perfect manhood (*MC*, II, 17); the weaning of the soul and its transformation into dry bread (*MC*, III, 28); its recovery " through temptations, aridity, and other tests " (*DN*, I, 6); the " long " night of the senses (*DN*, I, 14) " and its speedy passage under God's direction " *(ibid.)* ; the pleasant respites between these dark nights — " for days and years " (*DN*, II, 1).

281

Secondly, *God alone is in charge of this mysterious process.*
He prolongs it or shortens it as He chooses. He conducts
weak souls through the dark night " very slowly and without
severe temptations, " so that they " reach perfection late in
life or not at all. " He humbles others by " severe " or
" lengthy " tests. And He purifies the nobler souls " which
can endure greater suffering " by the " most penetrating and
severest " trials (*DN*, I, 14). The only determining factor
is " God's will, " and it involves not only " the degree of
union " which He chooses to give the soul, but also the state
of the soul — its degree of " imperfection, " its courage, and its
liberty " steeling it against suffering. " [16] Thus the goal of
mystic experience " contains " within it the means of achieving
it. The time of the mystic journey is essentially a time of
eschatological realization.

Ecstasy : Death and Resurrection

The specific goal of mystic experience is determined by Christ.
The mystic must die and rise with Him.

A. Meaning of the Assertion

It is a complex problem because death and resurrection are not
only successive *stages* in mystic experience but also simultaneous
components of this experience. Mysticism begins with a kind of
death and ends in a kind of resurrection. The two phases are
necessarily linked together even as far as the Beatific Vision.
Concerning spiritual marriage St. John says : The mystic
" must enter the darkness of suffering and crucifixion, the

[16] Cf. *LF*, II, 5. This text integrates the various other texts of the saint.
The mystic's progress stems from God's will and his own generosity; but
the latter trait stems from God also. His lack of progress comes from his
own frailty and cowardice for which God is not responsible. The intersection of these two causes remains a mystery for us. Hence the well-known
phrase : " Only God knows. "

road to life," so that he may enter "the fullness of God's wisdom and treasures" (*SC*, 36, 5). This process contains all that man can do with God's help and all that man can become under God's direction. The starting point is always man's *lowliness* and *imperfection*. This distinction is the key to the road which St. John marks out. [17]

Man's imperfection is the result of original sin and his own sinful actions. It is not just a shell covering man. It is *an intrinsic disorientation* of the soul and its powers, the privation of an original purity. Lowliness is an essential condition of a human spirit that has not been glorified. It is a mark of *the ontological gap* between creatures and their Creator. Creatures are bound by certain limits. Man by himself cannot unite with the transcendent being, the "Most High." Imperfection and lowliness form the starting point of man's journey toward God. Our imperfection must be destroyed and our lowliness must be banished through human actions and divine grace. Activity and passivity are inextricably linked in mystic experience. The dominant traits of this experience are well known. They group themselves into certain significant *kairoi* — the dark night of the senses and of the spirit, various degrees of loving union, especially spiritual betrothal and spiritual marriage — which anticipate the Beatific Vision.

B. DEATH AND RESURRECTION

Death

The first experience for the mystic, as for Christ, is *death*. St. John cannot find words too strong to depict the awesome process of purification — negation, denudation, uprooting, even destruction. We are familiar with the inevitable process (*MC*, I, 13). The mystic passes through a period of unknowing,

---

[17] Not only in *MC* and *DN*, but throughout his works; for example, *SC*, 25 : Man feels miserable in the sight of God's beauty because of "his many faults and imperfections" and "because of the lowness of his natural, human condition."

non-tasting, non-possessing, and non-being to reach a new level where he can know, taste, possess, and be everything. "To arrive at everything, seek to be nothing" *(ibid.)*. Of course, he is referring to spiritual abnegation, not to ontological destruction. But it is a thorough abnegation. All our sinful, "natural" *human ways* of knowing, tasting, possessing, and feeling must be altered to permit our union with God. And this alteration can be experienced only as a kind of real death. St. John expresses it by the word "night." [18]

Man is a living body and all bodily activity must be overcome and purified because *nothing corporeal can experience God*. [19] All sense-knowledge, sense-inclinations, and sense-feelings are to be cast aside. Man's free will must not place its love or its pleasure in these things. For sense realities are imperfect dross incapable of bringing us to God even when they are touched by divine sweetness (*DN*, I, 1). To stop at these things is to stop short of God. The principle is absolute. If the senses are not completely purified so that tangible realities convey the soul directly to God, then all sense-realities must be rejected. Otherwise, the senses will develop at the expense of the spirit (*MC*, III, 26). But man is a spirit too. Nothing is accomplished unless man's spirit is purified. The senses are the inferior part of man. They are the more superficial part of man, while the spirit is the nobler, deeper part (*MC*, II, 3). *The senses are really purified in the dark night of the spirit* (*DN*, II, 3). Man must enter this dark night and begin again. The three powers of the soul — memory,

---

[18] We should really make a thorough study of the symbolic significance of the dark night. But it would be an immense task. For example, in *MC*, I, 2 : " the soul's passage to divine union " is called Night, and this word refers to its starting-point (renunciation), its goal (God Himself), and its motivating force (faith). Here Night symbolizes *a structure*. In *MC*, II, 2, Night has three moments : pre-midnight (the dark night of the senses), midnight (faith), and dawn (supernatural illumination). Here Night designates *a journey in time* with a definite structure.

[19] We have developed this point in our " Note sur l'affectivité sensible chez saint Jean de la Croix, " *L'Expérience Chrétienne*, pp. 312-323. Eng. trans. *Christian Experience* (New York : Sheed, 1954).

understanding, and will — must be emptied and reformed if the soul (a purified spirit) is to be united to the pure spirit of God. The soul " knows itself in a human way but not as God knows it " (*DN*, II, 17). When it reaches the point where it no longer knows, loves, or possesses anything naturally and cannot do so supernaturally, there is nothing left. All that remains is a yearning, a devouring hunger, and an unquenchable thirst stirred up unceasingly and secretly by God. The soul realizes its essential impurity so well that it feels *forever* unworthy of God. It has been granted a view of God's grandeur and majesty. The view is " shattering " and " overwhelming. " But it cannot attain this vision and so it feels rejected by God and cast into hell (*DN*, II, 5-6). In reality it is experiencing a private purgatory, [20] torn between two emotions. It feels such a strong love for God that it " would give a thousand lives for Him. " But it also feels profound misery because there is nothing which can make it worthy of God. It feels worthy of rejection by God and His creatures (*DN*, II, 8). Only the words of the Psalm (72, 22) can express its feeling : " I am brought to nothing, and I knew not " (*DN*, II, 8). It is a situation similar to that of a drowning man. He sinks, rises, and then sinks again. The past is a tale of misery and horror. The present is filled with sorrow. The future can only be one of desolation. *The synthesis of time approaches the spiritual plane.* If it were not part of a rebirth into a new creation, the soul could only collapse. [21]

Resurrection

However, it does not collapse, because God subjects it to the " dark night of fearful contemplation " to raise it to divine life. First, He grants it an obscure taste of Himself. A small glow begins to sparkle in the darkness, and it brightens into the dawn of Paradise. It is the night which precedes the dawn; it begins

[20] Cf. *DN*, II, 12.

[21] Thus this testing period has some resemblance to certain pathological states.

imperceptibly and continues to grow. Through the two dark nights, God fits the senses and the soul for the act of contemplation in which the *knowledge and love of God are linked.* It is a state of *loving knowledge* (*LF*, III, 3), otherwise known as divine union itself. God has imperceptibly " transformed " the powers and the virtues of the senses to the spirit, so that now the spirit " grows and senses " while the senses are " dried up and empty. " The change was so radical that the soul could not " immediately " feel the full spiritual delight (*DN*, I, 9). The de-creation was so violent that the re-creation was unbelievable and incomprehensible. Now as the soul grows purer and more transfigured, it becomes aware of the transfiguration. As the soul mounts the ladder of love, the stages become clearer (*DN*, II, 21). It cries out to *discover Your Presence* (*SC*, XI), because it wishes to see God in the fullness of His being and His grandeur. In its yearning for glory the soul *senses* the hidden Being who communicates Himself by " rays of light mixed with dark " and dominates the soul as its center. This desire to see God, which St. John likens to that of Moses (*SC*, XI, I), cannot be realized on earth, and the soul cries out : " May the sight of Your beauty kill me. "

Faith has been " clarified " and " illuminated. " But it still *remains the only means* of attaining the Beatific Vision, because it conceals within itself the wondrous Visage of the Beloved (*SC*, XII) and etches His features on the soul. The soul desires to see " *the truths* of faith, " because they signify " *the Presence of the Beloved* and His loving gaze. " [22] This mutual exchange of glances, this radiant communion and union with the Word and the Trinity mark the period of spiritual nuptials. First there is the betrothal, the period when God in His generosity visits the soul with " wondrous conversations " and " marvelous gifts. " St. John portrays this period in terms of created realities — flowers, wind, embraces, wines, wine-

---

[22] *SC*, XII. It would be hard to find a more striking expression of *the necessary role* played by the truths of faith in establishing *immediate personal contact* between the soul and God.

cellarer. The divinized soul " drinks in God " through every pore (*SC*, 18), and desires to do only one thing — to love (*SC*, 20). But all this is merely a preparation for the highest state, spiritual marriage (*SC*, 28), in which the soul is completely transformed and " becomes, insofar as it can here on earth, God by participation. The two give themselves to each other completely so that they become two beings in one spirit. In their love they do not change essentially, yet each seems to be God. " Man " tastes the sweetness of God's glory in his soul and is transformed in Him " (*SC*, 28, 5). St. John sums it up in the words of St. Paul : " I live, now not I : but Christ liveth in me " (Gal 2, 20). [23] It is a time of imperturbable *peace*. The soul is hidden in intimacy with its Beloved, isolated from all created things and " guided " by God " toward Himself " (*SC*, 35, 3). Two subjects are united in a mutual dialogue of love which surpasses any kind of " psychological " description. " I shall be You in Your beauty, and You will be me in Your beauty, because Your beauty will be mine " (*SC*, 36, 3). The transformed soul lives in the Trinity, shares in the spiration of the Holy Spirit, and carries on " its acts of knowledge and love in a divine manner " (*SC*, 39). It is a time when God adopts His children fully as Our Lord promised and as St. Peter affirmed. [24] It is a foretaste of *the next* life in *this one* (*SC*, 39, 1).

C. ECSTASY

We have reached the heart of mystic experience. The dark Night is a passage to Light; after death comes resurrection. The soul's journey must be described as *an ecstatic movement*. St. John knew about this ecstasy from tradition and from

[23] To repeat : John excludes any ontological fusion of the creature with the Creator; " participation " permits union and excludes the possibility of fusion; union and unity are the two distinct poles of mystic life— union of substances, unity of love (or " of spirit ").

[24] Cf. Jn 17, 10. quoted in *SC*, 36, 3; 17, 20-24 in *SC*, 39, 1; also 2 Pt 1, 2-4, quoted in *SC*, 39, 1.

personal experience. He places its focal point in the spiritual nuptials. But instead of describing his own ecstasy, he refers to other writers, [25] particularly to the words of " Blessed Teresa of Jesus, our mother " (*SC*, 13, 1-2). He never ceases to say that ecstasy is the essential thing. The soul *departs from itself* and its lowly manner of thinking, willing, and sensing, *in order to enter* on high in a divine way. Thus " even its first responses to stimuli may be divinized. " This is the *distinctive negativity* which marks the dark night and its moment in time.

Time of Uprooting

This transition is, first of all, a time of uprooting. The soul departs from itself. It is plunged into darkness that it may be flooded with light; it is humbled that it may be exalted; it is emptied that it may be filled with God and enter " complete spiritual freedom " (*DN*, II, 9). All contradiction, [26] which would impede the development of the spirit, must be eliminated. The divine light which floods the soul surpasses all human powers. It never focuses on one " particular " activity alone (knowing or sensing) but affects everything. In every phase of this process there is *only one law* : the base soul functioning on the lowly level of nature, must pass beyond this state and function in a divine way. It must undergo a kind

[25] We might think that the time had passed when mystic ecstasy was equated with the trances occurring among primitive peoples. But J. Duvignaud, ethnologist and novelist, makes this very equation (*Pour entrer dans le XXᵉ siècle*, Paris 1960). After noting several traits of voodoo, he says : " The interior voodoo of Ruysbroeck and John of the Cross leads to Christian symbolism,... " (p. 176). It is a distressing statement for an ethnologist to make.

[26] The basic texts on this passage are found in *DN*, II, 6-9. In reading St. John we are often reminded of Hegel. Père Morel *(op. cit.)* mentions this in several places. In his experiences John discovers " contraries " which Hegel systematizes in his work. Cf. G. Grégoire, *Études hégéliennes* (Louvain-Paris 1958), " L'universelle contradiction, " pp. 54-140. However, it would be extremely difficult to compare John and Hegel or to re-interpret John's work in the light of Hegel's.

of *substantial change* in its very depths. The divine light must dazzle it, scorch its foundation, and consume its possessions so that its memory, intellect, and will may be reborn and " divinized, " and so that it may acquire a " new and blessed life " filled with the " glory of divine union " (*DN*, II, 9). This is the ecstatic experience at the heart of the mystic's activity and suffering. It takes place in the depths of man, in his " very substance " (*DN*, II, 9); it eventually uproots every inclination of the old man to which the soul was so " strongly wedded " (*ibid.*, 6). But this is *akin to killing the soul*. In this dark night of negation God rebuilds the powers of the soul. But at the beginning of this ecstatic movement, everything grows strange, because man's soul is alienated from itself and its natural way of functioning (*DN*, II, 9).

At first, then, the soul is uprooted from its normal condition in time. *God exercises an extraordinary eschatological hold on the soul.* He regulates this mysterious frightful passage in which the soul no longer possesses its past or its future and finds itself engulfed in a present of unspeakable distress. In the state of ecstasy the normal rhythm of spiritual action fades away. A terrifying process of birth begins because the soul is deprived of any kind of support from the senses or the spirit (*LF*, III, 3). Moreover, the soul *can no longer inaugurate time* because it has been delivered to God who inaugurates in it a new, mysterious, purifying time. The soul can *only accept* the new time in complete ignorance of the mysterious process which has transformed it. The soul consents to what it cannot understand. It is no longer the measurer of its temporal existence and its existence is no longer naturally structured and free as it once was. The soul now exists in time without knowing or understanding. In a sense it no longer exists in time at all, because the most basic and essential components of temporal existence now elude it. Compared to ordinary human time, this new time is *not time* at all. [27]

[27] Cf. *LF*, III, 3. At this point the journey is not measured by light but by darkness; by inactivity rather than activity; by God rather than man.

For it is bestowed supernaturally from above as divine contemplation is. It is a terrifying situation for the human psyche, which feels that it has been radically altered, deprived of its normal conditions, and enmeshed in an unspeakably torturous time-span. Its only recourse in this darkness is to believe through faith that this period is rooted always in a transforming love and given meaning by divine contemplation.

Time of Changes

Ecstasy is also a time of change. This is true of Christian life as well as of mystical experience. It is not a time of steady movement in only one possible direction (like that of a robot) but a time of *opposing movements* among which there are unforeseen destructive forces which deprive the soul of its secure roots in the human condition. It is a time *of continual adaptation*, with the usual high and low points.

God allays the terror of these nights by comforting graces, patches of light, and " breathing spells. " The dark night of the senses ends in a period of joy (*DN*, II, 1), when the soul journeys with care-free happiness toward God. It contemplates divine things joyously, spontaneously, and peacefully, and this contemplation rebounds on the senses. Only a few stormy periods — " hours or days " — interrupt this state. But the senses have adapted to the spirit only partially, and this adaptation is to prepare them for more suffering. Far from being " adults, " the wayfarers are only children in God's sight. They can become perfect only by experiencing sudden changes in *two contrary environments*, night and day.

The dark night of the spirit is so shattering and overwhelming that God intersperses these " few years " (*DN*, II, 7) with " periods of solace " during which the soul leaves its prison, breathes freely, and finds peace and intimacy with God once again. The striking characteristic of this changing state is that the soul is so *absorbed in the present moment* of pain or joy that it cannot " imagine " anything else. The contrary experiences do not link up *(ibid.)*. At each moment the soul believes completely that it is either lost or saved

290

(ibid.). During this " midnight " the soul continues to live in a state where " God strips it of its old covering " (*DN*, II, 2, 13). But sometimes it experiences explosive periods where strong enthusiasm and violent pangs alternate with each other *(ibid.)*. At other times it experiences nightmares and holy days in which good and bad angels vie for its consciousness. The devil may look at it or touch it in a " frightening communication between spirits. " The soul would die from this if God did not visit it " with spiritual favors and great joy. " He Himself or His good angel substantially communicates with it in an omnipotent divine way (*DN*, II, 23).

Then the soul has contrary experiences in the midst of light. They are all the result of the wondrous conscious presence of the Beloved. Sometimes He inflicts ever deeper wounds (the last is " akin to a death blow, " *SC*, 7). Sometimes He fills it with a longing for death because He reveals Himself and yet hides Himself, gives Himself and yet refuses to give Himself (*SC*, 9-11). Sometimes He penetrates so deeply into the soul that He " almost wrenches it from the body " (ecstasy) or intoxicates it with the Holy Spirit for hours and days (*SC*, 17). Sometimes He communicates Himself to the intellect, the will, or all the powers (*SC*, 18). The only determining factors in all this are the varied experiences themselves, which are ordered toward greater union and peace.

Regenerated Time

Finally, mystic experience becomes a time of rebirth when the soul is truly transformed. *This is the fulfillment of human time on earth* because in it human time participates in eternity " insofar as it can here below. " The soul has entered into union, and together with God it forms " one spirit and one love " (*SC*, 28). It has found a permanent state (*SC*, 31, 2) which precludes the sudden changes and tragic " angers " caused by the devil, the passions, joys and sufferings (*SC*, 30-31). It has been " stripped of all conflicting states

291

and annoying activities " (*SC*, 31, 2), purified in its material and spiritual parts, and secluded with its Beloved. Now alone with God (*SC*, 22-35), it has entered divine bliss (*SC*, 39, 2) which, for St. John and the Bible, is the fullness of all good things. But even *in the midst of this peace the ecstasy continues.* For the soul still longs for communion with God and the Beatific Vision. The suffering of purgation has disappeared, but the longing grows into a desire for death.

The last " sail " is still untorn. The soul is still united to the body and only death will break this union at the appointed hour. Thus death, too, has been transformed. It has become a thousand times more desirable than life, because now, *to die means to see God.* When the soul is wounded by love before the spiritual nuptials, it desires death. For these wounds heal only if they bring death (*SC*, 9-13). Death is " like a friend or a spouse, " and the day of death is like betrothal or marriage. The soul cries out : " Let the sight of Your beauty kill me! " (*SC*, II, 2). At the time of spiritual marriage, this desire becomes even more intense. The soul begs for the perfect consummation of divine union (*LF*, I, 5) because " its thirst is not yet sated. " It still " hungers after God " and begs Him to shatter its earthly bonds. But the soul is beyond pain and in perfect accord with God. And so it pleads : *Do this, if it is Your will.* It discovers once again the words of St. Paul (Phil 1, 28) and lives according to the *Father's* perfection (*LF*, I, 5). It begs for death only because God indicates that He wants it to live in glory : " I ask for what You want me to ask and nothing else " (*LF*, I, 6). Death is seen, not from the viewpoint of time but from that of eternity, and it has lost its sting. Each divine communication is a depth of light, and so ecstasy is *a passage from one light to the next* (*LF*, III, 4), *a journey to eternity.* [28] But mystic

[28] That is why we do not find in St. John's works the " hatred of time " which R. Otto noticed in the works of Eckhardt. In *Mystique d'Orient et Mystique d'Occident* (Paris 1951), Eng. trans. *Mysticism East and West* (New York : Collier), we read (p. 77) : " Time prevents us from approaching the light (of true knowledge). *Nothing is more contrary to God than time,*

292

life is perfected by Infinite Love. And St. John integrates the three phases — *divinization, communion,* and *union* — in an extraordinary phrase : " God loves the soul in Himself, with Himself, and with the same love He has for Himself " (*SC*, 24, 4). Ecstasy has no other purpose than to ensure the soul's passage from a *human* to a *divine* mode of spiritual existence, from apparent existence to real existence.

Eternalization and Temporalization

" Eternity " is a word which St. John seldom uses. He reserves it for the Beatific Vision in heaven. And so he uses other words to express its characteristic features — divinization, union, glory, beauty. His main concern is to describe a storm-tossed ascent which cannot be completed on earth. In short, he describes an ascent which is a complex process of eternalization and temporalization.

A. Two Inseparable Movements

These two processes are inseparable. God takes the initiative throughout the journey and calls the soul to union with Himself, to divine transformation, to eternalization. Man must respond to this call. He will not make it " unless he has courage and stout legs and *resolves boldly to march forward* " (*Max.* 8). But the journey will take time. Thus in its journey toward eternity, the soul begins a new existence in time. This is clearly evident when the soul enters the dark night of the senses and " God changes the powers and activities of the senses into spiritual ones " (*DN*, I, 9; esp. *LF*, I, 4). He submerges the soul in a time of sorrow, purgation, and darkness

attachment to time, contact with time, and even the atmosphere of time. " But for St. John time also is *a gift of God.* In time the soul is purified so that it may see God. Only *a sinful attachment* to time keeps us from God. But Eckhardt has more to say (cf. OTTO, *ibid.*, pp. 203, 120-211); his fine phrase, *God is the God of the present,* is certainly not anti-temporal (cf. *Traités-Sermons,* Aubier, p. 42).

which it can scarcely endure. But He does so in order to immerse it in the mysterious state of " obscure knowledge, " where all individual objects and activities give way to pure love and true knowledge of God. The soul " *departs from all created things and journeys to eternal realities* " (*DN*, I, II). It is a real temporal existence. For, in the grip of an unknown future which it already senses, the soul realizes the base defilement of its past in the sorrow of the present. Henceforth " if it does not turn back, it must draw near to the inaccessible God " (*LF*, III, 3).

At the same time, this experience is *the beginning of an eternal existence.* First, detachment from every kind of existence unworthy of God is realized only when the soul is imbued with a kind of general, non-individualized elan which is " one pure act " beyond particular acts (*MC*, II, 12). It is a secret divine communication, which pierces through to the very substance of the spirit (*ibid.*, 14) and plunges it into an " extra-temporal oblivion " (*ibid.*). Then the same flame, the " tender and loving " Holy Spirit, engulfs and consumes the soul's imperfections and " shortcomings " to transform them and manifest Himself by communicating " His riches, His glory, and His delights " (*LF*, I, 4). The soul has entered eternity.

B. ETERNALIZATION

This new *existence in eternity* is the *source* of a new *temporal existence.* The soul on earth is substantially transfigured by its contact with God's very substance. It is completely adopted by God and touches the Word in the flame of the Holy Spirit (*LF*, II). The soul has gone beyond all the " means " of reaching God, and God Himself has become the " guide and the means toward Himself " (*SC*, 39, 1). It is propelled directly toward God by the flame of the Holy Spirit (*LF*, I). Insofar as it is possible here below, the soul reaches its center, the Beatific God (*LF*, I, 3), and concentrates all its affection on its Beloved. It is immersed in a state of *permanence*, which excludes the sudden changes of the testing period [29] and anything that could trouble its peace. It has entered a deep interior life which is characterized by stability. It shares in the very unity of God through mutual love, but it is not absorbed by God in any pantheistic sense. In effect, the soul has found once again the crystal purity of the state of original justice and of Baptism (*SC*, 38, 2). It has returned to its source and is immersed in the unity of its Creator. Hence all its powers and all its activities " are *made divine* " (*LF*, II, 6). The soul is united to God so that their two wills are only one and their two loves are only one (*SC*, 38, 2), because it shares in the eternal communication of love between the Father and the Son *(ibid.)*. The soul has been delivered from its natural " baseness " which was like death. It is " dead to all that it was by nature " and " alive to what is divine in it " (*LF*, II, 6). Therefore, the *only motivating force of its activity* now is *the impulse communicated to it by the Holy Spirit (ibid.)*. Its powers and their objects are divinized; its memory, understanding, and will are God's too; its imperishable substance, incapable of becoming God, is, however, " immersed in God, so that it becomes divine by participation " *(ibid.)*. Through this metamorphosis all the necessary conditions are again present *for a re-establishment of psychic functioning* in accordance with its nature but at a level beyond its natural power. That is why the impulse which re-establishes this functioning is a process of eternalization.

St. John describes one more communion between the soul and God — the final act of eternalization — in terms of *torches* and *shadow* (*LF*, III, 1-2). The torches are the divine attributes — omnipotence, wisdom, goodness, beauty — in all their splendor. These torches are revealed as distinct attributes, as related to one another, and as related to the simple essence of God. They are identical with His essence and manifest it; so that all these torches, in the last analysis, are the single

[29] Cf. *SC*, 30, 32, 39.

torch, God's essence. Now, just as everything here on earth casts a shadow — of greater or lesser intensity — so these divine torches cast their shadow by being manifested to the soul and communicated to it. Just as God " cast a shadow " on the Virgin at the conception of the Word, so each divine attribute " casts a shadow " on the soul. The power of God's beauty casts a shadow on the soul, a shadow which is a participation in God's power or beauty. These shadows " glow clearly " with splendor. They are " the very shadow of God. " But God does not unveil Himself. The divine attributes remain shadowy, but the presence of these shadows enables the wayfaring soul " to taste God's glory in the shadow of His glory " (*LF*, III, 2).

Moreover, all these " bright " shadows, like the torches, are gathered up in the single Flame " of God's essence. " When the soul receives these divine splendors, it is elevated to a kind of knowledge and love which are but one unifying force. In this union the soul discovers one or another torch, as God wills. The soul notes its particular nature, its individuality, and its relationship to the others. But this multiplicity is reduced to unity each time, because the soul sees the substantial identity of all the torches and their " concentration " in " the infinite unity and simplicity " of the One Being (*LF*, III, 2). Thus the soul is *submerged in the infinite unity* of God and *eternalized by this divine communication*. It finds itself in " the valley of delights " which spring from Him who is the " brightness of eternal light, and the unspotted mirror of God's majesty, and the image of his goodness " (Wis 7, 26; Heb 1, 1-3; cited *ibid.*).

C. Temporalization

The mystic, however, remains a pilgrim on earth. He does *not yet* live in *eternity*. He lives *only a process of eternalization*, which seems to be submerged in its goal at every moment. His life still bears three characteristics of existence in time.

296

The mystic does not escape from this world. The more he deepens his union with God, the more *he recovers the universe and cosmic time*. The purification of the soul at once gives him a new outlook not only on himself but also on creatures. Created things become a marvelous revelation of God (*SC*, 4-7). They reveal themselves and their true nature by their very presence. *They become what they* really *are* — wondrous links with God, created in the image of the Son and trans-figured by His Incarnation and Resurrection *(ibid.)*. They reveal God's grandeur and beauty. But angels and men are " creatures " also. And such a wondrous manifestation of divine grandeur leads the soul to the realization that it " understands nothing. " It " knows not what they say. "

At the time of spiritual betrothal, St. John describes a loftier, more radical kind of temporal existence. It does not ascend from the world to God, but rather *descends from Him to envelop and regulate the world as God Himself does*. It presupposes that the soul has been submerged in the peaceful night, in " a state of obscure divine understanding " which " borders on a new dawn " (*SC*, 15, 2). In this state the soul contemplates creatures. It sees that they manifest the unique, simple Wisdom of God. They are " gifted with a certain resemblance to God. Each in its own way displays the divine qualities in it " (*SC*, 15). Together they form a harmonious ensemble, a " silent concert " for the senses, and a " sonorous solitude " for the spirit. " Sweet music " and " silent quietude " unite to form this environment *(ibid.)*. In short, the soul sees each creature springing from God and " exalting Him according to its capacity for participating in Him " *(ibid.)*. Then, when the soul is immersed in the spiration of the Holy Spirit (*SC*, 39), it discovers among other things " in this new springtime, " not the universe as such but " God insofar as He is the source of life and existence for all creatures. " It knows " their source, their time-span, and creatures them-selves in Him. " To talk of the universe — " this charming

297

grove " — is to speak of " God and all the creatures in Him. "
It is to see creatures in their relation to God, but *from the
viewpoint of God* who causes them to exist in harmony. It is
" to know by way of contemplation " *(ibid.)*.

Finally, St. John describes another experience which is
even rarer, more mysterious, and more wondrous (*LF*, 4, 2)
— the awakening of the Word in the soul and the soul's longing
for God. The Word stirs its beloved soul by touching it at
its deepest point. This awakening is a participation in the
knowledge of the creator — " All things were made by him. . .
In him was life " (Jn 1, 3-4). It calls attention to the divine
beauty of the material and spiritual cosmos. All things seem
to stir and live in the aromatic splendor of this transforming
epiphany. The soul still sees the many individual creatures,
but *from the viewpoint of the One God.* The soul " knows
that God is all things in His Being but on an eminently higher
level. And so it knows creatures better in Him than in
themselves. " It knows creatures through God rather than
knowing God through creatures. This " different way of
knowing is *essential.* " Through the unforeseeable ebb and
flow of this blessed knowledge, ecstasy comes in contact with
the created world. This knowledge is a part of the soul's
beatitude and its transformation; it continues the process of
eternalization. After the rejection of all sense-images, they
are restored through the contemplation of their source. Thus
this experience is usually described by poems filled with
symbolism. This is scarcely an a-cosmic viewpoint but
rather a pan-cosmic viewpoint in which everything is recreated
and divinized. The transfigured soul is in a radically new
kind of time and measures the universe *from the divine viewpoint.* Man's consciousness begins a time of inconceivable
plenitude " because his soul and body have been transfigured
as far as it is possible here below. " Man's desire for God,
his love of God, and his communion with God have united
to bring this about. The old view of the universe fades into
the divine view. Through God, the mystic sees the true nature
of the universe, its activity, its source, and its final end.

As Abbé Wehrlé once wrote, *knowledge of the truth has become the truth of knowledge*. This radical change results in a *cosmic time* which is *completely spiritualized*. It feels the very pulse of the universe because it is one with temporal creation itself — insofar as this is possible here on earth. This explains why this communion with the cosmos is still a " perfect solitude " with God, and why this new process of temporalization implies an amazing process of eternalization.

Temporalization and God

The process of eternalization *is always* linked with God. St. John, in accordance with tradition, views the possession of God as a kind of progression toward Him, even in Paradise. The gap between the finite and the infinite remains. Thus, the closer the blessed come to God, the more they realize that God is incomprehensible. The soul advances across an infinite " expanse " (*SC*, 7, 5; *LF*, III, 3). But here on earth the soul does not have a vision of God. Its *advance* is *an unconditional necessity*, and the successive points of near approach constitute the essential significant moments of mystic experience. At these moments the soul feels that God is coming toward it. They are sudden visits filled with surprise and shock, in which the Holy Spirit embraces it (*LF*, I, 1; 6). The soul is plunged into the Trinity (*LF*, I, 3) and made to feel, touch, and taste eternal life (*SC*, 37, 5; *LF*, II, 4). [30]

But God does not undergo motion. He is not immobile but rather immovable. And St. John knows this. *It is the soul which moves to Him, through Him, and in Him*, because it has not yet reached " perfect glory " (*LF*, III, 2). And in its movement it grasps God so clearly [31] that " God Himself seems to move " (*LF*, IV, 3). *The ecstatic process does not*

[30] It is the same when the Word stirs in the soul and restores the universe in it (*LF*, 4, 2).

[31] On the immediacy of this knowledge see J. MARÉCHAL, *Psychologie des Mystiques*, II, pp. 342-344, 345-347 (Eng. trans. New York : Benziger, 1927); M. DE LA TAILLE, " Théories mystiques, " *RSR* (1928), pp. 297-325.

cease until the last hour. On the one hand it places the soul *in time*, because these " movements " (or instantaneous acts, *LF*, I, 6) succeed one another in an ordered progression. On the other hand, the ecstatic process places the soul *in eternity*, because these acts derive from the one simple Being, who touches the substance of the soul with His own substance, andth us gives it a participation in His simplicity and eternity.

Temporalization and Love

Finally, the most solitary mystic is never alone, because the closer he is to the One, the closer he is to all those who are vivified and enlivened by the One. The soul began its journey in a dark night of agony. It goes on, utilizing all its powers and gradually concentrating them " on one activity — love " (*SC*, 20, 5). Through love it performs " perfect, pure works for Christ " (*SC*, 21, 5). When it has been transformed by love, one act of perfect love " is worth more than everything it did in the process of transformation " (*LF*, I, 1). The man who wrote these words was neither a moron nor a prophet. He zealously chose poverty, abnegation, and suffering for the sake of Christ and His Church. He wore himself out in loyal service until he died. That is why he knows that love is the summation of everything. Creation, Incarnation, Passion and Resurrection are only " moments " or " phases " of love. The man who is united to this glowing source in spiritual marriage, finds himself immersed in salvation-history (*SC*, 29). He is to participate in it more than others and " lose his skin for Christ's sake. " [32]

The most evangelical brotherly love results from this love of God. St. John demonstrated it throughout his life. He showed such deep tenderness [33] toward his friends, his confreres, his nuns, his noble friends. Of his brothers, the

[32] BRUNO DE JÉSUS-MARIE, *Vie de saint Jean de la Croix*, p. 250. Eng. trans. *St. John of the Cross* (New York: Sheed, 1957).

[33] Even though certain texts may seem harsh and inhuman. On the first *Cautela*, for example, see the references and remarks of P. LUCIEN, 1334-1335.

300

poor, he wrote : " From too much delight with pleasant things comes a horror of the poor — and this is against the doctrine of Christ " (*MC*, III, 25). He did everything out of love for Christ. He was a missionary to workers, a spiritual director, an assistant bricklayer, a defender of the truth. In the prison at Toledo he was beaten, mocked, and insulted as a fool, " more often than St. Paul, " he said laughingly. In the midst of filth and vermin he sang the praises of his Beloved until the last days of shameful persecution. " If at the end of our days, we shall be judged by our love of God " (*Max.* 80), said John, then " *the man who does not love his neighbor, hates God*" (*Max.* 108).

The shining example of his life and work, his teachings and his writings, have only one purpose — to help souls follow Christ in poverty and nakedness in order to attain transformation in God. To the Carmelites of Cordova he wrote : " It is God's will that you live in the warmth of poverty, that you may come to appreciate the ideal you have professed — the naked Christ. Thus souls which feel a vocation to your order will know what they are to become. " [34] He knew very well that *when a soul has been transformed, other souls and the entire universe begin a process of transformation.* That is the end-product of the highest form of charity. Thus we see the close relationship between the process of eternalization and the process of temporalization in the experiences and the teachings of St. John. The mystic is not shut up in himself. Instead, he opens out to the infinite insofar as faith takes hold of him. St. John himself demonstrated this in his own work. The Carmelite reform was orientated toward conformity with the suffering and Risen Christ, and was inspired by the spirit of both contemplation and apostolic work. The mystic consciousness develops in time, and so others were destined to perceive more clearly the social, apostolic role of contemplation. St. Teresa of the Child Jesus, a spiritual daughter of John and one of his most illustrious exemplars, has translated this aspect of

[34] BRUNO DE JÉSUS-MARIE, *op. cit.*, p. 328.

mysticism into words and deeds with wondrous simplicity and profound directness.

The mystic is deeply influenced by the Bible. Indeed, the Bible came to be the saint's only text. [35] We do not see a detailed exegesis but rather the spirit of a text. For this school of mystic thought, the *central* theme is the death and Resurrection of Christ. The motivating *force* of mystic experience is faith understood in the biblical sense. For man cannot see God here below. The soul's progress is a continual *journey* toward God, an " exodus " and an " ascent, " a death and a resurrection experienced with Christ. For the mystics, *the great " spiritual types "* are (even more than St. Paul) Abraham, Moses, David, Job, Jeremias. *The great symbols* are biblical — night, water, fire, betrothal. [36] J. Baruzi has pointed out that the *tragic* note in the works of St. John of the Cross derives from the Old Testament. Its concern for *epiphanies* comes from St. Paul and St. John, and represents the culmination of the book of Wisdom and Canticle of Canticles. Everything is incorporated into a long and venerable tradition. [37] St. John sees the history of his soul in the history of God's people, and his experiences are connected to the experiences of Christ. It is not surprising that mystic time, as delineated in St. John's writings, is biblical time [38] in all its fullness, as experienced in the pure consciousness of a saint.

[35] Cf. the solid studies of J. VILNET, *Bible et Mystique chez saint Jean de la Croix* (Paris 1949); H. SANSON, *Écriture et esprit* (*op. cit.*, I, chap. IV); J. BARUZI, " Saint Jean de la Croix et la Bible, " *Histoire générale des religions* (Quillet, 188-191).

[36] J. Vilnet counted 597 quotations from the Old Testament against 327 from the New Testament.

[37] This has been clearly noted by H. SANSON, *op. cit.*, p. 153, notes 1 & 4. But to see St. John in true perspective on this point one must consult the erudite work of H. DE LUBAC, *Exégèse médiévale*, 3 vols. printed.

[38] The late A. GELIN, whose critical prudence understood the meaning of divine things, noted the trials of Job, through which he approached the " *Ipsissimus Deus*, " and did not hesitate to say : *his journey is the same as that of John of the Cross* (*LV*, 22 (1955), p. 17).

302

12

Death and Time

L'âme est partie, on rend le corps à la nature.
La vie a disparu sous cette créature;
    Mort, où sont tes appuis?
Le voilà hors du temps, de l'espace et du nombre.
On le descend avec une corde dans l'ombre
    Comme un seau dans un puits.

The soul is gone, the body returned to nature.
Life has slipped away from this creature.
    Death, where is your support?
Outside time, outside space, outside number.
It is let down into the darkness by a rope
Like a bucket into a well. [1]

---

[1] V. Hugo, "Pleurs dans la nuit," *Contemplations.* Compare the harsher view of Claudel in *Positions et propositions*, I, pp. 43-51.

Man " before the grave. " We must consider the last sad phase of human time, the moment of death. From its first day to its last, man's being is measured by this movement toward death. Here the irreversibility of time reveals its darker aspect and menaces us by its inexorable march. In the meaning of death we shall discover the aspect of time which it perfects.

The Meaning of Death

Death and Man

First, death is *the complete contradiction* in our existence, the " impossible possibility " which no man can escape. Man is a composite of body and soul. A living body, by definition, is corruptible. Birth, procreation, death — that is the cycle. An infinite " biological " existence would be absurd and shocking. But a spiritual soul, by definition, is incorruptible and immortal. It is a spirit and, as such, cannot give way to disintegration. [2] It is in the image of God and " communes with the angels. " It could only cease to be if God annihilated it. Man, therefore, is a living contradiction. He is made to die and not to die. In the midst of an existence which is gradually disintegrating, he instinctively wills to endure forever. [3] This is the most tragic aspect of death as " the separation of body and soul. " It mutilates man's being, because it opposes the nobler divine part of man's nature, his immortal soul. The soul makes man a unified entity. Death, therefore, affects the whole man. It crushes him and removes him from human existence as such. This fact cannot be erased from man's consciousness. It is the threat which pervades man's development and his decline, the inexorable

[2] On the problem of immortality see, for example, J. MARITAIN, *Sort de l'homme* (Cahiers du Rhône), chap. I; " De l'Immortalité de l'Ame, " *Lumière et Vie* (Nov. 1955), cahier 24; R. TROISFONTAINES, *I Do Not Die* (New York : Desclée, 1963).

[3] On this contradiction see St. THOMAS, *ST*, Iª-IIªᵉ, 85, 6; and *CG*, IV, 81.

contradiction in temporal existence. As Rilke said : *Flowering and withering are inseparably linked in our consciousness.* [4] It is one indication of man's complex nature.

Yet, despite this contradiction, death is *the fulfillment of man*, because it involves the spiritual act in which he makes his ultimate determining choice. [5] This violent separation strips the soul, delivers it, and opens up new vistas. And through it the soul's destiny is determined forever. This compensates for the seeming contradiction. If we acknowledge that death is *natural* for man, that he can only be delivered from it *supernaturally*, then we cannot regard it as a *purely negative*, destructive process which is contradictory to the nature of man. It would then be a meaningless necessity, an absurdity. But it does have meaning even though it is difficult to fathom. And its meaning resides in the connection between these two aspects, contradiction and fulfillment. This final moment of man's temporal existence derives its ultimate meaning from the state of man at the time. It can be horrible or wonderful, as the case may be.

Death and the Sinner

For fallen man, death is not just a paradoxical reality. It is the painful wages of sin (Rom 6, 23). God did not make death and He wanted to deliver man from this terrible contradiction.

---

[4] *Duiniser Elegies*, IV.

[5] This idea was vigorously expressed by MERSCH, *Théologie du Corps mystique*, I, 316-317. Eng. trans. *Theology of the Mystical Body* (St. Louis : Herder, 1951). It is repeated by R. TROISFONTAINES, *op. cit.*, and is basic to the view of K. RAHNER in *On the Theology of Death* (New York : Herder & Herder, 1961). The words of M. BLONDEL are very fitting : " So many people live as if they were never going to die. For them death is an illusion. They really should live as if death were the only reality. When one grasps the infinite domain of death, everything is changed! Yet, even the philosophy of death is quite undeveloped! Men have tried everything to suppress the thought of it. Few people have examined it and many would like to deprive it of the very characteristics which should be attributed to it. They do not realize that death can and should be the supreme act " (*L'Action*, 1893, p. 384).

He elevated man to a state where the physical was subsumed in the spiritual, and human nature in its entirety was subsumed in the " supernatural. " Man was made a son of God — never to know death. Man's body was saved from its natural corruptibility because his soul was united to God. But when the first man sinned, he and all his descendants lost God's friendship and the gifts it entailed. He now trembled before God, [6] and his body was again subject to the law of nature. In this being composed of body and soul, bodily death was *a consequence, a sign, and a prediction of eternal death.* [7] Whether men today know it or not, death is the final end of a sinful creature. That is why it is such a terrible thing. Our despair, revulsion, and horror of death stem from this. It is not only a shattering contradiction, but also a threat which menaces the soul even as it strikes the body. It is an enemy by definition — *inimica mors* — the last enemy which the Lord will conquer (1 Cor 15, 26, 54-57 & Ap 20, 14-15).

We glimpse the nature of this death, paradoxically enough, in the death of Jesus Christ. He took on Himself our sinful state. In God's sight He became — not a sinner, for that would be impossible for God's Holy One — but " sin for us. " He accepted the weight of our faults and endured the punishment. In His agony " He began to fear and to be heavy. And he saith to them : My soul is sorrowful even unto death " (Mk 14, 33-34). His sorrow finds expression in the terrible cry : " My God, my God, why hast thou forsaken me ? " (Mk 15, 34). Christ's holiness is not affected. He still com-

---

[6] On the dread of sinful man before God in the Old Testament, see A. M. DUBARLE, *Le Péché originel dans l'Écriture* (Paris 1958), pp. 22-26.

[7] Note how many patriarchs died a peaceful death. After their full measure of earthly days, they are peacefully reunited with their fathers while their name is carried on in their children. But the terrible nature of death gradually becomes more apparent. Man sees sin as the terrible rupture which makes him a shade in Sheol. On the exegesis of the Pauline texts, see A. FEUILLET, " Mort du Christ et mort du chrétien, " *RB* (1959), with a bibliography. Specifically, see p. 184, note 1, for the change in perspective noted here.

munes with the Father. He is still the well-beloved Son. But He has chosen to face an accursed death *to warn* us and *deliver* us. The death of a sinful man is a well-deserved condemnation. The Cross tells us so.

This is a second trait of the human condition which cannot be eradicated, even for redeemed mankind. *Apart from Christ*, death is *really* experienced as a contradiction and a condemnation. The two factors reinforce each other. The contradiction is felt as a punishment, and the condemnation affects man's deeply ingrained will-to-live. The two factors are felt to be an insufferable injustice, because a sinner cannot recognize the "justice" of God. They lead to things we know all too well — savage revolt, nameless despair, and a fierce refusal to look into the face of death.

This explains why death mars human time with an incredible anguish, why the irreversibility of time becomes a fearful approach to eternal damnation, why this inexorable moment menaces the whole span of man's temporal existence.

Death and Christ

It would be blasphemous to end our analysis here. The death of a Christian is not the death of a sinner but the death *of a redeemed sinner*. It is subsumed in the death of Christ. It is a *death with* Christ, a death which opens out on salvation and resurrection. This is the true face of death.

Christ the Deliverer

Christ died to deliver us from the condemnation to eternal death and from the fear which enslaves the sinner (Heb 2, 14-15). He has conquered death, the child of sin, because He has conquered sin itself. He has undergone death to destroy it. He has overcome this radical contradiction by elevating us to a participation in His risen life, in "life eternal." Death has not yet been *completely eradicated*, but it has been *completely transformed*. Christ has delivered us all to the Cross because He, the Head of mankind, the Center of the redeemed universe, the Savior, " bore us all in Himself " during His sacrifice. Thus " if one died for all, then all were dead " (2 Cor 5, 14), [8] and all are saved from the satanical power of death. [9] It is love, not damnation, which envelops men and restores them to God. It envelops them as individuals : He " loved me, and delivered himself for me "; as members of the race : He " loved us, and hath delivered himself for us "; and as members of the Church : He " loved the church, and delivered himself up for it. " [10]

This infinite blessing affects our personal life at Baptism, where with Christ we " are dead to sin, but alive unto God " (Rom 6, 11). The power of the Risen Christ dwells in us that " we may walk in the newness of life, " that each day we may cast sin farther away and crown our lives with the divine *agape*. The life of a Christian in time is a paradoxical one. He is dead to sin, yet must die to it each day; he lives in God, and must live for Him each day; he is the battleground of an eschatological struggle in which Christ the Conqueror faces the vanquished devil, that He may triumph once again in the freedom of a regenerated heart. By immersing himself ever more deeply into Baptism and Christ, the Christian grows with Christ and brings about His victory even in death.

Christ the Enveloper

Insofar as he lives in Christ, the Christian is totally enveloped by Christ *both before and after death*. Before death, He is the life-giving, saving Lord. After death, He calls, judges, purifies, and transfigures the life He has given. Here below, He communicates the seed of immortality, especially in the Eucharist. Up above, He will be the source of the glory which will transform our soul and our body. The Eternal Himself is present before and after death. So at our death Christ is present as the Savior who protects the Christian from the last

[8] On this text, see A. FEUILLET, *op. cit.*, p. 483 ff.

[9] See the reflections of H. RIESENFELD, " La descente dans la mort, " *Aux sources de la tradition chrétienne* (Neuchâtel-Paris 1950), pp. 211-221.

[10] Gal 2, 20; Eph 5, 2. 25.

assault of the evil one, revives his flagging spirits, and leads him from the time of testing to his eternal reward. He is the Mediator through whom and in whom every Christian experiences death. Externally, death still seems to be a terrible process of annihilation. But internally it is the mysterious maturation of the new creature in Jesus Christ. " This is the will of my Father that sent me : that every one who seeth the Son and believeth in him may have life everlasting. And I will raise him up in the last day " (Jn 6, 40, cf. 54). " I am the bread of life. . . This is the bread which cometh down from heaven : that if any man eat of it, he may not die " (Jn 6, 48. 50).

As far as the Christian is concerned, he is already dead to sin through Baptism. He has escaped its dominion. His being is not rooted in sin nor does it tend toward sin. His free will is truly liberated. The baptized person in spirit dwells in the kingdom of the risen ones. He is " alive from the dead " (Rom 6, 13), living *already beyond this world through grace.* Because he lives in Christ, God has " raised us up together, and hath made us sit together in the heavenly places " (Eph 2, 6).[11] In Christ and with Christ he straddles the shores of death. But his death to sin is a *spiritual* one which does not alter the mortality of his body. It is a *supernatural* death which he achieves by faith but which he cannot perceive directly. *The effect* of this death on his earthly life *depends on his own free will.* He must immerse himself in Christ's death and resurrection and strive to die to sin if he is to rise with Christ.

Christ the Transfigurer

In theory, then, corporeal death is transfigured for the Christian. It is *suffused with the blessing of Christ* and cannot

---

[11] St. Paul did not arrive at this doctrine immediately. In Romans salvation is yet to come; in Ephesians and Colossians it is here already (cf. S. LYONNET, " Note sur le plan de l'Épître aux Romains, " *Mélanges Lebreton*, I, pp. 301-316). In both cases, however, the tension remains. In Romans the baptized person is already risen, but in Colossians he must still be conformed to Christ (Col 3, 1-4).

be separated from Him (Rom 8, 31, ff.). It is the beginning of the Christian's direct definitive communion with Christ. The " perfect " Christian, like St. Paul, [12] can only long to be dissolved and to be with Christ. He takes up the hymn of St. Francis of Assisi in his last days :

> Blessed be my Lord, for our sister bodily death
> From whom no living man can escape.
> Cursed are those who die in mortal sin.
> Blessed are those found obedient to Your holy will,
> For the second death will do them no harm.
> Praise and bless my Lord . . .

Leaving aside the saint, who is the ideal but also the exception, we must say that the Christian is a divided being. He is still a sinner even though he has already been redeemed. He can still commit mortal sin, and he is tarnished by daily faults. He does not know when or how he will die. The dreaded hour of judgment is not known by this being who may be tarnished by only one sin. Death always has two possible results, condemnation or reconciliation, union with God or fixation in evil. As the Christian well knows, *death is overcome only in Jesus Christ.* Everything depends on his union with Christ. Everything depends on how deeply the theological virtues are rooted in his soul and how strongly the divine *agape* influences his action. The divine power within him must " absorb " death and transfigure it. For everything depends on his union with Christ in sacrificing to the Father and gradually attaining eternal life. His body is disintegrating, yet it is linked to the body of Christ by the sacraments. The Christian knows that the universe is tinged with glory and that his mortal body is planted in the earth like a seed. Together with all the saved, he will rise in a glorified universe, the new heaven and the new earth. [13]

[12] Cf. J. DUPONT, *Sun Christô* (Paris-Bruges 1952), pp. 171 ff

[13] Cf. Is 51, 16; 65, 17; 66, 12 (these texts connect this renewal to the messianic age); Mt 19, 28 (the palingenesis); Ap 21, 1-2. On St. Paul, see S. LYONNET, " La Rédemption de l'univers, " *Lumière et Vie,* 48 (June, 1960), pp. 43-62.

310

The Time for Hope

Death and Christian Liberty

At the moment of death the Christian exercises his free will. He is the master of his own will and he can make his earthly existence what he chooses to make it. In short, *three roads* are open to him.

First, he may choose to be disloyal to Christ. He becomes a stranger to Christ, living without Him and apart from Him. He orientates himself toward a death which will be a contradiction and a punishment by living a dissipated, destructive existence. His soul is already filled with rebellion and despair, or at best, with an angry resignation to his fate :

> Maigre immortalité, noire et dorée
> Consolatrice affreusement laurée
> ....
> Qui ne connaît et qui ne les refuse,
> Le crâne vide et le rire éternel! [14]

Secondly, the Christian may *want* to be faithful to Christ. But he is vacillating and imperfect. Egotism and generosity, " vigilance " and " sleep, " alternate confusingly. For him death is twofaced. Damnation and salvation get the upper hand alternately. His life is a mixture of fear and hope.

Finally, the Christian may really *remain* faithful to Christ. His fidelity may not be perfect, but it is deep-rooted. His life depends on Christ and is directed toward God. There are peaks and lowlands along the way, as St. John of the Cross says, but the road runs directly to the Risen Christ. When the Christian lives a life of " spiritual " sacrifice (Rom 12, 1-2)

---

[14] Paul VALÉRY, *Le cimetière marin.*
> Frail immortality, dark yet glittering,
> Our grim-faced consolation
> ....
> Who has not seen and set his heart against
> The bony skull fixed in an eternal smile!

and love like that of Christ, he lives an earthly existence in which death loses its terror because it becomes his eternal passage in Christ to the Father.

Death and God's Sovereignty

But there is *no real passage from earth to heaven* by human means alone. Man must submit his free will to God.

The death of the Christian is in God's hands alone. The Christian does not know the hour of his death. He does not know how he will be judged and so he does not know the ultimate value of his own death. " I am not conscious to myself of any thing, yet am I not hereby justified : but he that judgeth me, is the Lord. Therefore judge not before the time; until the Lord come. " [15] The Christian works out his salvation " in fear and trembling, " *reverencing* the divine judge and *trusting completely* in the Father. Death is God's final definitive seizure of human time. It completes the eternal plan of predestination, because God alone can complete what He has started. He has saved men from the kingdom of darkness and brought them into the Kingdom of His well-beloved Son. Now He alone can transplant them forever into eternal life. The mystery of final perseverance is a divine gift, the last act of Christ's saving mercy. It enables us to " be found in him, not having my justice, which is of the law, but that which is of the faith of Christ Jesus, which is of God : justice in faith " (Phil 3, 9). The adult Christian expresses his conversion by continuous adoration. And his final choice too is expressed in adoration of the one holy Lord and Savior.

Furthermore, the death of the Christian is always *enveloped in the mystery of Christ and in the mystery of the Church.* It is not the death of an isolated individual, but of a member of the Church. This explains many baffling things. Many

---

[15] 1 Cor 4, 4-5. Paul is referring to his apostolic activity; but the preaching of the Gospel is the heart of his personal mission, and therefore, of his Christian existence. With due restrictions the words are applicable to all Christians.

312

sinners die in peace because countless others have borne their sins and pleaded for them through the unique oblation of Jesus Christ. When a saint ends his earthly labors and goes to the Father, the entire Mystical Body mounts toward its eternal fulfillment. That is why at times the saint does not feel joy but rather suffers the agony of others together with Christ. Instead of leaving this world, he remains here, torn between the desire for death, " a far better thing, " and the " necessity of abiding in the flesh " to continue his work and nourish his own in the joy of faith (Phil 1, 23-24).

All the saints experience the joy of redeemed liberty and many have spoken about it. It is a time of service or of happiness, as God wills. The saints, more than others, know the meaning of Christ's words from the Cross : *My God, My God, why have You forsaken Me?* and *Father, into Thy hands I commend My spirit.* They share these experiences as God wills, and according to their role in the Church. St. Teresa of Avila, who had fought so hard for the honor and the love of God, died saying : " Lord, it is time to see us ! " St. Térèse of Lisieux, who desired so much to save souls, murmured : " I would not have believed one could suffer so much. Never ! Never ! " and died saying, " My God, I love You. " St. Bernadette, who saw the Lady from heaven and did so much penance for sin, pleaded : " Pray for me, a poor sinner, a poor sinner, a poor sinner. " These different words speak of an identical hope, for they come from souls already dead and risen with Christ through love.

Man's Liberty and God's Sovereignty

Yet *many days are needed to prepare our death* and to realize the eternal plan of predestination. This is the supreme importance of our time on earth. In order to enter eternal life, it is necessary, as Simone Weil said one day, " to press time on our heart until it crushes it. " [16] God does not sound

---

[16] Cited by A. CORNELIS and H. LÉONARD, *La Gnose éternelle* (Paris 1960), p. 89.

the call of death until our free will has prepared its response. At the last moment the Cross of Christ can save a man who has abandoned and rejected God all his life. But this does not mean that God damns someone who has always tried to serve Him. The Cross of Christ even more clearly indicates this. No one " merits " the grace of dying well. It is the final gift of God's infinite mercy. But man can dispose himself for it by his prayers and the whole conduct of his life — *Suppliciter emereri potest*. Even within the divine plan of predestination, free will has something to say. Death may be the unknown hour of judgment, but it is also the supreme act of our free will. We decide what our death will be, and prepare for it by the free orientation of our whole life. Our *life* is a mystery which we place in the tender hands of our Father. Our death remains a mystery to us. We can never look beyond death even when we approach its border. Yet, we *anticipate* our death by our labors as a Christian, by our death and resurrection with Christ in the sacraments and in our own souls. Truly, " we are to some extent our own fathers. " We fashion our own death,

— *Death, the secret child, already quite developed.* [17]

And the act of dying is the final act of self-generation. Temporal existence blossoms into eternity. When man " weighs anchor, " [18] it is the sovereign God who " detaches " him, carries him and receives him. Bodily death [19] for the Christian becomes *the sacrament of death in Jesus Christ*. The Christian's death is enveloped and transformed by the divine plan of predestination and the redemptive work of Jesus Christ. The condemnation becomes a means of redemption; the contradiction becomes a means of self-fulfillment.

[17] This phrase is from VALÉRY, *Jeune Parque*.

[18] Does St. Paul mean the same thing when he uses this infrequent word *(analuein)* three times? (cf. Phil 1, 23; 2, 17; 2 Tm 4, 6). Cf. A. FEUILLET, " Parousie, " *DBS*, col. 1384.

[19] Whatever may be the bio-psycho-spiritual processes involved and the consequent scientific and philosophical problems.

314

Mensurabiles Dies Meos

Let us summarize once more the characteristics of time. " O Lord, make me know my end. And what is the number of my days " (Ps 38, 5). Time is the measure of our journey on earth, and death ends this journey. The measure is completed and ended by God who established it. Our days on earth were *measurable*. Now they are *measured*. Death is the moment when man, whether he wishes it or not, must submit to the divine measure which constitutes his being. But man has freely " filled " this measure and given it meaning and value. He is a *mensura mensurata*. Temporal existence implied that man was distant from his final end and absent from his full self. Now the end is here, and man suddenly discovers

what eternity has made him. [20]

Time allowed him to make himself what he chose to be; now the end is here and his self-fulfillment is completed. Time derived its value or lack of value from our free choice; now it has become a meaningful whole or an empty abyss, depending on our acceptance or rejection of God. At the hour of death, time, as a *sovereign* measure and a *personal* measure of human existence, is ended.

But man opens his own temporal existence in the mysterious point of his supra-temporal *ego* which already participates in eternity. At the moment of death his *ego* stands firm in its ultimate choice and settles its course by the final act which determines everything. Man is then snatched from his fragmented existence in time and enters the *fully unified* existence of eternity. The spiritual *ego* has reached the instant of *complete maturity* through the instant of disintegration.

---

[20] We present this famous but often distorted verse because it aptly expresses the dazzling vision we are trying to suggest. However, Mallarmé envisioned a nebulous eternity in which man was present in a poetic way (compare the view of Edgar Poe) to human generations. We envision a *real* eternity in which man is present before the face of God.

From the earthly point of view, death is a terrible uprooting. As one medieval mystic exclaimed :

> *All that is* mine *turns into* dust,
> *And being separates from nothingness,*
> *From time and place and sense ;*
> *I tread the narrow unmarked road*...[21]

But, in fact, death is the time when the spiritual *ego* truly realizes itself. It comes under God's careful scrutiny, yet His justice is enveloped by His infinite love. Man sees himself fulfilled and reunited to the eternal idea which he represents. In Jesus Christ, *he measures himself as God measures him and judges himself as God judges him.* His acceptance or rejection of God is made eternal, and his existence is perfectly unified forever for good or evil. This unification takes place *in Jesus Christ.* Hence, if he has rejected God, his *ego* is cut off from its life-giving source and excluded from communion with God and men. But if he has accepted God, his *ego* is brought to maturity in Christ. He unites with other men in eternal communion with the Three-in-One. We have heard the frail cry of the newborn infant and the last gasps of the dying. But we cannot know the cry, the expression, and the vivacious sigh of the creature being born in eternity in the act of dying. We know only that his complex temporal existence is revealed in a flash, that his earthly life is fulfilled in eternity. His earthly life has prepared all this, but it was secretly sustained by eternity because " He who is to judge us dwells in us to save and pardon us *in our time of trial.* " [22] If a man dies in Christ, his soul is taken into bliss and into the eternal inter-cession of the One who always stands before God as our representative. Far from being separated by an *insurmountable absence*, the soul is plunged once more into the march of men on earth. There it lives in joyous rapturous maturity.

---

[21] A thirteenth-century hymn cited in *Hadewijch d'Anvers*, p. 137, note. 2.

[22] Elizabeth of the Trinity, *Spiritual Writings* (New York : Kenedy, 1962), p. 95. The italics are mine.

But now we are in the time-for-hope, cradled in the hands of the *Christ-God*. [23] He insures our passage to the Father. And the most appropriate sign of this *In manus tuas* is Viaticum, the last communion on the tongue of the dying. Christ becomes the food for our journey, the remedy of life, the source of immortality, the living bread from heaven which leads us to Paradise. [24] The Church takes the words of Jesus seriously : " He that eateth my flesh and drinketh my blood hath everlasting life : and I will raise him up in the last day " (Jn 6, 55). To receive Viaticum is " to die in the Lord " in the strictest sense of the word. It is to be led by the Way to the last crossroad; by the Truth, to the last deceitful temptation; by the Life to apparent annihilation.

Thus we see that at the final lonely hour the Christian is surrounded by the Trinity and the family of God's children. [25] This is the wondrous meaning of the prayer *Proficere :* " Depart from the world, Christian soul, in the name of God the Father who created you; in the name of Jesus Christ, Son of the living God, who suffered for you; in the name of the Holy Spirit who has been poured out on you. . . " All the saints are there to protect and receive their brother; the Virgin Mary is there so that " he will no longer fear the terrors of death, " but " go joyously to his Father's house in heaven "; the angels are present " to conduct him to paradise " and

[23] A familiar expression in the oriental liturgies.

[24] Of course, these biblical expressions do not imply any local motion in Christ. They merely indicate *the primacy and the sovereignty* of His presence and His activity. The law of the Church, which is very strict on this point but often overlooked, stems from the Council of Nicea (*Can.* 13, *DB*, 57). The Council appeals to the " ancient law of tradition " and insists on the urgent need of receiving " the last and very necessary viaticum. " On the rites and prayers for the dying see J. C. DIDIER, *Le chrétien devant la maladie et la mort* (Paris 1961). The Church has also severely condemned the recurrent practice of giving communion to the dead.

[25] The following texts are taken from the prayers for the departing soul in the Roman Ritual.

to push back " Satan and his devilish hordes " into " the abyss of eternal night "; St. Joseph, the Patriarchs, the Martyrs and the other saints are there too. Because the King is there, the whole celestial army is there. The priest gives Viaticum and commends the soul to God. Through the invisible presence of these people, death in Christ and the Church proves to be a deeply sacred act filled with joy, sorrow, and peace. It is *the last act of holy abandon by man's free will.* Truly, " Blessed are the dead, who die in the Lord " (Ap 14, 13).

Thus we see the frightening complexity of the time for death, this essential dimension of Christian life. It is not a time of dread or of unconcern, but *a time of hope in Jesus Christ.* It is the moment in which Baptism is completed by the final Easter. [26] Our first birth is completed by our re-birth. We were initiated into eternal life at the baptismal font. Now we enter into the fullness of that life. The time for salvation gives way to the state of salvation. To be sure, there is still a time after death. [27] For the souls in Purgatory it is a time of expiation and purification. For unrepentant sinners it is a time of rejection. When God is not loved, eternity is a kind of time measuring the pain of the damned. [28] It reminds us that death is still a judgment, and that our free will can still institute a time of eternal condemnation in spite of God's grace. But the Christian beseeches God to save his fickle

[26] This point has been clearly underlined by J. C. DIDIER, *op. cit.*, pp. 105-106, 118-119.

[27] Here we are not concerned with death in itself. Thus we avoid discussing the state of the soul and its possibilities at the moment of death. There have been many controversies but now one can read the solid and irenic article of Msgr. P. GLORIEUX, " In Hora mortis, " *MélSR* (1949), pp. 199 ff.

[28] St. Thomas does not hesitate to say that " in hell there is no real eternity, only time " (*ST*, Iª, X, 3, 2m). — Cf. also " De Spe, " *Q UNICA*, 4, 3m : " The continuing state (continuatio) of beatitude does not involve any notion of future, because *insofar as one is blessed, he participates in eternity*, in which there is no past or future; that is why the state of beatitude is called eternal life (cf. 9m). " It is a real *living state* of immeasurable fulfillment beyong any activity of movement or rest which constitutes past and future *for us.*

318

free will; he begs Mary and the saints to intercede for him at the hour of death; and he hopes that Christ will save him from the devil and bring him to Paradise. The Christian's time-for-death is *affected intrinsically* by all this.

In many eucharistic liturgies the grace of a happy death is implored. The Eastern Christians say: " We ask for a Christian end to our life in joy, honor, and peace, and we seek a strong defense before the tribunal of Christ. " [29] The Western Christians say : " Grant that we be saved from eternal damnation and numbered in the flock of your elect, through Jesus Christ, our Lord. . ." " May the reception of Your Body, O Lord Jesus Christ, which I, though unworthy, dare to receive, not lead to judgment and condemnation, but through Your love be a protection for soul and body. . ." The hour of death is the *Parousia for the individual, which anticipates the universal Parousia.* We understand the striking meaning of the *Anima Christi,* in which many Christians down through the ages have voiced a plea for their first and last hour :

> *At the hour of death call me,*
> *Bid me come to Thee,*
> *That with Thy saints*
> *I may praise Thee for all eternity.   Amen.*

For the Christian, death is objectively the moment of final decision and final conversion, of the last birth and the last act of service when everything is put into the Father's hands. Subjectively, it is the moment when our sacrifice with Christ is consummated in a flash. Our personal salvation-period is definitively accomplished and we make our supreme act of hope in the night :

IN TE DOMINE SPERAVI
NON CONFUNDAR IN ETERNUM.

---

[29] Offertory prayer in the liturgy of St. John Chrysostom. Cf. MERCE-NIER, *La prière des Églises de rite byzantin* (Amay-sur-Meuse 1937), I, p. 248 (cf. pre-Communion prayers, p. 257).

N.Y. 21. — Printed in Belgium by DESCLÉE & Cie, ÉDITEURS, S.A., Tournai — 10.703